THE
MARINE FISH
Health
& Feeding
Handbook

Produced and distributed by
T.F.H. PUBLICATIONS
One T.F.H. Plaza
Third and Union Avenues
Neptune City, NJ 07753
www.tfh.com

Printed and bound in China.

Library of Congress Cataloging-in-Publication Data

Goemans, Bob.
The marine fish health & feeding handbook : the essential guide
to keeping saltwater species alive and thriving / Bob Goemans and Lance Ichinotsubo.
p. cm.
Includes bibliographical references and index.
ISBN 978-1-890087-95-1 (alk. paper)
1. Marine aquarium fishes. 2. Marine aquariums. I. Ichinotsubo,
Lance. II. Title. III. Title: Marine fish health and feeding handbook.

SF457.1G64 2007
639.34'2--dc22
2007040212

Co-published by
MICROCOSM LTD.
P.O. Box 550
Charlotte, VT 05445
www.microcosm-books.com

Design by Linda Provost
Color by Digital Engine

Front Cover: Queen Angelfish (*Holacanthus ciliaris*) Collage © Ralph A. Clevenger/CORBIS
Back Cover: Top: Queen Angelfish (*Holacanthus ciliaris*) normal and with HLLE, illustrations by Joshua Highter/Microcosm
Middle: Feeding juvenile Scrawled Cowfish (*Acanthostracion quadricornis*), photograph by Matthew L. Wittenrich
Bottom: Net-caught Neon Wrasse (*Halichoeres melanurus*), Philippines, photograph by Matthew L. Wittenrich

THE MARINE FISH Health & Feeding Handbook

THE ESSENTIAL GUIDE TO KEEPING SALTWATER SPECIES ALIVE AND THRIVING

Bob Goemans AND Lance Ichinotsubo

with a Foreword by Martin A. Moe, Jr.

PRINCIPAL PHOTOGRAPHERS
Matthew L. Wittenrich,
Dr. Gerald Bassleer, Dr. Vincent Hargreaves,
Nelson Herwig, Alf Jacob Nilsen, David Vaughan

ILLUSTRATIONS
Joshua Highter

MICROCOSM

tfh

PROFESSIONAL
SERIES™

All aquarium hobbyists belong
to a family of caring individuals;
ultimately, brothers and sisters in many regards,
joined in a commitment to marine husbandry.

We dedicate this book to them and to others
who wish to enhance their stewardship
of the animals we keep.

Bob Goemans & Lance Ichinotsubo

Contents

Contents

The goal: vibrant, healthy fishes. Female Shortfin Lionfish (*Dendrochirus brachypterus*) begs its keeper for a treat of live grass shrimp.

Well-kept fishes display natural behaviors: Hancock's Blenny (*Acanthemblemaria hancocki*) darting out of its hiding cave in a barnacle shell, attracted to plankton passing in the aquarium water column.

Acknowledgments

We wish to gratefully acknowledge and thank Dr. Gerald Bassleer, Dr. Vincent Hargreaves, Nelson Herwig, Alf Jacob Nilsen, and David Vaughan for their support and photographic contributions to this book, which provide visual depictions of the various diseases, parasitic organisms, and conditions discussed in the text. There's much truth to the old adage, "A picture is worth a thousand words," and we are sure that every aquarist and marine fish dealer will appreciate the photos and accurate identifications from these experts.

We also wish to thank David Vaughan for proofing an early version of the text, which was very helpful in organizing the structure of the book and helping tweak some of its content. We sincerely thank Martin A. Moe, Jr., who penned the Foreword and reviewed the final manuscript. His immense knowledge about this hobby and his willingness to help us put forth a new contribution to the health and welfare of our animals are to be commended.

Designer Linda Provost, principal photographer Matthew L. Wittenrich, and illustrator Josh Highter deserve our warm thanks for the engaging look of this book. We thank the peer reviewers and Microcosm editorial team—Mary Sweeney, Kelly Jedlicki, Louise Watson, John Sweeney, Judith Billard, and James Lawrence—for their editing, proofreading, suggestions, and guidance in producing this work. We appreciate the enthusiastic support of the folks at T.F.H. Publications, who instantly understood the need for an up-to-date book on the subject of marine aquarium fish health and feeding.

Last, but not least, we wish to thank our spouses, who spent many lonely evenings and weekends during the past several years while we were gathering and organizing our information and photos. They fully supported our work effort, as they realized that what we were forging was the culmination of a dream to provide a handbook that could be widely utilized to improve the health and welfare of marine aquarium fish.

Bob Goemans & Lance Ichinotsubo

Juvenile Longhorn Cowfish
(*Lactoria cornuta*) in a Philippine
facility ready to be shipped, with
rubber block protectors (fashioned
from old flipflop soles) on its
vulnerable horns.

A Sense of Caring
for the Lives of Marine Fishes

From reef to aquarium, finding success by doing things right

The success and the future of the marine aquarium hobby depend on four very different groups of people.

A successful collector of wild fishes is a steward of the reef environment and caring harvester of healthy marine specimens. A successful wholesaler eliminates diseased and drugged specimens, educates collectors, discourages trade in organisms not suitable for home aquariums, and knows how to properly ship all kinds of marine organisms all over the world. A successful retailer keeps a clean, disease-free shop, has healthy, well-nourished fish and invertebrates, can knowledgeably service the needs of beginning and advanced aquarists, and educates customers about the function of systems and the needs of all types of marine organisms.

Finally, a successful amateur aquarist, the core and focus of the marine aquarium hobby, is one who understands how aquarium systems work and expends the effort to properly care for the animals that he or she maintains. The common threads that run through the efforts of all these successful professionals and hobbyists are great respect, appreciation, caring, and proper maintenance of the animals that give us enjoyment, satisfaction, and delight, and perhaps a livelihood as well. But all the love, care, and respect in the world will not counteract a lack of basic knowledge about keeping fishes healthy in a captive environment.

Do you have a medicine cabinet? Sure you do. It probably contains aspirin, band-aids, antibiotic ointments, and perhaps some prescription drugs. Do you know how to use them? Of course you do. You have learned what each of these

Local aquarium shop fishkeeper hand-feeds dried seaweed to a hungry batch of newly imported Yellow Tangs (*Zebrasoma flavescens*) showing signs of malnourishment.

"Who hears the fishes when

is used for, how much to use and when, and when it is no longer useful. You wouldn't just take some medication and hope for a good outcome; you want to know that you are doing the right thing. And you do the same for Rex and Felix, your dog and cat. You have the right food for them, you have medications for fleas and ticks and internal parasites, and the veterinarian is only a phone call away if the situation is more serious. But what do you do for the fish and invertebrates in your aquarium? Unfortunately, nutritional, environmental, and medical care for our marine friends often depends on a hope-this-works, shotgun approach, and the cure can be worse than the malady.

Rex, Felix, you, and the kids all have something in common: all are terrestrial vertebrates, and at an early age we become familiar with the requirements for the health and well-being of these organisms. But aquatic marine organisms—fish and invertebrates—are another story. If something isn't right, if they show signs of disease or distress, you first have to know what is wrong, and then you have to know how to fix the problem, and this isn't always easy. Your local aquarium shop may help, but if not, there aren't many veterinarians on call for sick fish or shrimp, and information on the Web can be confusing and conflicting.

But suppose you could sit down with two guys—one a long-time, extensively published marine hobbyist and the other a professional aquarist with broad experience in the operation of marine aquarium shops and the development and maintenance of commercial marine systems—and ask them how to care for your aquatic animals from birth to old age and how to identify and cure disease? In a way, this book allows you to do just that.

Bob Goemans and Lance Ichinotsubo have combined their considerable knowledge and experience in the world of marine aquaristics to write a book about the care and maintenance of marine fishes in home aquarium systems. The result is a comprehensive instruction manual for the acquisition and routine and emergency care of your aquatic family. Not only do Goemans and Ichinotsubo know what they are talking about, they also care deeply about the marine animals that are the essence of our hobby. It is much more than just a business to them. The success of everyone who makes keeping marine organisms a hobby or a business depends on this level of caring and commitment.

Wholesalers and collectors will benefit greatly from the information in this book, but the retailer and the hobbyist, the people on the receiving end of the chain that stretches from the reef to the aquarium, are the book's main focus. For them, having access to the authors' expertise could mean the difference between success and failure. It is likely this book will become the most valuable item in the marine aquarist's medicine cabinet.

Martin A. Moe, Jr.
Islamorada, Florida

MARTIN A. MOE, JR. is the author of *The Marine Aquarium Handbook: Beginner to Breeder, The Marine Aquarium Reference Book: Systems & Invertebrates,* and other titles.

they cry?" —*Henry David Thoreau, 1906*

Harlequin Tuskfish
(*Choerodon fasciatus*):
a showoff specimen
caught in various poses
as it interacts with an
aquarium viewer.

Fishkeeping as if Fish Matter

"Fish are not disposable commodities, but a worthwhile investment that can be maintained and enjoyed for many years, providing one is willing to take the time to understand their requirements and needs."

Lance Ichinotsubo:

There is a mystique about marine aquariums. They conjure up thoughts of Paradise—South Pacific islands, beautiful coral reefs, tropical rainforests, aquamarine waters, and romantic sunsets. Having been born in Hawaii, I am extremely fortunate to have grown up in just such a paradise and to know it's much more than a fantasy. We lived very close to nature and were always taught respect for our planet and all its inhabitants, in our schools as well as at home.

From the very beginning of my involvement with marine aquariums in Hawaii, as both a hobbyist and a professional, it has been my desire to provide our fish with the best possible environment in which to live, and to keep them as robust and healthy as possible. This is an ideal and it can sometimes be a challenge. As anyone who has kept fish—or any other pets, for that matter—knows, things can go wrong, disease can happen, untimely deaths can and do occur. With fish, most problems can be traced to severe stress: the rigors of shipping, prolonged poor nutrition, exposure to aggressive tankmates, sudden or long-term changes in water conditions and quality. Fish shipments from far-flung tropical places are filled with animals that have been stressed, perhaps severely.

For example, a recent shipment of fish to a local Florida retailer of my acquaintance resulted in over 50 percent mortality within 48 hours of their arrival. After performing an examination of some of the mortalities, I determined that at least eight different diseases afflicted this one shipment of fish.

The remaining fish were saved, but only after careful diagnosis and in-depth therapeutic procedures were performed. We will be covering all of them in this book, and in doing so, we hope to show you that the effort of diagnosing and treating fish maladies is a worthwhile and effective undertaking.

As a case in point, a puffer named E.T. was a member of our family for more than 20 years, and in that time she suffered more than her share of illnesses, some of them serious. With the care and attention she received whenever she was under the weather, she was able to overcome diseases that otherwise would, almost certainly, have killed her. Fish are not a disposable commodity but a worthwhile investment that can be maintained and enjoyed for many years, providing one is willing to take the time to understand their requirements and needs.

"What caused this fish to die?" This is the question I always ask myself when there are losses. For some time now, I have felt that those involved in the marine aquarium hobby need some way of obtaining accurate information about how to take better care of their animals when things go wrong. "Perhaps many fish could be saved if I could collect and share the things I've learned," I thought. Then my friend Bob Goemans asked me if I would be interested in writing a book with him about marine fish health management and feeding. We designed our book to offer insight to others who might be experiencing the same challenges that virtually all aquarists face from time to time. We hope that our success in dealing with diverse fishkeeping challenges will provide inspiration and guidance to help keep your fish in the best health possible.   ⤙

Lance Ichinotsubo
Margate, Florida

Bob Goemans:

I date my own quest for healthier aquarium inhabitants to 1950, when I became the first person in the United States to have and use an undergravel filter, then called the

A Striped Burrfish (*Chilomycterus schoepfii*): A puffer similar to this engaging specimen was an Ichinotsubo family pet for more than 20 years, thanks to timely treatment of various health challenges.

"French Invisible Filter." As a very young member of a local aquarium society in Queens, New York, I was fortunate enough to be present when a speaker from Europe at one of our monthly meetings introduced a device he said would revolutionize aquarium keeping. I won the bid for the filter and found that when I used it, the fish in my 10-gallon freshwater aquarium seemed healthier. This success led me on a path that continues today, to search for improved ways to care for our aquarium animals.

In our nearly 90 years of combined experience in the aquarium industry, Lance and I have encountered almost every possible situation within the gamut of aquarium-keeping. From the most incredible, state-of-the-art, fully equipped fish mansions to the most neglected and derelict fish graveyards, we have had to deal with a multitude of conditions.

Using the techniques we have described in this book, we have been successful in reversing even the worst conditions that we have encountered. Many required detailed diagnoses, disease treatments, and water quality upgrades.

We have written this book as a tool for others, and we intend it to be a readable, easily used body of information that will stimulate awareness about the probable causes of poor animal health and provide restorative methods. We hope it will be an aid to hobbyists, aquarium shop owners and personnel, and others in the aquarium profession.

We have chosen to divide our book into three sections that reflect our view of how fishes can be kept healthy. The first section is dedicated to the all-important topic of selecting, acclimating, and getting a fish or group of fish into your home aquarium in good shape and without disease or attached parasites. It includes an overview of water conditions necessary for the maintenance of good health. The second section covers foods, feeding, and nutrition, and their significance in promoting long life and good health. Finally, our third section gets to actual diseases and conditions, including all of the ailments that most amateur

aquarists will ever encounter. We provide symptoms, remedies, and ways to prevent reoccurrence. We are pleased to be able to provide photographs from several well-known scientists to help visually identify the diseases discussed.

We trust that what you are about to read and view will enhance your knowledge of marine fish husbandry. This is a discipline that begins with patience and doing a lot of things right; we hope you will take into account the full picture of how to keep fish alive and thriving, and how

to keep devastating problems out of your home aquarium. Fish disease and ill health are never the first considerations for new aquarists, but we hope those who are serious about the health and welfare of their marine aquarium fish will find the essential facts, advice, and guidance they need within these pages.

Bob Goemans
Tucson, Arizona

The home reef aquarium of Pieter Suijlekom in the Netherlands, with a profusion of healthy fishes and corals.

Secrets of Helping Fish Thrive

What it takes to keep your marine charges vibrant and healthy

Coming face to face with a healthy marine aquarium for the first time, most of us are dazzled by the brilliant colors, captivated by the graceful movements and diversity of shapes of the fishes, and fascinated by the often bizarre forms of invertebrate life. A saltwater aquarist is born when the desire to have something similar, or even grander, is kindled.

Those new to the hobby of marine fishkeeping often want to create their very own slice of the ocean quickly, preferably overnight—but if that's the way it's done, the road ahead is usually filled with many obstacles. So what are those obstacles, and what will it take to steer clear of them?

Doubtless the most troubling hurdle any fishkeeper can encounter is having one of his or her prize specimens fall ill or meet an early demise. Unfortunately, when a single fish shows signs of disease or parasites in a marine aquarium, there is a good chance that its tankmates may follow. A whole community of fishes can be lost with astonishing speed if nothing is done. Such an event, in fact, is a leading reason many people lose heart, consign the tank to a yard sale, and take up a less challenging hobby.

Many cataclysmic health problems can be traced to owners who fail to take their time in choosing, acclimating, feeding, and tending their fishes. It's an often-repeated saying that "Nothing good ever happens fast in a marine aquarium." If you learn only one thing from reading this first section, let it be that the three most important words in marine fishkeeping are patience, patience, and patience. Prevention of the most deadly marine diseases is largely a matter of keeping them

Diver with net-caught Copperband Butterflyfish (*Chelmon rostratus*) in the Albay Gulf, in the Philippines. Local divers here have moved away from the use of cyanide for capturing coral reef fishes, good for the environment in source countries as well as healthier specimens for the marine aquarists who buy them.

out of your tank in the first place, as we shall see.

The intent of this first section is to chart an easy path around the most common fishkeeping pitfalls and to outline the general conditions that affect the health of aquarium inhabitants. The formula is simple enough:

1. Start with a healthy fish.

2. Get it into your home aquarium in good condition and free of disease and parasites.

3. Keep it in good, pollution-free water with the proper environmental conditions—steady, appropriate temperature, lighting, oxygen levels, and aquascaping.

4. Ensure that it has the right mix of tankmates and is not being bullied, constantly harassed, or driven into hiding at feeding times.

5. Be sure it has the right foods, in the right quantities.

The all-important first step begins with your local aquarium shop, where you should seek out the healthiest animals possible. Recognizing what is and isn't healthy takes some experience, and hopefully you will gain much of it from this book.

Stress Factors

Stress has the same effects on animals as it does on humans—it tires us and wears down our resistance to fight many illnesses. Go diving or snorkeling on a healthy coral reef and you will seldom see an unhealthy fish. In the wild, the big challenges in most cases are competition and predation, not disease. For an aquarium fish, however, stresses never encountered in nature can be major factors in triggering various diseases and maladies.

Where a fish is concerned, it all begins in the wild when it is captured. Instinctively, it goes into a "fight or flight" response, which is a basic animal survival strategy. In most cases, it panics and in the course of trying to flee, shuts down non-essential processes, such as digestion and the immune system, for the immediate use of energy for escaping. Additionally, we now know that the stress enzyme, cortisol, is produced by all animals in large quantities during stressful times. Although not yet fully understood, this flood of cortisol may be one of the reasons why an animal's immune system response is lowered when it is stressed. After capture, the fish will endure days or weeks of transport, living in plastic bags and crowded holding tanks with multple exposures to diseases in multiple systems, often without food for the entire period.

With its immune system stressed, the fish may not be able to cope with the parasites or bacterial infections that it would have normally and safely dealt with in the wild. Parasites and secondary bacterial infections take advantage of the window of opportunity from capture to destination (your aquarium). This is sufficient time for disease-causing organisms to multiply to epidemic levels.

Reduction of stress in the home marine aquarium begins with having a stock-ing plan for your aquarium. What is it that you want to replicate? A tank holding a colorful mix of relatively peaceful species from the Indo-Pacific? A small species tank for a pair or trio of clownfish? Perhaps a rambunctious predator tank with grouper, triggerfish, and moray eels?

The most successful marine aquarists have a plan for each tank and stay with it. Rather than falling for the most tempting new fish at the local aquarium store every time you visit, take the time to know as much as possible about the various species you are considering. Putting incompatible fishes together is one of the surest routes to serious health problems and/or lost community members.

Selecting Livestock

Picking healthy and appropriate livestock from the incredible range of choices available requires that the hobbyist invest some time, not only in formulating an overall stocking plan but also in observing potential purchases at the store. The local aquarium shop owner and his or her staff can be a great resource, and the responsible fish retailer will strive to match the right fishes to the right systems and owners, especially when helping newcomers get off to a sound start. The hobbyist who has no such local expertise

Stress Management Checklist

- Stock your system slowly.
- Be sure all animals are healthy before introduction to the show tank.
- Don't overcrowd. Resist the temptation to add just one more fish.
- Prevent rapid or extreme changes in temperature or specific gravity.
- Use a timer to keep daylight:nighttime hours (photoperiod) predictable.
- If possible, ramp up light intensity for daylight and slowly dim lights at night. Don't simply turn bright lights on or off, especially in a dark room.
- Know the dietary needs of all animals.
- Feed a variety of foods for marine fishes.
- Replicate "reeflike" conditions of water movement and aquascaping.
- Limit external noise and vibrations transmitted to the aquarium.
- Be sure all the inhabitants are compatible tankmates.
- Avoid using household cleaners, paint, and insecticides near the tank.

Healthy Copperband Butterflyfish exhibits all the desirable signs: alertness, bright colors, clear eyes, perfect finnage, a rounded fullness to its body and a greedy interest in feeding.

natural-born predators. Do not expect to house large, carnivorous species with a school of small, defenseless fishes and see them to conform to some sort of polite rules of captive behavior.

A mix of bottom dwellers, open-water swimmers, and some that roam the nooks and crannies will help provide a more socially balanced environment and a more visually appealing aquarium.

Also, having a balance among the three basic types of food consumers, i.e., omnivores, carnivores, and herbivores, will add to the stability of the environment and reduce the stress threat.

Remember, fishes that are not compatible with each other or with certain invertebrates in the wild will not exhibit any better behavior in a closed system.

Knowing the aquascaping preferences of your fishes is also a good tool for reducing stress. Many species need rocky hiding places to feel secure and will do very poorly in a sparsely decorated tank. Others may need deep sand beds for burrowing or even burying themselves at night or when frightened.

Some texts suggest rearranging the aquarium aquascaping when adding a new or aggressive fish to a closed system in the belief that the problem fish will spend its time redefining its own territory and not battling others. We prefer not to add stress to our animals or ourselves by rearranging the aquascaping. And when introducing fish, try adding more than a single newcomer so as to divide the attention of the established inhabitants. A temporary plastic divider can also be used to introduce a new fish.

If your goal for the community includes aggressive fish,

to call upon will have to consult books, online sources of information, and other aquarists. (See Selected Bibliography and Sources & Contacts, pages 222-223.)

COMPATIBILITY When choosing fishes that will need to coexist in the confines of your aquarium, it is important to know their adult sizes, diets, temperaments, and the special needs of each species. This is no small matter, and it can become a lifelong course in self-education and one of the great rewards of being involved in marine aquarium-keeping.

Bear in mind that many marine fish are more territorial than freshwater fish. Many are naturally very aggressive in the wild and even more so in a closed system. Some are

"Bear in mind that many marine fish are more territorial than freshwater fish. Many are naturally very aggressive in the wild and even more so in the closed system. Some are natural-born predators."

add them last and provide numerous hiding places for those that are not so aggressive. Always feed your fish before adding a new tankmate and dim the lights before introducing newcomers. Better yet, feed the tank and then add the new fish after the lights have gone out. Aggression usually ceases with darkness.

Also, give some thought to not adding similarly shaped or colored species. Different species of anthias, fairy wrasses, and flasher wrasses may end up in conflict, unless the aquarium is huge, with the less aggressive fishes driven away from food and eventually perishing. If there is aggression, try putting a mirror next to the aquarium to divert some of the attention. Temporarily separating a troublemaker in the aquarium with a plastic barrier may also be helpful. And always try to prevent overcrowding, which fosters territorial problems.

PROBLEM BEHAVIORS When it comes to certain behaviors, there are inherent factors that are not going to change. Qualities that give fish a survival advantage in the wild can give the home aquarist ongoing grief, especially in average- to small-sized tanks.

Some fish are too big and/or too rowdy for many aquariums, needing large, open expanses of water for their active swimming behaviors. Obvious examples are the larger surgeonfishes/tangs, some of the wrasses, parrotfishes, big puffers, groupers, and others.

There are species that are simply too industrious for the average tank. The Rockmover Wrasse, for example, will gather pieces of live rock and rubble and create its own aquascape. Convict Eel Blennies will move vast amounts of substrate to build their tunnels. Moray eels may forage through rockwork and coral colonies at night, dislodging pieces that are not firmly anchored in place. These behaviors are fascinating to watch, but too disruptive for many aquariums, especially as the fish gets larger and stronger.

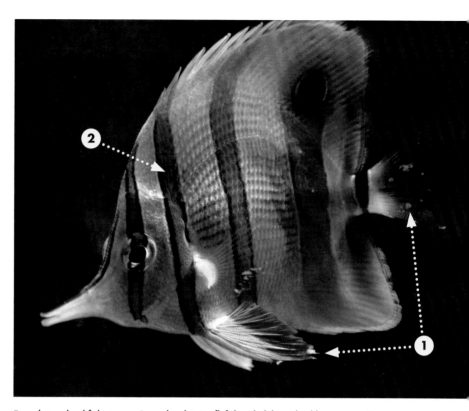

For sale in a local fish store, a Copperband Butterflyfish with dubious health prospects. Note suspicious tufts (1) on fins and tail and wasted muscles (2), suggesting malnutrition or starvation.

Active jumpers will be a problem if your tank is not covered. The dartfishes, for example, will be on the carpet in no time unless a cover is in place. In fact, many species will jump, and having a full hood or panels of eggcrate over the entire top will prevent almost certain fish loss.

Many grazers and omnivores can develop the bad habit, from a reefkeeper's point of view, of nibbling at coral polyps or the tempting mantles of giant clams. Some species of dwarf angelfish, for example, are well known to have this tendency.

Without a doubt, certain fish can become terrors in mixed company. There are some species of triggerfish that may, once they reach a certain size or age, undergo dramatic personality shifts and start to attack anything else in the aquarium. In fact, they will even bite the aquarium panel between them and you in an effort to take a piece out of their keeper. Some of the tangs or surgeonfishes seem

Volitans Lionfish (*Pterois volitans*) with a mouthful of live shrimp that it has just attacked. Such natural hunting behaviors can be fascinating and educational to observe, but not if the shrimp in question is a prized ornamental species, perhaps acquired at considerable cost. Choose large predatory fishes with care.

to live to be fiesty and can inflict serious damage on their less aggressive tankmates. Examples include the Yellow Tang, which can terrorize a small tank, and the beautiful Sohal Tang, which can be a menace even in large systems. Those species with reputations as bullies are generally well known, and you can avoid bringing an instinctive trouble-maker into your system by reading its profile in a reference book or two and/or asking the retail store staff before actually making a purchase.

It is much better to know about all such potential behaviors prior to purchasing the specimen, rather than trying to resolve the problem once the fish is in the aquarium.

PREDATOR ISSUES Some fish are going to look upon other fish and/or your favorite invertebrates as conveniently available food items. If a species relishes giant clam flesh in the wild, for instance, it is not likely to hold back in your aquarium just because its "master" paid a small fortune for that centerpiece "ultra" clam. Species that eat coral polyps or ornamental crustaceans and mollusks will obviously be unwelcome in most reef aquariums.

Certain butterflyfish will dine greedily on various invertebrates, including coral polyps and ornamental feather duster worms. Lionfish will eat some of their living tankmates, e.g., other fish and shrimp that will fit into their mouths. Frogfish (anglerfish) will do the same, although they can actually swallow fish larger than themselves. Therefore, it's a must to understand the disposition of the animal in question before adding it to the aquarium. Large carnivores, such as the groupers, eat so much and create so much nitrogenous waste that they are usually unwelcome in systems with delicate corals that demand very clean water at all times.

The same cautions hold true for some invertebrates. There are shrimp that feed exclusively on starfish, anemones that eat fish or sting nearby corals, and corals that sting other nearby corals. Indeed, an aquarium can be a dangerous place for some of its inhabitants.

FEEDING Usually, there is a wide variety of animals in the aquarium. Many have special nutritional needs. Understanding those needs begins with knowing whether they are carnivores, herbivores, or omnivores, which is explained in the Foods & Feeding section of this book. Some (such as tangs) are casual feeders, similar to cows grazing in a meadow. Others (such as puffers) are aggressive feeders, stuffing themselves whenever food is available. Some fish (such as smaller gobies) are shy and retiring, and cannot compete with aggressive fish when mealtime comes. Oth-

ers (such as obligate coral eaters, like certain butterflyfish) are specialized feeders, and their foodstuffs are not available or could easily far outweigh the cost of the specimen.

Orbiculate or Common Batfish (*Platax orbicularis*): Cute juveniles will outgrow most home aquariums within a year and can easily reach almost 20 inches (50 cm) in length, with height to match.

Without a dedicated keeper, animals needing special care are not among the best choices for average aquariums. Understanding their feeding behaviors and nutritional needs is extremely important, as it will influence their well-being and longevity.

SHORT-LIVED SPECIES Some fish and invertebrates have exceptionally short life spans. The Neon Goby, *Gobiosoma oceanops*, normally lives only about two years. The Seven-figure Pygmy Goby (*Eviota sigillata*) found on the Great Barrier Reef has been reported to "live fast, reproduce, and die

Dwarf Seahorses (*Hippocampus zosterae*): Seahorses represent many species of marine fishes that demand live foods and frequent feedings every day if they are to thrive in the aquarium.

young"—doing it all in less than two months. Generally, the smaller species that reproduce prolifically and live in dense schools tend to have shorter life spans. The cardinalfishes (Apogonidae) are a good example. In some studies the oldest specimens found in the wild were only in the two to three year range. Among the invertebrates, many of the highly intelligent small octopuses live less than two years, with females almost always perishing soon after laying their eggs. On the other hand, there are many records of marine fishes living between 10 and 20 years in aquariums where they are free of predators and receive good care. The majority of popular marine aquarium species can be expected to live 7 to 10 years with proper husbandry.

SOCIAL HABITS Some fishes, including certain butterflyfishes, angelfishes, and frogfishes, mate for life and may perish if separated from their partners. Fish-invertebrate matchups are also known: Prawn gobies tend to form long-term partnerships with pistol shrimps, and may do poorly in the aquarium if they have been separated. Still other fishes, such as the various *Chromis* species, need to be kept in groups or they tend to waste away. It always pays to study the natural history of a species before making a pur-

Hasty Stocking vs The Informed Purchase:
A large percentage of aquarium problems stem from hobbyists buying a new fish on impulse. Experienced aquarists always ask questions and do their research before acquiring a new species. How big does it get? How large a tank will it need when it reaches full size? What does it eat? Is it a likely bully or likely to be bullied by other fish in your existing community? Does it need special care or aquascaping? Is it likely to do well with the level of husbandry you can provide?

chase, and a number of good references are now available. (See Further Reading, page 232.)

SIZE It's a must to know how large animals will get, and also how fast they grow. The Common or Orbiculate Batfish juvenile may only be a few inches (5–7 cm) in height when first introduced. However, a year later it won't fit in a 20-in. (50 cm) high aquarium. Once a small

Filipino collectors bringing the day's catch of net-caught fishes back to shore in a small boat with a stablizing outrigger. The use of potassium cyanide to stun fishes for live capture is still prevalent in the Philippines and Indonesia, but various groups are helping local fisherfolk convert to sustainable capture methods.

juvenile becomes much larger, will it still be an animal that is desirable in the system? Size also relates to feeding, as larger fish require greater quantities of food, which in turn affects water quality. It could be that more expensive filtration equipment would need to be installed, possibly sooner rather than later. Larger fish may eat smaller fish and that needs to be assessed before it happens. This is especially true in systems with myriad hiding places, as removal of unwanted specimens can become very difficult.

METHOD OF CAPTURE To have the greatest chance of long-term success with any marine aquarium fish, start with the healthiest specimen possible. Ideally, find a source of net-caught fish from a responsible dealer who tries to avoid trafficking in cyanide-captured livestock. The healthiest stock comes from certified sources that pass high standards for safe and sustainable collection and careful handling and

shipping. Know the country of origin, if you can, and be wary of uncertified stock from the Philippines and Indonesia, historically the sources of the majority of cyanide-caught fishes. (See pages 76-77.)

POOR SURVIVAL Finally, it can be very challenging to keep some species alive. Either they fail to ship well, they have specialized (or unknown) nutritional needs, or they grow too large or otherwise are not easy for most home aquarists to manage.

Some others, such as the parrotfishes, simply never thrive in the confines of home aquariums and should not be caught and sold—or bought by informed aquarists. One detailed ranking of imported species is the American Marinelife Dealers' Association (AMDA) Ecolist, titled "List of Fishes Suitable for Keeping in Captivity," which was developed by many retailers, wholesalers, and others

Dragon Wrasse (*Novaculichthys taeniourus*) is a fascinating species, but far too rowdy for many aquarium situations. It grows to almost a foot (30 cm) in length and habitually turns and moves corals, stones, and rocky rubble.

who have lengthy first-hand knowledge of these species. It can be found online at *www.amdareef.com*.

Carrying Capacity

There are many "rules of thumb" regarding how many fish per gallon can safely be kept in an aquarium of a given size. We have found that people, including the experts, see this topic differently, and even those who ought to know better often fall victim to the "just one more pretty /interesting/ must-have fish" syndrome. One recommendation that is quite reasonable, yet far from ironclad, is this: Do not exceed one to two inches of fish (not counting the tail) per 10 gallons of water for reef aquariums, and twice that amount for fish-only systems.

A particular aquarium's biological load is really dependent upon the efficiency of the system's filtration, not just how many gallons of water the aquarium contains. Once the number of fish exceeds the ability of the system to extract or assimilate the waste produced, pollution results.

Regardless of what form that takes—excessive nutrient levels, low oxygen content, or rampant algae growth—fish can become stressed and sessile invertebrates such as corals will also suffer and become smothered in algal overgrowth.

Because there's no easy rule about carrying capacity, factors such as how dependent the system is upon its live rock and sand bed for biological filtration, and the efficiency of its circulation, waste removal, and skimmer, must be taken into consideration. And animal waste directly affects the filtering capacity of the system, so cleanliness and detritus removal is important, as are periodic partial water changes.

The word "overcrowding" is widely used; however, its symptoms are infrequently recognized, as is the actual overcrowding. The assumption that there is always room for one more fish has been the downfall of many hobbyists.

Persistent traces of ammonia, rising levels of nitrate, yellowing of the bulk water, development of cyanobacteria mats along with loss of colors and appetite in some fish, and the worst case scenario, devastating disease outbreaks, are sure signs that the system as a whole needs more attention. The solution may be better general maintenance, water changes, use of activated carbon, increasing the skimming capacity, and vacuuming the sand bed. If it's overcrowding, that should be quite evident and easy to rectify.

Although heavily stocked, David Saxby's reef aquarium has the volume (over 3,000 gallons, including a 1,500 gallon sump) and a world-class array of filtration equipment and circulation devices to make it all feasible. Overcrowding is most often a factor in smaller systems, but some species can become large and problematic even in very large aquariums.

Coral reef in the Maldives, nature's model for a healthy marine aquarium: pristine water, constant temperatures, steady salinity, regular light patterns and low to zero dissolved nutrient levels.

Water: The Font of Good Health

Creating and maintaining the right aquatic environment for your marine aquarium fishes

Considering that their bodies are about 80 percent water and in places separated from the surrounding seawater only by a thin, permeable membrane, it should be evident that the well-being of marine fishes is greatly influenced by the quality of the water that envelops them.

Environmental Factors

In a marine aquarium, disease does not just happen, nor does it drift in on a breeze. Pathogens typically enter when a new fish, live rock, water, or other matter from another aquarium is introduced.

However, certain environmental conditions can contribute to animal losses, allowing disease to break out in a tank even when no new sources of pathogens have been introduced. For fishes and many of the invertebrates we strive to maintain, factors that need to be watched include temperature, lighting, water flow/oxygenation, biological filtration, organic loading, and a number of other measures of water quality.

Lack of attention to these husbandry and maintenance basics can set the stage for two hazards that reduce or end the life span of fish: New Tank Syndrome and Toxic Tank Syndrome. In each of these conditions,

7 Key Targets for Water Quality

Temperature: 74–80°F (24–27°C)
Dissolved Oxygen: ~ 6.0 ppm
Specific Gravity: 1.023–1.025
pH: 8.1–8.2
Ammonium/Ammonia: 0 ppm
Nitrite: 0 ppm
Nitrate (reef): 2.0–5.0 ppm
Nitrate (fish-only): 5.0–20.0 ppm

Aerial view of the Great Barrier Reef, central Queensland, Australia, with deep blue ocean offshore providing daily flushing of clean, oxygenated water in the form of waves and tides.

fish colors fade, body film or fungus may develop, respiration increases, appetite dwindles, and fish may hide most of the time. Death usually occurs within a short time. In both cases, treatment consists of improving water chemistry along with physical factors—adjusting temperature and/or water flow, reducing bioload, and correcting inadequate biological filtration.

A good way to begin looking at these environmental factors is to start with the fishes' ability to regulate the amount of dissolved salts inside their bodies.

Osmoregulation

The quantity of dissolved salts in the water that surrounds marine fishes is of extreme importance because their internal salinity is lower than that of the surrounding seawater. That's because marine fishes constantly take in seawater and purge salt via specialized active-transport cells in their gills. As an interesting side note, the opposite is basically true for freshwater fishes, as they retain the very low levels of salts found in freshwater and internally store it in

"Marine fishes constantly take in seawater and purge salt via specialized active-transport cells in their gills... If the salinity gets too high or low, the marine animal may become stressed or may not survive."

their kidneys. The higher the surrounding salt content, the harder marine fishes have to work to expel excess salts. If salinity (measured as specific gravity) is too high or low, the marine animal may become stressed or may not survive. Curiously, elasmobranch fishes (sharks and rays) have a more efficient osmoregulatory system than do teleost (bony) fishes because the osmotic gradient between seawater and blood is less for these animals.

To ensure the health of our marine bony fishes it is important to maintain the correct specific gravity of their environment. The specific gravity of natural seawater (NSW) is about 1.025. If you're maintaining a fish-only aquarium,

you may choose to keep the level somewhat lower, between 1.0175 and 1.020, reducing energy requirements while purging excess internal salts, reducing stress, and helping to reduce the level of aquarium parasites. In addition, the water will contain slightly more oxygen.

However, where reef aquaria are concerned, staying in the range of 1.023–1.025 is recommended because corals and invertebrates cannot regulate their osmosis as fish do.

Keep in mind that the salinity found in the oceans worldwide varies very little, with most areas ranging between 1.023 and 1.027.

Respiration

Most of us are probably aware of the importance of oxygen (O_2), a simple molecule containing two atoms of oxygen. Without it, almost all life ceases. (Exceptions include anaerobic bacteria.) About 21 percent of the air we breathe is composed of oxygen. It is an exceedingly important factor in our well-being and that of the inhabitants of our aquariums. And even though 21 percent of the air around us is composed of oxygen, even well-oxygenated water has a scant 3 percent oxygen content. More active and larger fish species require a greater share of the dissolved oxygen. And because water is 800 times denser than air, more energy in the form of adenosine triphosphate (ATP) is required to move it across the gills than it takes to move air across the lungs in humans.

A successful reef aquarium with a profusion of life forms depends heavily on excellent circulation to keep the dissolved oxygen level near saturation, or approximately 6.0 ppm, as it is on shallow reefs in the wild.

Once oxygen concentration in a tank falls below the optimum level, it affects growth, reproduction, and other functions, making our aquatic animals far more susceptible to various diseases. Should dissolved oxygen drop to insufficient levels, fish will suffer from hypoxia, gasping at the surface while their hearts beat slowly to conserve energy. If conditions don't improve, carbon dioxide poisoning results and the fish will slip into a coma, losing equilibrium and dying, typically with flared opercula (gill openings) and gaping mouths.

The hemoglobin in blood collects oxygen—from either the lungs of humans or the gills of fish—and delivers it to various parts of the body. This same hemoglobin then collects carbon dioxide and carries it back to the lungs or gills to be exchanged for life-giving oxygen. Since the blood flowing into the gills has a lower level of oxygen than that of the surrounding water, the oxygen in the water diffuses into the blood to correct the imbalance. And since the flow of blood is countercurrent to the water flowing over the gills, it enhances the process of carbon dioxide removal, which allows a fish to remove the majority of the oxygen from the water it pumps over its gills.

To maintain marine aquatic animals in the best condition possible, the hobbyist should strive to maintain dissolved oxygen at or close to saturation. Depending upon temperature and density (freshwater can hold slightly larger quantities of dissolved oxygen due to its lower salt content), water can only hold a relatively small amount of oxygen, as already noted. When water reaches the maximum amount of oxygen it can hold under normal circumstances, it is called "saturated." Under some special conditions, e.g., in waves breaking over exposed surfaces, with extreme agitation, or in pressurized reactors, water will briefly contain a greater amount of oxygen than normal, a condition referred to as "supersaturation."

In the wild, especially around coral reefs, the amount of dissolved oxygen is approximately 6.0 ppm. A correctly engineered and maintained trickle filter is a very good way to boost bulk water oxygen levels for fish-only systems, but generates too much nitrate for reef tanks. Protein skimmers are excellent oxygenators, while airstones and powerheads located at different levels in the aquarium help bring water to the surface where gaseous exchange (oxygenation) can occur. Also, keeping substrate and mechanical filter media clean will help reduce the demand for dissolved oxygen.

The use of quality lighting combined with macroalgae will help in some instances to remove some pollutants and add oxygen to the bulk water, if properly maintained. Overcrowding and/or overfeeding strain a system's ability to keep oxygen adequately replenished. Undergravel filters, which are fast disappearing from the marine hobby, remove oxygen from the water but fail to adequately replace it. In fact, many undergravel systems cause the aquarium to operate at about 5 ppm oxygen or less, and at this level some animals begin to experience mild stress. At levels below 5 ppm, stress will greatly increase and other harmful conditions, such as stunted growth and poor digestion, may result.

We consider the minimum acceptable oxygen level in aquariums to be no more than 1.0 ppm below saturation at its present temperature and specific gravity. Keep in mind that water holds a far greater amount of carbon dioxide than oxygen; therefore, its surface area is an ideal place for a gas exchange, i.e., ridding the water of its free carbon dioxide while gaining some free oxygen by simple diffusion as a result of differing partial pressures.

Those hobbyists who close off the surface area with glass or solid plastic covers are reducing the natural gas exchange. A solid cover greatly limits an aquarium's ability to make up for oxygen consumed in the various ongoing biological and chemical processes. Another practice that limits gas exchange is failing to use a protein skimmer or surface overflow to extract water for filtration. A simple, inexpensive surface overflow will consistently remove the thin film of organic contaminants (surfactants) that gathers on the water's surface and creates surface tension, thereby blocking gas exchange.

Maintaining a high level of dissolved oxygen will reduce stress levels and go a long way toward preventing viruses and parasites. Good oxygenation should never be taken for granted, especially since it is a fairly simple matter to analyze aquarium water for its oxygen content. Bottom line: It's a small price to pay when you have a large invest-

Kill Your Undergravel Filter:

Once popular among beginning saltwater aquarists, undergravel filters are fast becoming obsolete in the marine aquarium world. They tend to accumulate waste and deplete the oxygen content of a system, stressing the inhabitants.

ment in the aquarium. We don't usually suggest testing the dissolved oxygen content in a fairly new setup, but as the bioload increases and once the aquarium begins to mature, we suggest testing at least once every month. Knowing that the level of this important element is correct, both you and your aquatic friends will breathe a lot easier.

Again, the best tools for ensuring high oxygen content are aggressive water circulation, including keeping the surface agitated; protein skimming; moving water to external filters via surface skimming; use of trickle filters or a sump where water and air can actively mix; and not using tight-fitting solid covers. (Porous plastic or eggcrate is preferred, and will keep fish from jumping while allowing gas exchange.)

Water Chemistry

The global cycling of water (otherwise known as the biogeochemical cycle), starts at the ocean's surface where water evaporates into the atmosphere. Some time later, water vapor falls back to earth in the form of rain, snow, fog, or other precipitation, and that water eventually returns to the sea carrying various minerals and salts that it has absorbed along the way. For this reason and others, water has been described as the "universal solvent." It has been said that "fish never see the same drop of water twice," and this is largely due to the earth's cycling of water between sea, atmosphere, land, and bodies of fresh water.

The elements in seawater, and what many refer to as its saltiness, primarily come from two sources: dissolved ions/ matter in the returning runoff from land masses, and deep volcanic activity along the edges of mid-ocean tectonic

Marine biologist J.R. Kerfoot uses a handheld refractometer to measure salinity in a large Florida Institute of Technology rearing tank.

plates. These elements fall into three groups: major, minor, and trace elements. Major elements include those present at concentrations over 100 ppm, and include chloride, sodium, sulfate, magnesium, calcium, and potassium. Minor elements are present at concentrations of 1–100 ppm, and include bromine, strontium, boron, and fluoride. Trace elements are present at concentrations of less than 1 ppm, and include iodine, iron, lithium, molybdenum, nitrogen, phosphorus, rubidium, and zinc, to name just a few.

Natural Seawater

Natural seawater (NSW) represents about 95 percent of all water on earth, and its chemistry, both in the oceans and in aquariums, is complex. In the oceans, seawater contains almost every chemical element known to man. Nevertheless, many are of no known importance to the long-term health of aquarium inhabitants.

Aquarists who live near a supply of natural seawater and have the means to collect it are incredibly lucky. Freshly collected seawater can be used in the aquarium in place of synthetic salt mixes if introduced into the system within about 12 hours of collecting. If that's not possible, precautions need be taken, as seawater can quickly become toxic due to the potentially rapid die-off of its plankton. Freshly collected seawater may look perfectly clear, but it actually teems with microscopic organisms. These tiny organisms, animals, and plant wanderers, commonly called plankton, will die when their oxygen or food supply, usually each other, is consumed. The result can be a toxic, ammonia-laden soup.

If freshly collected seawater cannot be used quickly, it can be stored in sealed plastic or glass containers in a dark area for up to two weeks. Keeping it in darkness simply prevents unwanted algae growth. Prior to using the water in a tank, add one bottlecap full of regular household bleach to 50 gallons of freshly collected seawater and aerate for two days. Turn off the air pump and let the water settle for a day. Vacuum the sediment from the bottom of the container. Aerate again for one day and/or until no smell of bleach remains or use a dechlorinator, such as sodium thiosulfate, to be able to use the water immediately.

Try to collect natural seawater away from inshore areas where sewage, fertilizer, insecticides, heavy metals, and other pollutants tend to collect.

Synthetic Seawater

Most of us are not fortunate enough to be able to collect NSW and must rely on dry salt mixes. In the late 1970s and early 1980s, some salt mixes appeared to be deficient in some of the more important elements. Long-term success during that time was a questionable matter, especially where some invertebrates were concerned.

Many companies have made major improvements to their mixes over the past couple of decades. Some salt mixes are prepared especially for reef type aquariums and contain levels of calcium above that found in NSW.

Bear in mind, however, that higher than NSW calcium content in salt mixes may result in a white, snow-like precipitate of calcium carbonate in the mixing container when mixed with tapwater already high in minerals. Fortunately, though, the precipitate is harmless and there is no need to remove it from the mixing container or even be concerned if it enters the aquarium.

No two salt mixes are exactly the same, and we don't know of any brand that would not suffice for the average aquarium. For reef aquariums, the differences between brands may be more significant. Most importantly, make sure the mix contains sufficient amounts of the major elements, such as magnesium and calcium, and the trace elements. We suggest occasionally testing newly prepared batches of synthetic seawater for calcium, magnesium, and ammonia levels before use. At a NSW salinity of 1.025–1.026, the calcium level should be approximately 400 ppm and the magnesium level near 1280 ppm. No ammonia should be detected; if it is, the solution should be aerated until it dissipates.

Selecting a salt mix can be somewhat confusing these days, as there are lots of claims to decipher. Bear in mind that it is not just a simple matter of mixing a dry salt mix with freshwater to have the perfect seawater for your aquarium. Unless you have a laboratory at your disposal, the condition of your fauna and flora is probably the best indicator of the suitability of the water. Ideally, freshwater should be aerated overnight before adding salt and then for at least 24 hours before use.

Every once in a while someone asks if they can use the natural salts that remain from evaporated seawater and simply rehydrate them for the marine aquarium. Theoretically that should suffice, if all the elements that were in a given volume of seawater were rehydrated. However, that usually does not happen without a lot of care and testing to

Commercial synthetic salt, both dry and in liquid form, along with ever-growing arrays of chemical amendments and supplements to replicate the composition of natural seawater, are available from most retail fish suppliers.

Aquaculture researcher Zan Didoha uses a simple hobbyist test kit to get a pH reading from a water sample. pH is one of the essential measures of water quality in a marine aquarium, with most systems tending to become more acidic if wastes are allowed to accumulate and water changes are insufficient.

assure that all necessary elements exist in the correct portions before they are rehydrated.

One should keep in mind that salts tend to fall out in layers as pure water evaporates. When the dried salts are collected, especially over large areas, the material gathered may contain elements in amounts disproportionate to those found in the original ocean water. Reconstituting that selection of salts simply leads to seawater that is deficient or excessive in some elements. Also, due to coprecipitation, some compounds, especially metals, will no longer entirely dissolve. It is possible to find salt mixes formulated from dried or concentrated seawater, and some aquarists believe this approach provides a superior balance of components, including the many trace elements in natural seawater.

Salt Content

Two common methods are used in measuring just how much "saltiness" is in seawater: salinity and specific gravity. Other methods, such as refractiveness and chlorinity, are outside the realm of testing for most aquarists.

SALINITY The total amount of dissolved solids in seawater, of which 98 percent is sodium chloride, is referred to as salinity. It is measured in parts per thousand (ppt), and on average, natural seawater contains 35 ppt. Parts per thousand equal the total amount of solid matter in grams (g) contained in one kilogram (kg) of seawater. One gram per kilogram equals one part per thousand, since there are 1,000 grams in a single kilogram. Therefore, since seawater is 35 g/kg, it equals 35 ppt. You may also see ppt expressed as 0/00. Salinity is the proper unit to use when measuring the salt content in natural seawater in the wild.

SPECIFIC GRAVITY Specific gravity (SG) is the measurement used by most home aquarists, and it refers to the weight of dissolved solids in seawater. If we weighed one liter of seawater and one of distilled water, we would find the seawater to be slightly heavier. In fact, if we slowly poured seawater into a container of distilled water and were able to keep it from mixing, the seawater would sink to the bottom. The fresh water would stay on top, like oil floating on the surface of water. This phenomenon is what causes underground fresh water to sit on top of salt water (known as a lens) in the aquifers of some areas in Florida, for example.

The more dissolved salts in water, the higher its density, or SG. Distilled water has a SG of 1.000 since it contains no dissolved salts. NSW has an SG of approximately 1.025, depending somewhat on where in the world it's sampled, but most reef areas are very close to this level. Because the density of seawater varies with temperature, it was necessary, many years ago, to take a reading on a test instru-

❗ Inaccurate Hydrometers:

Beware of very cheap, small floating glass hydrometers that often give highly inaccurate readings. Invest in a good floating-arm hydrometer or, better yet, a refractometer.

ment called a hydrometer and then cross-reference it with a temperature chart to determine correct specific gravity. Nowadays, the old-fashioned glass floating hydrometers are generally considered passé.

Safe and easy-to-use pre-calibrated plastic swing-arm hydrometers have become the choice of most aquarists. For most reef aquariums we prefer a SG of 1.023–1.025.

Most hobbyists measure the salt content of seawater as specific gravity, using an affordable plastic hydrometer with a floating arm. A more expensive handheld refractometer, rear, measures salinity or SG with greater accuracy.

Sometimes a slightly higher SG may be kept, particularly if Red Sea species are being maintained, and 1.026–1.027 should be considered.

Specific gravity is the proper term to use when one measures the salt content in aquariums, especially when one is using artificially mixed seawater.

Because the terms salinity and specific gravity are both used by aquarists, there is a formula for converting salinity to SG. Simply multiply the salinity by .0008 and then add 1.0. To convert SG to salinity, subtract 1.0, then multiply by 1250 (e.g. SG 1.026 - 1 = .026 X 1250 = 32.5 salinity).

TESTING SPECIFIC GRAVITY There are two common utensils used for testing SG: the floating glass hydrometer or the more convenient clear, plastic box-like hydrometer. If you choose to use a floating glass hydrometer, don't put it directly in the aquarium, as it is fragile and is meant to be used with a protective clear cylinder. Also, a low-cost floating hydrometer can render a very inaccurate reading. Plastic floating-arm hydrometers are quite accurate and are not expensive.

A third type of hydrometer, called a refractometer, is a small, handheld, telescope-like device that is much more

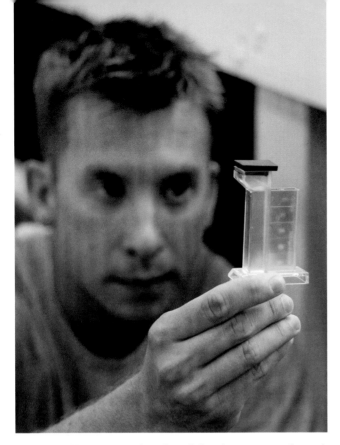

Affordable hobbyist water test kits allow side-by-side comparisons of treated sample water with graduated transparent color chips to obtain readings.

costly (about 10 times) than a plastic hydrometer. Nevertheless, it's an extremely accurate device and, if it fits your budget, well worth owning.

No matter what instrument is used, it should be rinsed in freshwater after each use so that salt residue will not interfere with the next measurement.

pH

Our marine fish have evolved in very stable alkaline waters and are called "alkalophiles." In contrast, most freshwater fishes come from neutral to slightly acidic waters.

pH stands for the phrase "pondus hydrogenii," or weight of potential hydrogen ions, and is measured on a logarithmic scale from 1 to 14. By definition, pH is the negative logarithm of the concentration of hydrogen ions. Water with an equal number of hydrogen and hydroxyl

ions is rated at 7 and considered neutral. Anything below 7.0 (more hydrogen ions) is an acidic condition, and anything over 7.0 (fewer hydrogen ions) is an alkaline condition. As ammonia is oxidized and reduced to nitrite ($NH_3 - NO_2$), three hydrogen atoms are released into solution. This normal process is what causes the natural attrition of pH. The tendency in marine aquariums is for the pH to drop unless corrective measures are in place to keep the system alkaline.

In the wild, we have recorded pH levels as high as 8.9 in tide pools along the Mexican coastline. In marine aquariums, we have heard reports of readings as low as 7.4 and up to 8.7.

The more acceptable pH range for marine systems is somewhere between 7.9 and 8.6, with 8.1–8.2 the ideal range as it is in natural seawater on most coral reefs. Keep in mind that the metabolisms of the organisms generally kept in aquariums have adapted to the NSW range over millions of years. Those organisms that can survive in tide pools have adapted to wider temperature and pH ranges, but the same is not true for most of the specimens kept by aquarists. Therefore, either very low or very high pH levels can easily stress most aquarium species. Furthermore, the change or swing in pH range per day in closed systems should be no more than 0.2–0.3 units up or down.

The tendency is for an established aquarium to grow more acidic over time, and this is generally corrected by regular water changes and the use of inexpensive buffers. There are many products on the market that can assist one in maintaining a proper pH range, and their instructions should be followed closely. Test pH weekly, once in the early morning and again after the system has been well lit for a few hours. It's best to test your pH sample immediately after removal from the aquarium. Transporting an aquarium water sample to a local store for a pH test may result in an inaccurate reading.

Ammonium/Ammonia

It's a little-known fact that ammonia is probably the number one fish killer. (And you thought it was people.) Am-

Testing kits and devices from a number of manufacturers and suited to different budget levels are available from all good aquarium retailers. At minimum, the marine hobbyist will test specific gravity, pH, ammonia, nitrite, and nitrate. Reef aquarists also need to keep track of calcium, alkalinity, and phosphate.

monia can burn delicate tissue and result in permanent gill damage. Here are some health consequences of exposure to ammonia:

- Internal organs can be damaged
- Blood vessels can hemorrhage
- Eyes can be burned or scarred
- Stress levels can increase
- Nerves can be damaged
- The production of protective fish slime can shut down

Possible signs of excess ammonia include rapid breathing or unnatural darting around the aquarium. Compounding the problem, fish cannot excrete their own waste if the am-

monia level in the surrounding water is higher than that of the waste they need to void. This is a serious problem, since fish excrete upwards of 95 percent of their waste through the gills. These are all good reasons to occasionally monitor ammonia, and to better understand its effects on fish.

When this compound is discussed, we are generally referring to total ammonia or the sum of free ammonia (NH_3) and ammonium (NH_4), both in solution at the same time. The less dangerous ammonium ion is more commonplace at or near a neutral pH. Yet, as pH rises above neutral, ammonium is quickly converted to the more toxic free ammonia. In fact, the toxicity of free ammonia increases about

A healthy 180-gallon reef aquarium set up by coauthor Bob Goemans using a modified Berlin Method approach for maintaining high water quality: strong circulation, protein skimming, live rock and live sand for biological filtration, metal halide lighting, and judicious stocking of reef-safe fish species.

tenfold when pH rises from 7.0 to 8.0. Between a pH of 8.0 and 8.3 it can increase another tenfold, depending somewhat on temperature and SG. Therefore, the toxicity of ammonia is directly proportional to pH.

Whether in new or well-established aquariums that may have ammonium present, it's wise not to deliberately raise pH more than 0.1–0.2 units per day, as pH affects ammonia equilibrium much more than temperature and SG levels do. Users of kalkwasser, which can raise pH rapidly, should carefully consider this if they are not using carbon dioxide injection equipment to lessen its pH impact.

Here are some common ammonia sources and situations that can generate it:

- Most ammonia comes from animal waste products when they are released into aquarium water. Remaining ammonia content comes from the microbial decomposition of organic matter. Having an adequate biological filter that is correctly sized for the existing bioload will go a long way toward keeping free ammonia at very low levels, even in the pH 8.1–8.4 range that many hobbyists strive to maintain.

- If the local water company adds chloramine to your tapwater (call them to find out), you'll need to remove this source of ammonia before adding it to the aquarium. The chloramine compound is much more difficult to remove than simple chlorine, as it is strongly bonded to the chlorine. Chloramine removers are available from aquarium suppliers.

- Overfeeding, including excessive use of invertebrate foods, can cause ammonia spikes even in well-established aquariums. In newly set up aquariums the danger is even higher because bacteria may not have had time to become sufficiently established. In either situation fish can become stressed and may cease to produce sufficient body slime. They then become easy prey for parasites such as *Amyloodinium* (marine velvet) or *Cryptocaryon* (marine ich).

- The uninformed homemaker can create a source of instant ammonia in the aquarium. This is the person who goes around the home using an ammonia-based spray cleaner, happily cleaning all windows, counters, and every pane of glass in sight. Ammonia-based household cleaners contain free ammonia. Any aquarium in close proximity can directly absorb the vapor from these sprays. Forewarned is forearmed.

- Medications can greatly reduce the efficiency of biological filtration. They destroy or inhibit bacteria and

Some hobbyists abandon basic testing for ammonia and nitrite after their tanks have become established, but these tests are useful in assessing a number of different potential problems.

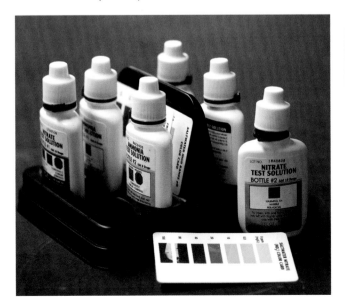

this can trigger a rise in the ammonia level. If your tests reveal any level of ammonia, the safest thing to do is refrain from adding any further bioload to the system until the source of the ammonia has been found and removed or rectified.

AMMONIA TESTING RECOMMENDATIONS

- Test during start-up of the new system and prior to adding its first fish and/or invertebrates
- Test prior to and after adding to the bioload, including the addition of live rock (whether cured or not)
- Test the freshwater used for a water change or evaporation make-up
- Test newly prepared seawater, as some salt mixes generate ammonia
- Test the aquarium prior to water changes, especially if a change has not been performed recently
- Test when you notice that an animal has perished or is missing in the aquarium
- Test after adding a medication
- Test after adding to or modifying system equipment
- Test when you notice cloudy water
- Test during power outages
- Test every few months, even in a well-established, stable aquarium

Ammonia: The Smoking Gun:

Any sign of ammonia in a well-established aquarium is like smoke rising from a forest. Where there's smoke, there's fire.

Just what level of ammonia is lethal is a tricky question. It seems that tolerance levels differ greatly among different organisms and species. Nevertheless it is safe to say that any detectable level of ammonia should be cause for concern. A level of 0.1 ppm can be deadly for some animals, while others can withstand up to 0.6 ppm or higher. However, none can continue for long without some kind of damage or health consequences. Keep in mind that any sign of ammonia in a well-established aquarium is like smoke rising above the forest. Where there's smoke, there's fire. Where there is fire, there's danger.

Nitrite

Once ammonia becomes oxidized, it forms a compound called nitrite (NO_2). Nitrite is sometimes believed to be as toxic as ammonia, but this is not the case. The confusion comes about because high levels of nitrite naturally follow high levels of ammonia in newly started aquariums. Because the damage done to fish during the accumulation of ammonia doesn't show until the nitrite portion of the nitrification cycle, the common and understandable viewpoint was that nitrite is also a very toxic substance.

Fish take in nitrite through chloride cells located in the gills, and since there is an abundance of chloride ions present in saltwater, and because chloride cells have a preference for chloride, the uptake of nitrite in fish is blocked. On the other hand, nitrite is highly toxic to corals and invertebrates. Nevertheless, high levels of nitrite in the blood stream can oxidize hemoglobin, causing the formation of methemoglobin. This compound colors the blood chocolaty-brown and makes it unable to carry oxygen. Methylene blue is a first-aid remedy in such situations and can help with oxygenation. The discovery of a nitrite reading in an established aquarium is an important indicator that an ammonia source is or was present. Any nitrite level should be a signal for further investigation.

As with ammonia, nitrogen is usually the product of the digestion or decomposition of protein. In closed sys-

A fat and healthy breeding pair of Shortfin Lionfish (*Dendrochirus brachypterus*): Predatory fishes with big appetites can place considerable pressure on the filtration system of the aquarium, and the aquarist will need to ensure that all highly toxic ammonia is being effectively converted into nitrate.

tems and elsewhere, the nitrogen element is constantly distributed via the animals' waste products. If it were not for bacteria, the hobbyist would have to perform almost daily water changes to keep fish from creating an environment where they would soon perish in their own toxic waste compounds. Fortunately both for humans and animals, there are beneficial bacteria that convert these hazardous waste products to less toxic compounds through the chemical principal of oxidation/reduction. These bacteria allow us to keep fish in captivity safely.

Most aquarists are familiar with the high nitrite spike during start-up of a new tank, but what about conditions in established aquariums that result in minor nitrite readings? Possible causes to consider:

- An inadequately sized biological filter or improper water flow (usually too fast) through biological filtration media can result in a system that never seems to fully complete the nitrification cycle. As a rule of thumb, there should be a flow equal to a turnover rate of four to six times the volume of the system water per hour through a biological filter, such as a wet/dry filter. If poor water flow is not the problem, the amount or type of biomedia may not be sufficient for the bioload in the system. This type of situation can occur in some of the hang-on-the-side filter units where the area for biomedia is extremely limited. If testing shows either ammonia or nitrite in your system, a larger biological filter (or more live rock) may be needed.

- Overfeeding can cause temporary spikes in ammonia levels. Overabundance of food from a too-generous hobbyist can lead to poorly metabolized waste products that contribute to poor water quality. Understand the nutritional needs of your animals, then meet those needs, but do not exceed them.

- In systems that use denitrification devices, water tests may show slight levels of nitrite. This is generally caused by an incorrect water flow rate through the device. Sometimes, such devices have been known to revert nitrate back to nitrite. Reread the instructions and adjust according to manufacturer recommendations.

- Increases to the bioload, dead or dying animals, and

Target Zero:

Any sign of nitrite in a marine aquarium is an indication that there is a source of ammonia and insufficient biological filtration. The safe target for nitrite is zero.

....

medications can contribute to the causes that bring about ammonia, which then leads to nitrite. If experiencing any levels of nitrite, do not add any further bioload until the source of the problem is resolved.

As for testing, once a day is sufficient during start-up. After the aquarium has been conditioned, normal maintenance should include occasional nitrite testing—at least once per month. A low level of nitrite, e.g., 0.1 ppm, can indicate problems as noted above and should get your attention. Zero nitrite should be your target.

Nitrate

Few hobbyists were concerned about nitrate (NO_3) levels in the early days of the marine aquarium hobby. Fish-only aquariums, some with levels of well over 100 ppm, were considered within normal bounds, as fish did not seem to be affected. Some fishes, such as lionfish, damsels, triggers, and moray eels, could withstand extremely high levels of nitrate without exhibiting even the slightest sign of discomfort. Nitrate seemed harmless.

As more scientific evidence became available, concentrations as low as 20 ppm were reported to cause high mortality rates in certain types of fish fry or their eggs. Other articles pointed towards levels of nitrate between 30 and 100 ppm affecting the respiration of some invertebrates. Yet, there is still very little well-defined scientific data on how nitrate affects the species hobbyists keep in their aquariums.

Nevertheless, once the interest in reef aquariums began in the mid 1980s, nitrate became a compound of major interest. Reefkeepers became aware that excessive levels of this compound could stress delicate fishes and prize invertebrate specimens, and/or help generate unwanted forms of algae. Most current information indicates that we should keep nitrate in the reef aquarium at a much lower level than

Protein skimming or foam fractionation is a filtration method of choice for most marine aquarists today. Skimmate waiting to be cleaned out and discarded, above, represents dissolved organic matter extracted from apparently clear aquarium water. Too much skimming is seldom a problem, although the towering skimmer shown right at the Interzoo trade show in Germany is best suited to a commercial-sized facility or huge tank.

we would allow in a fish-only aquarium. Recommendations vary, but a reasonable rule of thumb is to keep nitrate from exceeding 5.0 ppm in the reef aquarium.

We recommend that a newly set up aquarium be tested prior to stocking. If the nitrate level is found to be higher than 5.0 ppm, a major water change should be considered. When adding to existing bioload, we suggest testing once a week. After the bioload is steady, monthly tests will tell if general maintenance needs to be improved.

As for controlling/reducing nitrate accumulations, there are several approaches:

• A heavy growth of macroalgae is sometimes helpful in keeping the nitrate level low. Algae will act as a sponge and absorb nitrate, then as a reservoir to contain it. When you harvest the macroalgae you are exporting nitrate from the system. The use of lighted refugiums to culture macroalgae is ideal for this.

• If tapwater is going to be used for water changes or evaporation makeup, it can be a source of nitrate. Using reverse osmosis or ion exchange resins to treat freshwater is a good idea, and almost essential for reefkeepers. Reverse osmosis units will remove about 90 percent of the nitrate present in tapwater. Removing as much nitrate and other nutrients as possible from tapwater before it is used in the aquarium simply makes sense.

• Equipment is available that can accomplish the removal of nitrate directly from aquarium water. Most are small biological filter systems that use special additives to promote a biological denitrification process, while others may use small electrical currents or oxygen starvation methods. They are somewhat beneficial, yet maintenance intensive.

- Overfeeding and overcrowding contribute greatly to nitrate accumulation. The greater the number of fish, the more food is fed, and of course the more waste products are generated. This is probably the initial cause of high nitrate levels in most aquariums, and the remedy is clear.

- The excessive use of protein-based foods could quickly add up to a nitrate problem. Pay special attention to your animal's nutritional needs and feed a variety of foodstuffs that contain the proper levels of protein.

- Collecting the foam that flows into the collection cup of a protein skimmer removes organic matter before nitrifying bacteria can break it down into nitrate (prior to mineralization and deamination.) Without a doubt the protein skimmer is one of your most important pieces of equipment, both for fish-only and reef aquariums.

- The quality of salt mixes is much better these days than in times past. However, do check a low-cost or new brand before using it to be sure it is not a nitrate source.

- Water changes are fine for the newly set up system where nitrate may be elevated from the initial cycling period. For long-term nitrate control, water changes are not a cost-effective approach. It would simply take massive water changes on a steady basis to keep a serious nitrate problem within an acceptable range. In reef aquariums, nitrate accumulates inside live rock or in the depths of a sand bed. Using water changes to reduce nitrate levels may seem effective the first day, but nitrate will flow out of the rock and sand bed back into the water. Within a day or two the aquarium nitrate level will be almost back to where it was prior to the water change. It's important to get to the root of the problem.

Nitrate Watch:

Once considered harmless, nitrate is now known to fuel blooms of nuisance algae and, at higher concentrations, is suspected of impacting animal health.

To confuse matters, there are two different methods for reading nitrate. Some nitrate test kits measure the nitrate ion and others measure nitrate-nitrogen. Nitrate is a compound, or combination of elements. One molecule of nitrate is composed of one nitrogen atom and three oxygen atoms. Since the atomic weight of nitrogen is 14.01 and the atomic weight of one oxygen atom is 16, the weight of one nitrate molecule equals 62.01, or $14.01+16+16+16$. Therefore, a test kit that reads the nitrate molecule will show a reading 4.4 times higher than a test kit that reads nitrate-nitrogen. Reader letters frequently fail to mention which their kit measures. Even mentioning the brand of test kit would be helpful. When we refer to nitrate levels, it always relates to nitrate-nitrogen unless otherwise noted.

As for NSW, it has very little nitrate: Nitrate-nitrogen = .03 ppm at or near fringing reefs where many of our prize stony corals grow. In and around shoreline areas, nitrate readings rise slightly and certain kinds of invertebrates, such as soft corals, exist without problems. It's unfortunate that there are no specific scientific studies on just what levels of nitrate affect the invertebrates kept in aquariums. But experience is a good teacher and as noted above, we recommend nothing greater than 5 ppm nitrate-nitrogen for the average reef/invertebrate aquarium. For the reef aquarium containing more delicate small-polyp stony (SPS) corals, our goal is less than 2 ppm. In a fish-only system, keeping nitrate below 20 ppm is a good target, and the less the better.

Keep in mind that the level of nitrate is an indicator of overall microbial balance. If the quantity of microbes that normally and effectively use nitrate is equal to or greater than the microbes that produce it, the system has achieved balance through equilibrium. If nitrate accumulates, the aquarist must recognize where the system imbalances are and be willing to correct them. Some are easier than others to correct, but without a good microbial foundation, system adjustments may be expensive and time-consuming. If not adequately resolved, unwanted forms of algae will benefit and flourish.

Finally, it has often been said that nitrate does not have any major impact on fish health, yet there is now some

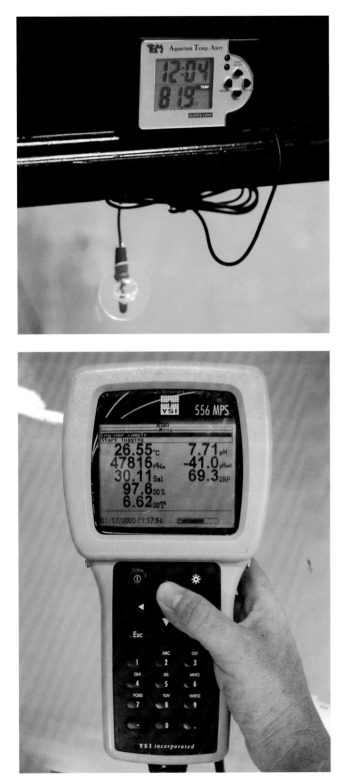

Top: The alert aquarist's best friend: a digital thermometer allows an instant safety check whenever you pass by the aquarium. Bottom: Professional YSI multiparameter digital water testing meter gives simultaneous readings of temperature, conductivity, dissolved oxygen content, pH, ORP, and salinity.

evidence that Yellow Tangs are sensitive to excessive build-ups of the compound, as they have been seen to lose some of their yellow coloration when nitrate levels were far in excess of 20 ppm. Further research is needed, but common sense tells us that fishes will do best in a low-nitrate environment similar to the waters where they live in the wild.

Chlorine/Chloramine

Many water companies are now adding ammonia as well as chlorine to disinfect drinking water. This combination produces chloramine, a very stable substance that is deadly to fish and corals. Chloramine is so stable that aerating the water will not remove it, as it does chlorine. As a background note, it has been found that when chlorine is used to disinfect municipal water, a compound known as trihalomethane (a known carcinogen) is formed, so the trend is to move away from chlorine.

Fortunately, the removal of chloramine is not difficult and can be accomplished by adding a solution of sodium thiosulfate, which is normally sold as a dechlorinator. The dechlorinator should be added to the freshwater before adding a salt mix. Also, the dechlorinator only breaks up the chloramine and removes chlorine, leaving behind the ammonia. One can either use a water conditioner, which is designed to remove both chlorine and ammonia, or simply aerate the solution as needed and test with an ammonia test kit before using. You can also use activated carbon to filter out chloramine, but the filter must be replaced on a timely basis. A properly maintained RO/DI unit will also remove virtually all chloramine from tapwater.

Temperature

The majority of fish and invertebrates we keep in our aquariums come from tropical coral reefs where tempera-

A new reef system in a retail shop: Long-term success in keeping fishes and invertebrates healthy starts withn the deceptively simple-sounding term, "Water Quality" — maintaining all key water parameters within safe bounds.

other metabolic functions. Too-low temperatures slow the animal's activity, which reduces uptake of nutrients and can lead to reduced growth rate or death. Higher than normal temperature actually results in a greater than normal need for food, which generates more waste and leads to a higher pollution level.

Dissolved gases are also affected by temperature. Cool water contains more dissolved oxygen than warm water, which directly affects the respiratory rate of the animals. Equipment like trickle filters, which have a very good air flow through their packing media, will cool the water temperature by one or two degrees by producing a higher than normal evaporation rate. This phenomenon is known as evaporative cooling.

For very short-term high temperature problems, placing ice in a plastic bag and floating it in the aquarium may temporarily resolve the problem, although it is not the ideal solution to an ongoing temperature problem. At higher temperatures, hypoxia can occur, reducing the amount of oxygen available to the fish. This condition can cause fish to die prematurely, and often does.

The long-term solution for high temperature problems is either air conditioning for the room or a chiller for the aquarium. A chiller is initially more expensive than a window A/C and does not provide the same benefits to the aquarium viewer. Electrical costs will be lower for a chiller than for a room air conditioner because there is less area to cool, and temperature control for the aquarium will be more effective.

Over the years, we have noted that when fish experience a rapid or immediate change in temperature of more than 4°F (2.2°C) in either direction, they often develop a disease of some sort (marine ich, or a swim bladder problem) shortly thereafter. There is no doubt that there is a metabolic rate change when the animal experiences a temperature shock, but exactly what internal processes are initiated is unclear.

It should go without saying that one needs to monitor and control temperature. Extreme excursions from the normal range of temperatures, in fact, can lead to the loss of an entire collection of fishes and other livestock. Having an easy-to-read digital aquarium thermometer that allows a quick water temperature check whenever you pass by the aquarium is very good insurance in case a heater or chiller starts to malfunction. More sophisticated temperature alarm systems are also worthy of consideration.

Ozone

Many types and sizes of ozone generators are available to marine aquarists. Their use is advocated as a preventive measure to keep water quality from deteriorating and to kill various pathogens.

The normal molecule of oxygen (O_2) has two atoms, whereas ozone (O_3) has one additional atom. The extra atom is an intense oxidizing agent and highly unstable. It will react chemically and break down or change various organic and inorganic molecules and destroy parasites and bacteria. Flow of ozone is measured in milligrams per hour (mg/h). Ozone has a distinctive aroma, sweet or fresh, similar to that of over-ripe fruit.

The main reason for the use of ozone is to eliminate unwanted dissolved waste products by increasing the system's redox/ORP. Redox means "reduction/oxidation" and applies to a sequence of chemical events in which elements and compounds transfer or rearrange their electrons (oxidation/reduction). Elements and compounds that want to gain an electron are called "reduction agents." Those that want to give up an electron are called "oxidizing agents." The effectiveness of this process is measured by the minute electrical charge it generates in millivolts (mV) with an Oxidation Reduction Potential (ORP) meter.

This process is similar to resistance in electrical wiring: the more resistance, the less flow of electric current. The dirtier the water, the less ability it has to conduct electricity. High quality ocean water, e.g., around outer coral reefs, has an ORP of 350–400 mV. Most of the corals we keep in our aquariums come from lagoon areas where ORP is 200–300 mV.

There are both positive and negative consequences associated with the use of ozone, as shown below.

POSITIVE ATTRIBUTES
- Provides crystal-clear water as it oxidizes suspended matter and dissolved organic material (increases redox readings)
- Oxidizes nitrite
- Oxidizes compounds that would ultimately turn into nitrate
- A small amount of ozone flowing through a protein skimmer changes some organic material into more surface-active compounds, enhancing efficiency
- Reduces microalgae problems
- Kills bacteria and free-swimming parasites in skimmer reaction chamber
- Encourages healing of wounds on both fish and invertebrates by killing bacteria

These are great benefits, but the old saying, "more is better," is definitely not the rule with ozone.

NEGATIVE ATTRIBUTES
- Free ozone, the ozone that you can readily smell in the room, may cause headaches, nausea, depression, and possibly eye disorders in humans
- Too much will kill nitrifying bacteria in filters
- Excessive use can cause severe damage or death to fish and invertebrates
- An excessive dosing rate used in a protein skimmer can greatly reduce effective foam production
- Can reduce the integrity of plastic or rubber products
- Can reduce or eliminate desired macroalgae growth
- Removes valuable trace elements from solution
- Cannot be used in conjunction with medications

Redox Readings

ORP	WATER QUALITY
<100 mV	Very Poor
100 - 200 mV	Poor
200 - 300 mV	Good
300 - 400 mV	Very Good
400 - 450 mV	Excellent
>450 mV	Risky

Ozone generators can help raise water quality by eliminating dissolved wastes. Success is monitored with an ORP meter reading in millivolts.

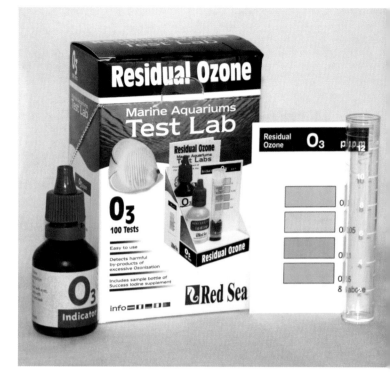

Using ozone safely is best done with a controller, top left, that switches the generator on and off to maintain a set ORP level. An air dryer, left, uses silica beads to condiiton air before it enters the ozonizer. A residual ozone test kit, above right, is used to ensure that ozone levels are safe.

Ozone also reacts with chloride and bromide ions in seawater and results in hypobromus acid. Therefore, the use of bromide is limited in some salt mixes to reduce this possibility.

When ozone is produced in areas of high humidity, the air flowing to the ozone-producing device should first pass through an air dryer, as moist air greatly reduces ozone production. Furthermore, ozone-safe tubing should be used between the device and the entrance to a dispersal device, often a protein skimmer. Bear in mind that the effluent from an ozone contact chamber must be passed over a bed of activated carbon to remove residual ozone before it returns to the aquarium. Even though residual ozone is fairly short-lived, usually less than an hour, it can damage fish tissue and invertebrates.

Various manufacturers make ozone test kits for those who want to test for residual ozone in the flow before and after the carbon bed. Properly controlled and metered amounts of ozone should not normally present any problems to fish and invertebrates.

Depending upon goals and maintenance practices, it is very possible to get by without the use of ozone. Before turning to its use, you can increase dissolved oxygen in the aquarium by increasing water circulation, reducing bioload, trying a more efficient protein skimmer, removing any tight or solid aquarium covers, placing some airstones under the trickle section of a trickle filter (if so equipped), and/or increasing the general level of maintenance. One could consider ozone use as something like an insurance policy—nice to have, but something you hope never to have to depend upon.

Ultraviolet Sterilization

The word "ultraviolet" (UV) is actually a description of the light wavelength found just below the visible portion of the spectrum, i.e., between the blue violet and x-ray wavelengths. This short 253.7 nanometer (nm) wavelength is very effective in destroying most free-floating bacteria, viruses, fungi, mold, microalgae and very small protozoans, providing the proper exposure is achieved. Correct dosage of this wavelength can break the DNA chain in some organisms, thereby preventing reproduction. It is also very effective in killing bacteria such as *E. coli* (*Escherichia coli*) in drinking water and is now being used to make various table meats safer for humans to eat. Typically, there is no harm to fishes in the aquarium or the chemistry of its seawater. However, UV radiation can alter or change the chemical structure or nature of some medications, and therefore, many manufacturers of medications recommend turning off your UV sterilizer during treatment.

UV energy is measured in microwatt seconds per square centimeter ($\mu W/cm^2$), with 15,000 $\mu W/cm^2$ considered

Watch Your Eyes:
Ultraviolet light can be very harmful to the eye. Never look directly at an unshielded UV bulb and be sure to use only a well-maintained and properly sealed sterilizer unit.

minimum for algae, bacteria, and viruses, and 35,000 $\mu W/cm^2$ considered minimum for effective destruction of larger protozoans. Although many bacteria and viruses are effectively killed at 15,000 $\mu W/cm^2$, some will require between 20 and 25,000 $\mu W/cm^2$. Higher concentration, 90,000 $\mu W/cm^2$ will eradicate most protozoans, since that level of concentration prevents replication of the parasites.

UV light, even at a distance from the lamp, can also have a detrimental effect on the human eye. Therefore, never look at a lit UV lamp. A blue light coming from the lamp does not mean it is operating correctly, as UV is invisible to the human eye. Since the effective distance of the organism-destroying wavelength from its source is extremely short, about one inch (2.5 cm), the water containing these organisms must flow very close to the surface of the lamp. UV sterilizers are fairly simple devices that consist mainly of a tube that encloses a germicidal lamp. Some units utilize a quartz or very thin glass sleeve to enclose the lamp and provide better lamp operating temperature, i.e., 104°F (40°C). The sleeve keeps water from contacting the lamp, which prevents bio-fouling of the lamp, making this aspect of lamp maintenance unnecessary. Having a sleeve does increase the unit cost, especially if it's a "quartz" sleeve.

Even though effective wavelength range is very important, so is dwell contact time—the time water stays inside the unit. Should water flow through too swiftly, there is simply not enough time for organisms to absorb enough energy to be effectively destroyed. In certain cases where it is difficult to kill larger parasites, e.g., protozoans such as *Cryptocaryon* and *Brooklynella*, decreasing the flow rate through the unit may help. Another important operating parameter is flow turbulence. Turbulent flow causes attitude changes in the positions of the organisms flowing through the lamp, rotating them and increasing their UV exposures. Mounting the unit in a vertical position with flow from bottom to top allows for improved internal turbulence and also allows any air bubbles to easily exit.

Manufacturers provide the data you will need to make the correct model choice for your aquarium and specific needs. However, beware of product over-rating, and do keep in mind that cleanliness of the sleeve and lamp is very important; if they are not properly maintained, their effectiveness will quickly diminish. Furthermore, allow only clear, prefiltered water to flow through a UV sterilizer, as that will lengthen efficient operating periods. Placing the UV sterilizer downstream of a mechanical filter is a good idea. More than one unit can be used if one large unit will not fit into the mounting area. Many aquarium stores use multi-unit assemblies to service their fish-only systems.

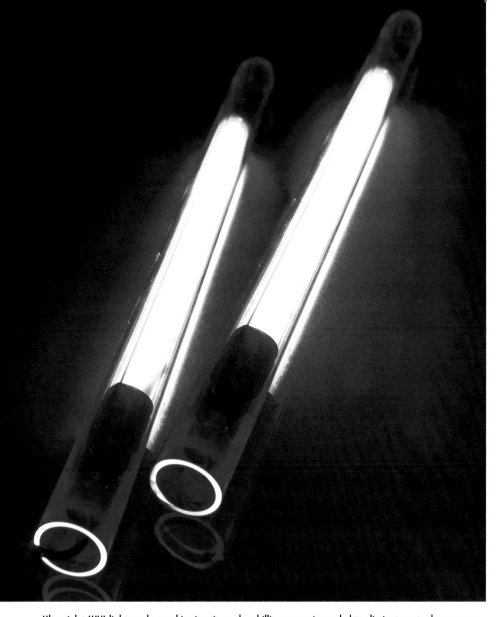

Ultraviolet (UV) light can be used in situations when killing power is needed to eliminate water-borne parasites, harmful bacteria, viruses, fungi and other pathogens. Never look directly at an unshielded UV bulb.

to prevent the formation of free-radical compounds.

When performing water changes it may be best to shut off the lamp if the flow of cooling through the sterilizer unit will be reduced. A very hot lamp could easily shatter when water begins to flow again. That would not only damage the unit, but also possibly cause personal injury and even harm aquarium inhabitants.

A UV sterilizer should not be run during start-up of a new system. It would kill off any nitrifying bacteria in the bulk water and lengthen the nitrification cycle. UV equipment is something like a lock on the door: Until someone breaks in through the window, it may just be creating a false sense of security.

In his 1979 book, *Seawater Aquariums: The Captive Environment*, Stephen Spotte notes that a study performed at the Steinhart Aquarium in San Francisco found that UV sterilizers reduced total bacteria count by 98 percent on well-maintained aquariums. Yet the mortality rate in those aquariums remained the same. Therefore, the steady use of UV equipment in fish-only systems is a debatable practice. It is even more questionable in a reef aquarium where many of the inhabitants are filter feeders. We have to ask ourselves if killing microorganisms in a UV sterilizer is a sensible approach for this type of environment. For the fish-only aquarium it may or may not be cost-effective, but we do not recommend its use on reef aquariums unless there is a particular, temporary need.

If UV equipment is utilized, it should operate around the clock, as numerous on/off operations reduce the lifespan of the lamp. You should be aware that some antibiotics are photosensitive and will be neutralized by UV radiation. If there is a need to treat with tetracycline or sulfas, do so in a separate treatment tank or turn off the sterilizer.

In a similar manner, copper drugs are affected by UV exposure, so turn off the UV sterilizer during treatment

Weights & Measures

Liquid/Weight/Light

1 Teaspoon	= 5 milliliters
"	= 100 drops
"	= 5 cc
1 Tablespoon	= 3 teaspoons
1 Fluid ounce	= 6 teaspoons
"	= 2 tablespoons
"	= 0.062 pint
"	= 0.031 quart
"	= 0.0078 gallon
"	= 29.6 milliliters
"	= 0.029 liter
"	= 1.8 cubic inches
1 Pint	= 473.2 milliliters
"	= 0.57 liter
"	= 16 fluid ounces
"	= 0.5 quart
"	= 0.125 gallon
"	= 28.87 cubic inches
1 Cup	= 48 teaspoons
"	= 16 tablespoons
"	= 8 ounces
"	= 237 milliliters
1 Liter	= 203 teaspoons
"	= 67.6 tablespoons
"	= 33.8 fluid ounces
"	= 4.23 cups
"	= 2.11 pints
"	= 1.06 quarts
"	= 0.264 gallon
"	= 1000 milliliters
"	= 61 cubic inches
1 Milliliter	= 20 drops
"	= 0.034 fluid ounce
"	= 0.2 teaspoon
"	= 0.066 tablespoon
"	= 0.002 pint
"	= 0.001 quart
"	= 0.0003 gallon
"	= 1.0 cubic centimeter
"	= 0.001 liter
"	= 0.06 cubic inch

1 Cubic Inch	= 16.39 milliliters
"	= 0.016 liter
"	= 0.55 fluid ounce
"	= 0.035 pint
"	= 0.017 quart
1 Grain	= 64.8 milligrams
1 Dram	= 1.77 grams
1 Gram	= 1 milliliter of water
"	= 15.4 grains
"	= 0.034 fluid ounce
"	= 1000 milligrams (mg)
1 U.S. Pound	= 16 ounces = 454 grams
1 Ounce (Wt.)	= 28.35 grams
"	= 438 grains
"	= 0.96 fluid ounce of water
"	= 0.06 pint
"	= 29.6 ml
1 Gallon	= 128 ounces
1 Cubic Foot	= 7.5 gallons
1 Liter	= 0.264 gallon
Liters to Imp. Gallons	x 0.22
Liters to U.S. Gallons	x 0.26
1 Kilogram	= 1000 grams
Kilograms to Pounds	x 2.205
1 Millimeter	= 0.03937 inch
"	= one thousandth of a meter
1 Centimeter	= 0.3937 inch
"	= one hundredth of a meter
1 Meter	= 39.37 inches
1 Lumen	= 10.76 Lux
1 Imperial Gallon	= 1.2 U.S. gallons
1 Foot Candle	= 1 Lumen
1 Lux	= 0.09299 Foot Candle/Lumen
1 Micron	= 1/1000 mm (0.000038 inch)
1 Gallon Seawater	= 8.3 pounds
1 Nanometer	= 1 billionth of a meter
1 ppm	= one second of time in 11.6 days
1 ppm	= 1 teaspoon in 1,302 gallons

How many times have you been instructed to add one milliliter of something, or three grams of something else? To help make some sense of the various systems of measurement used by aquarists, we offer these tables to provide conversions, along with other aquatic reference charts that may come in handy.

meq/1	CaCO₃(ppm)	dKH	meq/1	CaCO₃(ppm)	dKH
0.00	0.00	0.00	1.80	90.00	5.04
0.05	2.50	0.14	1.90	95.00	5.32
0.10	5.00	0.28	2.00	100.00	5.60
0.15	7.50	0.42	2.10	105.00	5.88
0.20	10.00	0.56	2.20	110.00	6.16
0.25	12.50	0.70	2.30	115.00	6.44
0.30	15.00	0.84	2.40	120.00	6.72
0.35	17.50	0.98	2.50	125.00	7.00
0.40	20.00	1.12	2.60	130.00	7.28
0.45	22.50	1.26	2.70	135.00	7.56
0.50	25.00	1.40	2.80	140.00	7.84
0.55	27.50	1.54	2.90	145.00	8.12
0.60	30.00	1.68	3.00	150.00	8.40
0.65	32.50	1.82	3.10	155.00	8.68
0.70	35.00	1.96	3.20	160.00	8.96
0.75	37.50	2.10	3.30	165.00	9.24
0.80	40.00	2.24	3.40	170.00	9.52
0.85	42.50	2.38	3.50	175.00	9.80
0.90	45.00	2.52	3.60	180.00	10.08
0.95	47.50	2.66	3.70	185.00	10.36
1.00	50.00	2.80	3.80	190.00	10.64
1.10	55.00	3.08	3.90	195.00	10.92
1.20	60.00	3.36	4.00	200.00	11.20
1.30	65.00	3.64	4.20	210.00	11.76
1.40	70.00	3.92	4.40	220.00	12.32
1.50	75.00	4.20	4.60	230.00	12.88
1.60	80.00	4.48	4.80	240.00	13.44
1.70	85.00	4.76	5.00	250.00	14.00

To calculate the amount of toxic ammonia (NH_3), the total ammonia ($NH_3 + NH_4$) must be multiplied by a factor selected from the chart below, using the pH and temperature from your aquarium. Test the aquarium water for ammonia. Read aquarium pH and temperature. Find factor and multiply to find the amount of true ammonia, as all test kits result in a reading that adds ammonium and ammonia together.

pH	Temp 72	Temp 75	Temp 79	Temp 82	Temp 86
7.0	.0046	.0052	.0060	.0069	.0080
7.2	.0072	.0083	.0098	.0110	.0126
7.4	.0114	.0131	.0150	.0173	.0198
7.6	.0179	.0206	.0236	.0271	.0310
7.8	.0281	.0322	.0370	.0423	.0482
8.0	.0438	.0502	.0574	.0654	.0743
8.2	.0676	.0772	.0880	.0998	.1129
8.4	.1031	.1171	.1326	.1495	.1678

Temperature (F)	Temperature (C)	Specific Gravity
86	30	1.021
84	29	1.021
82	28	1.022
81	27	1.022
79	26	1.022
77	25	1.023
75	24	1.023
73	23	1.023
70	21	1.024
68	20	1.024
66	19	1.024
64	18	1.025
63	17	1.025
61	16	1.025
59	15	1.025

Weights & Measures

Calcium

Ca (ppm)	CaCO$_3$ (ppm)	KH°	Ca (ppm)	CaCO$_3$ (ppm)	KH°
0.00	0.00	0.00	160.00	400.00	22.40
5.00	12.50	0.70	170.00	425.00	23.80
10.00	25.00	1.40	180.00	450.00	25.20
15.00	37.50	2.10	190.00	475.00	26.60
20.00	50.00	2.80	200.00	500.00	28.00
25.00	62.50	3.50	210.00	525.00	29.40
30.00	75.00	4.20	220.00	550.00	30.80
35.00	87.50	4.90	230.00	575.00	32.20
40.00	100.00	5.60	240.00	600.00	33.60
45.00	112.50	6.30	250.00	625.00	35.00
50.00	125.00	7.00	260.00	650.00	36.40
55.00	137.50	7.70	270.00	675.00	37.80
60.00	150.00	8.40	280.00	700.00	39.20
65.00	162.50	9.10	290.00	725.00	40.60
70.00	175.00	9.80	300.00	750.00	42.00
75.00	187.50	10.50	320.00	800.00	44.80
80.00	200.00	11.20	340.00	850.00	47.60
85.00	212.50	11.90	360.00	900.00	50.40
90.00	225.00	12.60	380.00	950.00	53.20
95.00	237.50	13.30	400.00	1000.00	56.00
100.00	250.00	14.00	420.00	1050.00	58.80
110.00	275.00	15.40	440.00	1100.00	61.60
120.00	300.00	16.80	460.00	1150.00	64.40
130.00	325.00	18.20	480.00	1200.00	67.20
140.00	350.00	19.60	500.00	1250.00	70.00
150.00	375.00	21.00			

Dissolved Oxygen at Saturation at 1.025 Salinity/35 ppt

Temperature (F)	Temperature (C)	Dissolved Oxygen (ppm)	Temperature (F)	Temperature (C)	Dissolved Oxygen (ppm)
59	15	8.1	73	23	7.0
61	16	7.9	75	24	6.9
63	17	7.8	77	25	6.8
64	18	7.6	79	26	6.6
66	19	7.5	81	27	6.5
68	20	7.4	82	28	6.4
70	21	7.2	84	29	6.3
72	22	7.1	86	30	6.2

Temperature

Fahrenheit	Centigrade
59	15
60	16
61	16
62	17
63	17
64	18
65	18
66	19
67	19
68	20
69	21
70	21
71	22
72	22
73	23
74	23
75	24
76	24
77	25
78	26
79	26
80	27
81	27
82	28
83	28
84	29
85	29
86	30
87	31
88	31
89	32
90	32

Natural Seawater Composition

	Constituent	Concentration (ppm)
Major Elements (Over 100 ppm)	Chlorine – Cl	18,980
	Sodium – Na	10,560
	Magnesium – Mg	1,280
	Sulfur – S	884
	Calcium – Ca	400
	Potassium – K	380
Minor Elements (1–100 ppm)	Bromine – Br	65
	Carbon – C	28
	Strontium – Sr	8.5
	Boron – B	4.6
	Fluorine – F	1.4

Trace Elements (Under 1 ppm)

Rubidium – Rb	*Chromium – Cr	Dysprosium – Dy
Aluminum – Al	Titanium – Ti	Erbium – Er
Lithium – Li	*Molybdenum – Mo	Ytterbium – Yb
Barium – Ba	*Vanadium – V	Gadolinium – Gd
*Iodine – I	Antimony – Sb	Praseodymium – Pr
Silicon – Si	Gold – Au	Scandium – Sc
Nitrogen – N	Silver – Ag	Holmium – Ho
*Zinc – Zn	Krypton – Kr	Lutetium – Lu
Lead – Pb	Xenon – Xe	Indium – In
*Selenium – Se	Bismuth – Bi	Terbium – Tb
Arsenic – As	Zirconium – Zr	Samarium – Sm
*Copper – Cu	Niobium – Nb	Europium – Eu
*Tin – Sn	Thallium – Tl	Protactinium – Pa
*Iron – Fe	Hafnium – Hf	Radon – Rn
Cesium – Cs	Helium – He	Technetium – Tc
*Manganese – Mn	Argon – Ar	Ruthenium – Ru
*Phosphorous – P	Neon – Ne	Rhodium – Rh
Thorium – Th	Tungsten – W	Palladium – Pd
Mercury – Hg	Germanium – Ge	Osmium – Os
Uranium – U	Rhenium – Re	Iridium – Ir
*Cobalt – Co	Lanthanum– La	Platinum – Pt
*Nickel – Ni	Neodymium – Nd	Astatine – At
Radium – Ra	Tantalum – Ta	Francium – Fr
Beryllium – Be	Yttrium – Y	Actinium – Ac
Cadmium – Cd	Cerium – Ce	

*biologically important trace elements

Healthy Goldflake Angelfish
(*Apolemicthys xanthopunctatus*):
a prized species that demands careful
acclimation and care to thrive.

Acquiring & Acclimating Fishes

Picking healthy specimens and getting them safely into your system

Buying and bringing home a live animal is undeniably exciting and one of the most-anticipated events for all aquarium keepers. Ideally, the process starts in earnest at a good nearby aquarium shop—your local fish store (LFS in the parlance of experienced hobbyists).

Having zeroed in on a desired fish species and assured yourself that you and your system can meet its needs, picking a good specimen or specimens can begin. The best way to ascertain the health of a fish while it's in the dealer's tank is to watch it carefully. If the fish has been in the store for several weeks or has been through quarantine, the risk of buying a problem is reduced, but observing its physical appearance and behavior before purchasing any fish is essential. You should be willing to spend as much time as is required (20–30 minutes or more) in an effort to select the best animal or animals possible.

Look for the following:

- Eyes should be clear and intact, not opaque. Be sure the eyes are neither popping out nor sunken in, as these conditions indicate possible disease conditions, and that they have normal coloration for the species.
- Verify that the fins, whether normally clear or pigmented, are not cloudy, discolored, torn, or ragged.
- Breathing should be relaxed, not rapid or labored. Smaller fish tend to have a faster gill rate than larger ones.
- Fish should not be hanging out in the corners of the tank. This usually indicates that a fish is either stressed or sick.
- Be sure the fish's colors are true (consult a reference book, if need be) and that

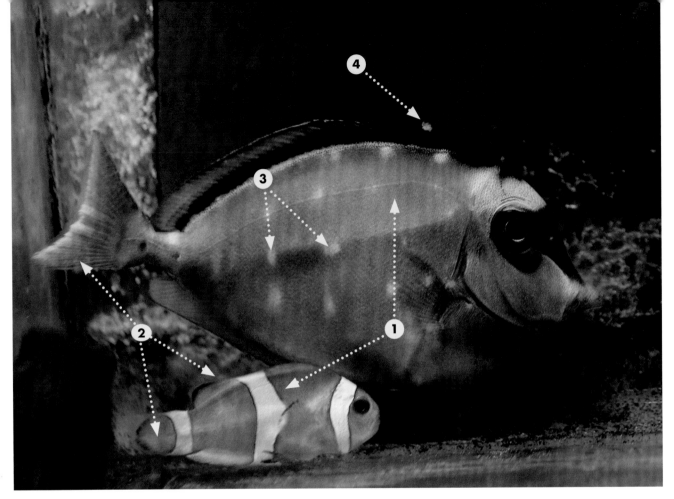

For Sale: Naso Tang (*Naso literatus*) and Ocellaris Clownfish (*Amphiprion ocellaris*) cower at the bottom of a retail store display tank showing multiple warning signs of stress and poor health: emaciated condition and sunken musculature (1), clamped fins (2), discoloration (3), a white tuft (3) and listless behavior.

there are no lesions or redness in, or under, the skin.

- Be sure there are no protruding scales and the body looks smooth, without any obvious bulges.
- Take the time to observe the fish's swimming behavior. It should not be shimmying or swimming with short, jerky movements.
- The fish should not be scratching on any substrate or other hard surfaces.
- Look for pinhead-sized white spots or a dusty-white appearance on body and fins. (See Section III, beginning on page 112.) If you see them, it is probably best to temporarily leave the fish with your dealer until cured.
- Be sure that the dorsal area just behind the head and the abdominal areas are not concave or pinched, which can

indicate severe malnutrition. A healthy fish should have a full and well-rounded appearance.

- Ask the dealer to feed the fish in your presence, preferably regular prepared foods similar to what you will feed on a routine basis. Be aware that almost any fish will eagerly accept live foods, yet may not feed on frozen or dried foods. If the fish does not eat, there may be something wrong with it.

The more time you spend observing various marine fishes, the better you will become at determining what is normal and what is not in a particular species.

If the fish looks good—alert, intact fins, normal colors, clear eyes, swimming normally, steady respiratory rate, no bruised areas, missing scales, or lesions—it may be perfectly okay. You might ask to place a deposit on the fish and let your dealer hold it for a minimum of 10 days. This 10-day window is advisable because the disreputable fish collection technique involving the use of cyanide is still prevalent in some parts of the world. Many cyanide-caught fish will die within that 10-day period. It's sad to say, but a cyanide-caught fish is better dead in your dealer's tank than in yours.

When purchasing a large fish, anything longer than about five inches, a good question for the person waiting on you is: "If I buy that fish, how are you going to catch it?" If the answer is "with a net," we highly recommend requesting that it be dipped out using a clear plastic container, whether or not the fish has a gill spike (preopercular spine). Netting of large fish induces extreme stress, besides possible body damage, and only adds to the coming upsets of being transported and introduced into a new aquarium.

According to author Martin Moe, we should also avoid fish that have long, white or brown string-like material or feces extending from the anus (the so-called "thread of death"). Although it may be a sign of malnutrition, intestinal worms, or protozoans, ultimately it may indicate cyanide poisoning, because a fish exposed to cyanide will sometimes slough off the internal lining of its intestines.

It is always prudent to ask about the environmental parameters of the aquarium in which your potential purchase has been kept. We like to ask about the water a fish is coming from, particularly specific gravity, pH, and temperature. Besides being being very helpful for the proper acclimation of your purchase, it can also tell you a lot about the standards of the dealer.

Of particular importance is the proper acclimation of ornamental shrimp, which are extremely sensitive to specific gravity changes and must be acclimated carefully. These animals will keel over quickly if given a SG shock.

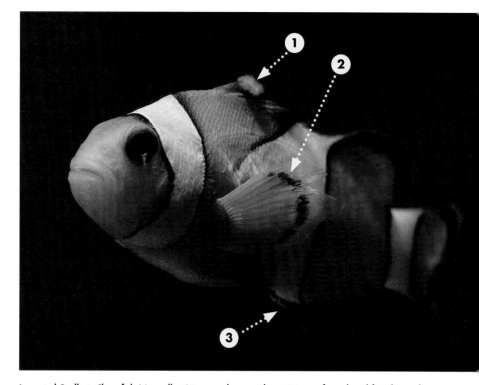

Imported Ocellaris Clownfish (*A. ocellaris*) in poor shape, with suspicious tuft on dorsal fin, clamped dorsal, pelvic and anal fins, and a thin white "thread of death" trailing from its anus.

Hobbyist Responsibilities

Consumers have a responsibility to educate themselves. They have a right to demand good quality livestock, sold to them in a healthy condition. They should have the option of buying captive-bred fish whenever possible. The most successful hobbyists make every effort to seek out responsible and reputable aquarium shops that employ good husbandry practices and maintain high standards at all times. These are the shops that deserve our trade, rather than rewarding dealers who offer cheap prices and low standards. And since it is oxymoronic to expect the best quality for the lowest price, consumers should expect to pay a little more for all of the time, effort, and expense responsible dealers must incur to provide a better product. If the dealer is quarantining his or her fishes and making a conscious effort to sell net-caught or certified animals, you have found a tremendous resource.

Hand-caught Pinstriped or Neon Wrasse (*Halichoeres melanurus*) in a barrier net. Harvested without the use of toxic sodium or potassium cyanide, such fishes have dramatically better prospects for survival and a long life. The availability of certified net-caught, sustainably harvested livestock is growing rapidly.

When shopping for new additions for your aquariums there are a number of other interesting and important considerations that will come into play.

Captive-bred Livestock

Purchasing captive-bred animals, whenever they are available, is a great option. Fish and corals of many species are now readily available and are being commercially produced for sale by many facilities, large and small. Although it is true that the selection in the past has been somewhat limited, and the prices somewhat higher than wild-caught specimens due to high production costs, captive-breds have many advantages. Fortunately, the list of facilities producing captive-raised species continues to expand and certainly the future holds great promise. Not only does

> *"It is now possible to stock an entire tank with fishes, corals, and various invertebrates that have been captive-bred. Having good sources of wild-caught fishes is important to all of us, but the fact is that captive breeding is going to play an important part in the future of the marine aquarium hobby."*

the marine ornamental aquaculture industry deserve our support for reducing the pressure on wild reefs, but their livestock is almost always significantly less stressed and more likely to adapt well to your aquarium. Many animals have spent a number of generations in captivity and have proved they can thrive with diet and conditions typical of a marine aquarium.

In fact, it is now possible to stock an entire tank with fishes, corals, and various invertebrates that have been captive-bred. Considering all the threats facing coral reefs, it is conceivable that at some point captive-bred or tank-raised animals may be the only ones available to us. Having good sources of wild-caught fishes is important to all of us, but the fact is that captive breeding is going to play an important part in the future of the marine aquarium hobby.

Sustainably Harvested Fishes

Collecting marine fishes with cyanide has been, and, sadly, continues to be a problem. (See pages 76–77.) The practice of stunning fishes with a nerve toxin started decades ago in the Philippines and has spread to Indonesia, two of the most important sources of livestock for the marine aquarium trade. Simply put, many fish live to swim again but never recover from a dose of cyanide, and large areas of coral reef have been killed by this poison. Reform is under way, but the practice is stubbornly persistent.

Additionally, the aquarium trade has been criticized for over-harvesting reef fishes and corals in some areas. The hobby also draws fire for collecting and selling certain species that seldom survive in captivity.

When first learning of all this, most hobbyists are shocked, and many of us are now determined to support non-destructive means of collection of marine livestock. It is in everyone's best interest that the collection of and trade

in marine fishes, corals, and other invertebrates be carried out in a sustainable way.

On the local level, we can help by asking our aquarium dealers if they are selling net-caught or certified livestock. Demand far exceeds supply at this time, but that situation is going to improve and getting non-cyanided, sustainably harvested stock will become easier in the near future. Survival rates for net-caught and certified fish are far supe-

Captive-breds, such as these Picasso Clowns (*A. percula*) from Oceans, Reefs and Aquariums, are consistently healthier than wild-harvested specimens.

rior to those of the conventionally caught product, so there is also a real element of consumer self-interest involved in this.

The conscientious hobbyist will take the time to learn about the needs and requirements of any animal he or she is thinking of buying. Saying no to animals that are unlikely to survive for long in our care makes sense both financially and ethically. A certified cyanide-free fish may fetch a 10–15 percent premium, but this is the best investment an aquarist can make.

If you can, find a dealer who is a member of groups such as the American Marinelife Dealers Association (AMDA), the International Marine Alliance (IMA), and the Marine Aquarium Council (MAC) and supports their philosophies, rules, regulations, codes, practices, and procedures.

Finally, know that the choices you make can have repercussions that go well beyond the confines of your tank. Consumer preferences do affect what your dealer stocks, which in turn can affect what fish are harvested (and how they are caught) in the wild by collectors. By voting intelligently with our dollars, we can have an impact on the overall health and well-being of the industry, as well as our environment. If both the hobbyist and the local shop owner agree not to buy or sell animals that have shown a lack of survivability in captivity, a powerful message is sent. At some point, it may result in a ripple effect, inhibiting collectors from harvesting these species in the first place because of a lack of demand. And if collectors refrain from removing such animals from the ocean, the perceived need for restrictive regulation may disappear.

Sight Unseen?

Purchasing livestock from mail-order companies can be a risky proposition. A fish you can observe in a local dealer's tank has many potential advantages over one that will be

Large Pakistan Butterflyfish (*Chaetodon collare*) on arrival from a major online livestock supplier. Shipping bag had leaked, leaving the fish in barely a quarter of an inch of water. This fish died during quarantine.

selected by someone else and has to go through the rigors of shipping before getting to you. Bad surprises can include everything from getting the wrong species, wrong sex, or tiny specimens, to buying fish that arrive chilled, shocked, tattered, on the verge of disease, or even dead. The fish you can get to know in a local tank, hand pick yourself, and buy from a dealer you know carries far fewer risks.

That said, there are certainly a number of good mail-order livestock sources. Those that guarantee live arrival, provide a reasonable health guarantee, and attend to ordering specifications will often be filling the needs of hobbyists living in remote areas where local shops do not exist or where the choices are poor. Keep in mind that mail-order shipments do require careful scrutiny of the stock purchased, as they are always far more stressed than animals purchased locally. Most of us are tempted to try mail-order sources, but unless there is some problem with your local

Small Goldflake Angelfish with exopthalmia (popeye) being treated in a basic quarantine/hospital tank. Such a utilitarian system, perhaps tucked into a basement or spare room, is an inexpensive but essential tool for the aquarist who wants to keep disease out of his or her main tank.

ing and homework and makes the most informed choices possible.

Coral animals should appear fully expanded and healthy. Stony corals should not have any exposed skeletal areas. If there are any broken areas, possibly from shipping, they should appear clean and freshly broken and should not contain any signs of microalgae (single-celled algae, appearing as a green or brown coating) growing on the broken surfaces. Established algal growth on hard coral usually continues to spread to healthy tissue. It's usually only a matter of time until the coral itself is overtaken and dies.

Soft corals should also appear fully expanded and healthy. Look for scars on the tissue material or bruises that appear to have some surrounding dead tissue. It could be a parasite has tunneled into the animal's flesh. Look carefully for external parasites, such as carnivorous nudibranchs (a type of sea slug) and mollusks, as they come in various shapes and sizes. Be aware

shops, it is usually safer (and ultimately cheaper) to select animals locally and personally, and to have your dealer special-order the rare ones he doesn't normally stock.

Invertebrate Purchases

An altogether separate dimension of aquarium keeping is the care and keeping of live corals and living reef systems. Although not the subject of this book, many ornamental invertebrates can also have an major impact on the health and well-being of our aquarium fishes.

A coral that "melts down" or dies suddenly can pollute an entire tank, causing a lethal rise in ammonia content. Some invertebrates are notorious fish eaters, including anemones, serpent stars, and crustaceans that can catch and consume vulnerable species. As one does when buying a new species of fish, the smart aquarist does some read-

that many of them mimic their prey to the extent that they look almost exactly like the host organism in shape and coloration, relying on camouflage for their survival.

Before venturing beyond fish, be sure you find out whether better lighting and water chemistry will be required. Make sure the dealer's tanks from which you choose your specimens are properly lit and maintained. Corals and other other invertebrates that come out of dimly lit or poorly kept sale tanks are prone to being shocked (and going into a rapid decline) when suddenly moved to a tank with bright lighting and the right water chemistry.

Quarantine vs. "Dump & Pray"

Quarantine comes to us thanks to the Plague, circa 1377 A.D., when ships and people coming into some European ports were not allowed entry until they had spent 30–40

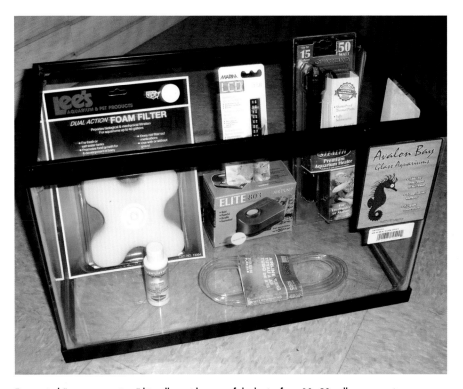

Economical "starter aquarium" kit will provide most of the basics for a 10–20 gallon quarantine system: glass tank, simple filter, heater, thermometer, air or powerhead pump, and chloramine neutralizer.

Many home aquarists, lacking a basic quarantine tank, take their chances and dump new arrivals in with the rest of their fish collection. Do this and if you happen to introduce a pest or disease, you will have to treat the entire population of fishes. In the case of aquariums containing only fish, this is less problematic than in a mixed-inhabitant aquarium containing vertebrates, invertebrates, and live rock.

Most disease treatments for marine fish spell absolute death for corals, invertebrates, and the beneficial bacteria inhabiting your filtration system, live rock, and sand. If you are unfortunate enough to introduce a diseased specimen into your mixed-inhabitant aquarium, you will be forced to separate the fish from all the other fauna for treatment in a separate system—a labor-intensive, time-consuming effort. The other option is to let the fish go untreated and hope for the best. This is, at best, a perilous option, as all the fish may be afflicted, causing a mass die-off and spelling disaster for the reef. Additionally, once certain parasites gain a foothold in a reef tank, they can persist for a very long time.

Ideally, quarantining would always result in successfully preventing contamination of your system; however, the reality is that though it greatly reduces this possibility, it does not entirely eliminate it. Still, the positive results of properly quarantining new additions far outweigh the extra time and expense required.

When the subject of quarantine arises it is usually in the context of fish, both captive-bred and wild-caught specimens. Nonetheless, fishnets, live rock, live foods, coral animals, and even natural seawater should be taken into account as possible sources of contamination. Most people who fail to quarantine assume that it will take up too much

days isolated on a nearby island and emerged disease-free.

To quarantine or not to quarantine—that is a question for every thinking fishkeeper and a subject matter discussed frequently among dealers and hobbyists alike. Does quarantining increase the chances of success? In our opinion, and the opinion of every public aquarist who keeps fish for a living, it most certainly does. Without quarantine, there is no telling what disease, parasite, unwanted alga spore, or organism might be transferred to a healthy display aquarium where it can run amok and cause untold, uncontrollable losses.

Quarantining allows you to manage and control sources of stress, one of the most significant factors in disease development. Reducing stress, as emphasized elsewhere, should be one of the main goals of an aquarist trying to avoid disease. There are different kinds of stress for fish, which will be explained in detail, and quarantine can help alleviate or remedy many of them.

Yellow Longnose Butterflyfish (*Forcipiger longirostris*) with early signs of marine ich (*Cryptocaryon irritans*), seen as white dots on tail. This fish is still eating and is a perfect candidate for treatment and holding in a quarantine system for three to four weeks while it recovers and all parasites are eliminated.

time and space and simply resort to the "dump and pray" method. Many say "it's too expensive," when, in fact, a basic quarantine tank can be set up for less than the cost of a single moderately priced fish. Quarantine is a surefire money-saver in the long run, and it can add significantly to your enjoyment of the aquarium hobby.

Failing to disinfect fishnets is one of the most common ways to transmit diseases between aquariums. For those with more than one aquarium and only one net, it is wise to sterilize the net after each use—a little household bleach or hydrogen peroxide solution in a bucket of water will do a nice job. Simply dip the net and flush it with freshwater. Better yet, have separate nets, buckets, siphons, rubber gloves, and the like for each tank.

If you use live organisms in your feeding regimen, you have another potential vector for disease. This includes the

Sources of Contamination:

Marine parasites can be transferred from tank to tank on rock, sand, nets, and human hands. Exercise caution.

feeding of small, live marine or freshwater fish (goldfish, mollies, and guppies) and small live shrimp. Often, these live foods, especially the freshwater feeder fish, appear to be in poor health and are questionable as safe food sources. (See Chapter 5.) If they are used, we suggest that they be placed in a small quarantine aquarium where they can be fattened up or enriched and made healthier before being used as an occasional live food source.

Because the health of many new coral specimens declines as a result of harvesting and transport, quarantining them before they are placed in the main system provides a margin of safety. That's not to say it is always required, since the chances of something being carried into the main show aquarium from coral can be insignificant.

You may choose to forego the quarantine of coral animals and introduce them directly into your aquarium. However, it is still necessary to use a proper protocol by slowly acclimating corals in a pail of water where the SG, temperature, and pH are gradually brought to match those in the show aquarium. During this type of acclimation period we have used Lugol's solution at a dosage of two to four drops per gallon to reduce the potential for pathogen introduction. Following acclimation, inspect your specimens for any abnormalities. Look for damaged tissue, nudibranchs, mollusks, and undesirable algal growths and carefully remove them before placing the new corals in their permanent home.

Curing Live Rock

Cycling, or curing, live rock in a separate holding vessel, such as an aerated plastic trash container, before introducing it will reduce the nutrient content imported into your tank and will provide an additional opportunity to further inspect it for any unwanted animals, dying sponges, or nuisance algae. (This die-off occurs as a result of the live rock being shipped for a long period of time in dry or barely moist conditions and possibly being subjected to wild shifts of temperature.) Without a doubt, the organic material from the die-off of sponges, small animals, and algae is better left in the cycling container than brought into the main show aquarium.

Curing live rock in a separate container doesn't guarantee that mantis shrimp, bristle worms, or unwanted algae spores won't make it into the main show aquarium.

Once established, a heavily populated aquarium, such as this large German reef system stocked with an outstanding collection of prized species, is extremely vulnerable to the introduction of new, non-quarantined stock.

seen or easily reached otherwise.

Because club soda is saturated with dissolved carbon dioxide, and these animals are aerobic, they can't survive in an oxygen-deprived, carbon dioxide-rich medium and will crawl out of the rock as fast as they can in order to seek out a more hospitable environment. A five-minute soak, completely submerged, should be sufficient to ensure the eradication of these undesirables. If you are processing a large quantity of rock, be sure to replace the club soda as it begins to lose its fizz, since this indicates the concentration of carbon dioxide is diminishing and it may be losing potency. For the most part, desirable organisms (such as coralline and macroalgae) will survive this treatment, and the trace populations that survived the shipping-induced die-off and the club soda soak will return to thrive on your rock.

Another effective method to extract unwanted pests is to place the rock in a vat or tank on a raised platform of plastic eggcrate or lighting grid, with some food or bait on the bottom. Mantis and pistol shrimp and crabs will drop down to feed and can be caught and removed.

Treating Natural Seawater

When it comes to freshly collected seawater, we recommend that it be used within 12 hours of collection. Beyond that point, seawater can become toxic due to the die-off of its plankton, requiring that other procedures be followed to make it usable in the home marine aquarium. Freshly collected seawater may look perfectly clear, yet it teems with microscopic organisms. These tiny organisms, animal and plant wanderers commonly called plankton, will die off when their food supply (usually each other) and oxygen is consumed. The result is an ammonia-laden soup, so it is always wise to test natural seawater for ammonia prior to use. If any ammonia is present, it should be detoxified by the use of an ammonia remover. If freshly collected seawater cannot be used quickly, it can be stored in non-

Prior to the curing process, simple methods of reducing the chances of introducing an unwanted hitchhiker into your show aquarium include physical inspection and removal, and the use of common club soda as a soak. Direct removal can initially be performed to opportunistically catch a few of the pests that happen to be on the surface, but the bubbling club soda soak will impact even the ones in the deep recesses of the live rock, where they can't be

Just arrived at a local fish shop after weeks in transit, this large female Maroon Clownfish (*Premnas biaculeatus*) is in need of immediate quarantine and treatment for ectoparasites emerging on its back—possibly *Brooklynella hostilis*—and apparent injury and infections on its lower lip and fins.

metallic, covered containers, in a dark area, for up to two weeks. Darkness simply prevents unwanted algae growth. Prior to using, the sediment that has settled on the bottom of the container should be separated from the water by vacuuming (siphoning) and the water aerated for 24 hours. When collecting seawater always try to do so away from inshore areas where sewage, fertilizer, insecticides, heavy metals, and other pollutants tend to concentrate.

If you need to store seawater for a longer period, it can be sterilized by adding bleach. This is accomplished by adding one bottlecap full of plain household bleach per 50 gallons of freshly collected seawater. You should then aerate the water for two days, then let it settle for a day. Vacuum (siphon) the accumulated sediment from the bottom of the container. Aerate once again until no smell of

bleach remains (which should take about a day) and then store or use as needed.

Fish Quarantine

In our many years of diving we have never witnessed diseased fish in the wild. Usually, healthy fish in a clean environment, such as an unspoiled coral reef, can ward off bacterial infections and attacks by protozoan parasites quite well. Nevertheless, no fish, no matter how well cared for from capture to its arrival at your doorstep, is as healthy as it was in the wild. Prior to your purchasing it, a fish has been stressed, usually starved, and has been held captive in many different questionable water conditions, none of which even came close to the pristine quality of its natural surroundings. So, no matter how good the fish looks, it usually isn't a happy one.

Remember, an unhappy fish is a prime candidate for parasitic infections, with the most common being *Amyloodinium*, *Cryptocaryon*, and *Brooklynella*, or various bacterial and viral infections such as *Aeromonas*, *Pseudomonas*, and *Vibrio*.

When you want to add a new fish to your collection, the choices are as follows: Quarantine it yourself, have the local dealer hold the specimen for 10–14 days while the animal has a chance to regain its stability, or dump and pray. Of these choices, quarantining the specimens yourself is the clearly preferable option. If you choose to leave the fish in your dealer's tanks for observation, you still run the risk of bringing home a disease.

If you are one of those hobbyists who want to save a particular fish that is languishing in a local shop tank, consider your motivation—if the conditions in that dealer's tanks are so deplorable, do you really want to patronize such a shop? If you do buy the fish under these circumstances, your three choices must be reduced to one—quarantine. If you purchase by mail order you have only two choices—quarantine, or release the fish into your display tank and hold your breath.

The quarantine tank can be as small as a 10-gallon aquarium with no sand bed. It should utilize a sponge or corner box filter, or an external hang-on biological filter, along with strong aeration and adequate hiding places for the fish. We think the outside hang-on filter is the better choice, as it is easier to service and therefore less stressful to the tank's inhabitants. A diatom (diatomaceous earth) filter can also be used alongside the biological hang-on unit, as it is very effective at removing free-swimming parasites. However, diatom filters do require frequent cleaning and are not designed for continuous service.

As for hiding places, any number of things could suffice, such as plastic flower pots, PVC fittings and pipe, non-calcareous rock, artificial coral, and the like. Offering hiding places helps to lower the stress fish may experience as they acclimatize to their new home. However, avoid bleached coral skeletons, live or coral rock, tufa rock, or any objects containing calcium carbonate, as explained below.

Adding some macroalgae, such as *Caulerpa mexicana* or *C. prolifera* and/or *Chaetomorpha*, may help somewhat to reduce a buildup of nitrogen-based waste products and at the same time provide a more natural-looking environment. Furthermore, the *Caulerpa* could also serve as a foodstuff, as these algae appear to be quite tasty where several species of fish are concerned. Keep in mind that many medications will kill algae and that the dim lighting of a quarantine tank is not ideal for long-term survival of plantlife.

If the fish requires a sand bed to tunnel or burrow into, that media should be composed of inert gravel or silica sand, which can be found in many different grain

The traditional drip method of acclimating fishes, with a slow addition of tank water to shipping water, may actually increase mortality, according to experts. Getting the fish into good water quickly is usually a better route.

For short trips, as from a local store to the aquarist's home, the bagged specimen may be floated in tankwater for 15 to 30 minutes to equalize the water temperature in the bag. Ideally, a new fish should be introduced in dim conditions and not floated under bright lights, which can quickly induce stress.

sizes. Calcareous substrates such as aragonite, crushed coral, dolomite, calcite, or any other calcium carbonate-type medium—including live rock—should not be used, as they may chemically attract and bind much of a copper-based treatment if it were to become necessary. Additionally, live rock would have become part of the seascape, so to speak, and its removal, which would become absolutely necessary if copper had to be added, would stress the fish further. Furthermore, it would then become necessary to add artificial decorations to take its place.

As mentioned above, the quality of the water in the quarantine tank should match that in the show aquarium, with the same pH and temperature and no ammonia or nitrite. (In fact, you may choose to fill the quarantine tank with water from your main system if it is disease-free.) As for SG, it may be as low as 1.010–1.013 if hyposalinity is being employed therapeutically, see page 135. This holding tank must have an operative biological filtration system, which can be achieved by using previously estab-

lished filters or by inoculating with live nitrifying bacterial cultures. The tank should have a hood or eggcrate plastic cover to prevent jumping. Normal room lighting is sufficient while in this transition mode, as it is best to keep a new arrival in lower lighting conditions initially. If a light is used, it should be on a timer (12 hours on, 12 off) and be of low wattage (7.5–15 watts).

Proper Acclimation of Animals

Now that you have set up a quarantine tank, it's time to head out to your fish retailer to select the new members of your aquarium collection. Applying the selection criteria outlined above, make your selection and rush your bagged specimens home as fast as the law will allow. Jesting aside, you should let your retailer know how much time it will take you to get your fish home. If necessary, steps can be taken to allow for extended travel time, such as bagging with oxygen and transport in an insulated box or cooler.

Hurried or careless transfer from one system to another can surely lead to the premature loss of fish and invertebrates, while proper acclimation techniques can lead to greater survivability and long-term success. And we think it is equally important for hobbyists and dealers to recognize and practice proper acclimation techniques.

Unfortunately, as with all controversial topics (and the aquarium trade has its fair share of them), just what constitutes "proper acclimation" is subject to many interpretations. In the chapter directed to professionals, we present a method with which we have been quite successful. (See Afterword, page 200.) Bear in mind that the dealer usually has more of a challenge, receiving fish that may have been bagged for many hours or even days and having to contend with ammonia-contaminated shipping water.

When a fish is placed in a plastic bag, the dissolved oxygen begins to be depleted by its respiration and the concentration of carbon dioxide begins to rise. As carbon dioxide increases, the pH of the surrounding water will begin to fall. Because the fish excretes waste into this water, and due to the small volume of water, a buildup of ammonia will occur. Fortunately, as the toxicity of ammonia is inversely proportional to the pH, it's more toxic at a higher pH, so the lower pH is actually advantageous and may not be overly troublesome in this situation. Also, the temperature may go up or down—usually down. All of these conditions are time-dependent, so the longer the fish spends in the bag, the further from ideal the conditions shift.

If the fish has not been in the bag very long (less than two hours or so) and the temperature in the bag and in the receiving tank are close to the same, then it might not be a bad idea to just remove it from the bag and place it in a properly established holding tank, preferably a quarantine tank. This tank should be darkened (lights off) and, if possible, should not contain any established fish that might attack a newcomer. It is always advisable to set up the receiving tank with a temperature and pH to match that of the bag water; however, it's not as critical as it is for specimens bagged for a longer time.

Keep in mind that fish are poikilothermic (or ectothermic), which means they have no real way of regulating

Beware the Bag Water:

Transport and shipping bags quickly become fouled with ammonia and may also be contaminated with chemicals and parasites. Never allow bag water into your display tank.

their internal body temperature, so it will vary based on their immediate surroundings. We recommend floating the bag containing the fish in the receiving system, particularly if it has been in transit for more than two hours. Generally 15–30 minutes is allotted to floating the bag. This will allow a more gradual equalization of the bag temperature to the aquarium temperature.

Nevertheless, what is most important is to minimize the time a fish spends in the bag. Since we prefer placing the new fish into a quarantine tank, we recommend the SG of the tank be kept at around 1.010–1.013. We find this not only helps to hold more oxygen in the water, but is also less taxing on a fish's metabolism and can retard the proliferation of ectoparasites. We do not recommend dripping or dipping tank water and mixing it with bag water.

Dr. Michael Stoskopf, a professor of aquatic, wildlife, and zoologic veterinary medicine at North Carolina State University, had this to say about acclimation at a recent national conference on fish health: "If you come across a dog suffocating with a plastic bag over its head...do you poke a hole in it and slowly administer oxygen, or do you pull it off and improve conditions as quickly as possible?"

Stoskopf says that extensive research clearly indicates that greater mortality is seen with drip acclimation. He favors equalizing the temperature and getting the fish into its new tank promptly.

Scott Michael, author of many books on reef fishes, agrees: "I used to drip-acclimate everything, but now I usually just want to get the fish out of the bag and into good water as quickly as possible. I float bags for no more than 30 minutes.

"For fish shipped overnight, I cut open the bag, pour off most of the water, and carefully slip the fish into its receiving tank. I try not to use a net. I believe this gives me better survival than long drip-acclimation sessions that can be stressful to many fishes."

Cyanide Fish Collection

Cyanide, used in the instant-death capsules of infamous Nazis, has been employed by unscrupulous fish collectors in Southeast Asia for decades. In dilute solutions, it can temporarily stun fishes, allowing them to be scooped up and later sold, if they revive, as live specimens for the aquarium trade or much-coveted live meals for Asian gourmets.

Because of its deadly side effects, cyanide collection of fish is banned almost everywhere. When the cyanide solution is squirted into a coral head, it is not discriminating about what animals are enveloped in its toxic cloud: In addition to the species being collected, it will knock down other fishes as well as killing coral poylps. Large areas of the once-prolific coral reefs in the Philippines and Indonesia have been killed by the practice of cyanide fishing for desirable species destined for restaurant fare and home aquariums throughout the world.

The use of cyanide in the collection of marine fish for the aquarium trade is being reduced, but it remains a disturbingly persistent practice, especially in the Philippines and Indonesia. Programs are in place to encourage collectors to use nets, but many of our ornamental fish are still captured with these poisons—sodium or potassium cyanide.

We know that fish caught with cyanide may continue to eat but not assimilate vitamins and minerals from their food. It has been reported that even sublethal exposure to cyanide can damage the digestive organs, including the liver. Such damage prevents the fish from digesting the foods eaten, leading to putrefaction and, ultimately, starvation.

Liver damage from cyanide has been linked to "Sudden Death Syndrome," a condition where fish die weeks or even months after being collected. A cyanide-collected fish can look perfectly healthy for varying lengths of time and then suddenly die. Most, however, succumb within one or two weeks of collection. The mortality rate of cyanide-collected fish while in the supply chain from reef to retailer has been estimated at 30 to 80 percent.

Fortunately, there is growing momentum to get collectors to switch to fishing with nets and for aquarists to demand healthy, cyanide-free animals. The Marine Aquarium Council, headquartered in Hawaii, is certifying fishers, exporters, importers, breeders, and retailers as they prove that they are complying with a rigorous set of best practices meant to ensure the sustainable collection and handling of marine animals.

Ask your local retailers if they are selling or can get certified marine fish and invertebrates. Several international bodies are working to sanction coral reef fish as being net-caught and sustainably harvested. These may cost 10–15 percent more, but are worth every penny. Certification is still in its formative stages, and there are other ways to find healthy fishes. Take into consideration where the fish come from, as there are many areas in the world where chemical collection of fish is not practiced, including the Red Sea, Hawaii, Australia, Africa, and the Caribbean.

Beware of fish originating from Egypt, since there are claims that Egyptian divers, having been trained by Philippine divers, are using cyanide to some degree.

If you are not sure where a particular fish originates, ask the shop owner or livestock manager. Let him or her know that you are aware of cyanide collection and you want to know the origin of your fishes and prefer to buy net-caught specimens.

Get What You Pay For:
Net-collected, certified, and captive-bred fishes often command price premiums of 10–15 percent, but their likelihood of long-term survival is dramatically higher than that of cyanide-caught specimens.

Conscientious collectors, exporters, importers, wholesalers, and local dealers are working hard to make cyanide collection a thing of the past. Informed consumers are the final link in a very long, complex chain of custody of these animals, and we can be a powerful force in saying "no" to cyanide and "yes" to better practices of shipping, handling, and labeling.

Lethal harvest: Diver squirts a cloud of potassium or sodium cyanide into a colony of *Acropora* sp. coral to stun reef fishes for easy collection. Still practiced in Indonesia and the Philippines, cyanide collection yields many fishes that will die early deaths and kills coral habitat in the process.

Foods
& Feeding

Hand feeding builds a bond between aquarist and fish: Keeper offers frozen shrimp to a young Scrawled Cowfish (*Lactophrys quadricornis*).

The Well-Fed Aquarium

Nutrition basics for a new age of marine fish feeding

In the world of marine fish feeding, there is no such thing as "the good old days." In decades past, saltwater fishes had to make do with rations created for freshwater tropicals and the old standby, frozen brine shrimp. Unenriched adult brine shrimp is not a particularly complete or nourishing food, and the old freshwater dry foods were often filled with cheap terrestrial cereal fillers such as wheat flour and fish meal of unknown quality.

Pioneering hobbyists had the right idea and avoided these inappropriate foods, opting instead to make their own, shaving and mincing shrimp and other marine seafoods from the fishmonger.

Today, the marine fishkeeper has access to a growing selection of very good foods with high quality ingredients designed to meet the unique nutritional needs of saltwater species. Many marine fish rations now include the essential fatty acids and natural pigments that help enhance and maintain good color.

While the choices we have available to us are undeniably better than they were, feeding remains a murky science and an unappreciated art for many hobbyists. Some observers believe that greater fish loss results from malnutrition, and even starvation, than from parasites and diseases. Some captive fishes can be very finicky in their eating habits and will refuse food until they simply waste away. Many others are not bold or aggressive enough to compete for food in an active community tank. These fishes often go into hiding, never to reappear. Still others will eat but slowly lose their color and become listless, the victims of malnutrition.

For the hobbyist determined to keep his or her fishes healthy and brightly colored, perhaps even to encourage breeding behaviors, feeding properly ranks right up there in importance with maintaining water quality. Fish live for just one or two things, depending on how you choose to count: to reproduce and to eat (so that they can grow and reproduce).

Unfortunately, most fish nutrition research has been done on the species consumed by humans, not the so-called "ornamentals" we keep in our home aquariums. Much scientific work remains to be done before we will know what makes the ideal diet for different captive reef fishes. (Science is not even close to agreeing on the optimal diet even for the most-studied species on earth, humans, let alone marine aquarium fishes.) We can, however, make some educated guesses.

Complicating the subject of marine fish nutrition is the fact that their diets vary by family, genus, and even species, and are affected by other factors such as age, temperature, and possibly by tankmates. Nevertheless, since most of us maintain a variety of fish in fish-only and reef systems, understanding their various nutritional needs is very important, since it will influence their well being and longevity. One should always look up the feeding requirements of a species before purchasing it. Some fishes demand live foods, others need to be fed numerous times each day, and still others have very specialized diets. If you can't envision meeting the nutritional needs of a new fish, save your money and the life of the animal and choose something else.

Diet Categories

Understanding the dietary requirements of individual aquarium fish species begins with knowing which of the three main feeding categories it fits into: carnivores, herbivores, or omnivores.

Carnivores require a greater percentage of protein,

Most known marine fish species start life as carnivores, but many mature into omnivores or herbivores. This larval surgeonfish, photographed by Matthew Wittenrich at Florida Institute of Technology, is equipped to capture tiny prey animals but will eventually become primarily a grazer of algal turfs.

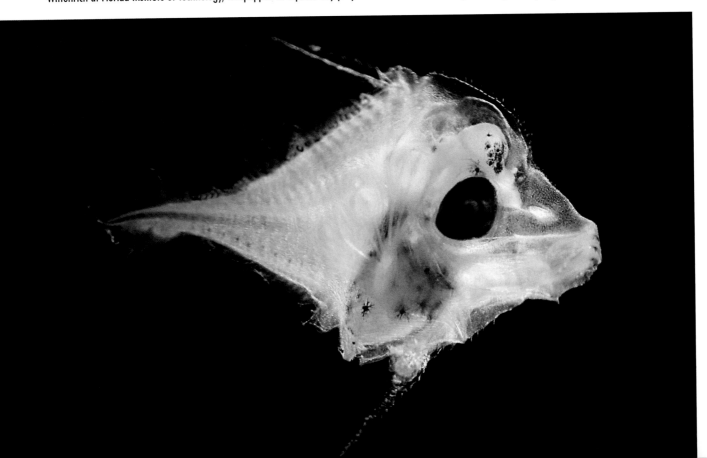

In fact, in closed systems herbivores should probably be thought of as omnivores, as they will consume meaty foods in addition to the marine green, red, and brown foods they require, such as algae and seaweed.

Carnivores are mostly meat eaters requiring a diet high in protein and amino acids. Products such as marine fish and crustacean flesh and other marine meaty foods should make up the bulk of their diet, which can be augmented with some plant/algae matter. Don't lose sight of the fact that some fish diseases and parasites (e.g., larval tapeworms) are occasionally transmitted via the consumption of fresh fish or crustacean flesh from the seafood counter. (See Chapter 5.)

Omnivores eat a variety of plant, algae, seaweed, and animal matter, and they make up the majority of the fish we strive to maintain in our aquaria. Their diet should contain a variety of meaty and plant-type foodstuffs. (In a sense, all marine fishes are omnivores, as the first foods of all marine

A toothy wrasse, this Harlequin Tuskfish (*Choerodon fasciatus*) displays the dentition of a classic carnivore, with large, sharp teeth for capturing, holding, and crushing meaty prey, some in hardened shells. Honeycomb Rabbitfish (*Siganus stellatus*), right, has small teeth and specialized mouthparts designed for nipping at macroalgae and grazing on tough algal turf beds.

whereas herbivores and omnivores need a more balanced dietary approach.

Herbivores are primarily vegetarians, yet they typically accept animal matter because in the wild they obtain animal proteins by ingesting them as a secondary food while consuming algae. A school of herbivorous tangs, for example, will greedily eat small crustaceans living on and within the macroalgae and algal mats that they consume.

A typical omnivore, this Potter's Angelfish (*Centropyge potteri*) cruises rocky substrates, grazing on microalgae but also hunting small crustaceans and taking the occasional meaty plankton item that drifts by. It is one of many omnivorous species that does best in a system with plentiful live rock.

fish larvae are planktonic animals.)

Once a fish's feeding category has been determined, its feeding behaviors should be taken into account: Is it shy, bold, finicky, secretive, nocturnal? Know where and how it takes its food: surface, bottom, open water, grazed from rock, or sifted out of the substrate. Keep in mind that some fish are plankton feeders, attracted only to food items drifting by in the water column. Others may only take their meals by picking them off the substrate. All these possible traits need to be taken into consideration in closed systems where there is usually a mix of different types of feeders. Be especially sure to note if a species typically needs live

foods and if it can be weaned off them and taught to accept frozen or other rations. Most can.

In a mixed-species tank, you will likely have to meet a range of feeding demands and will need to offer a variety of foods to suit all members of the community.

Food Composition

A basic understanding of the composition of different foods, including proteins, carbohydrates, lipids (fats), minerals, and vitamins, is helpful. Each of these nutrient groups confers particular health benefits.

PROTEINS Proteins are composed of various amino acids, including arginine, histidine, isoleucine, lysine, methionine, phenylalanine, threonine, and valine, that are essential for fish health. They are found in meaty and plant-type foods and provide for growth, tissue repair, and disease resistance. A lack of certain amino acids can result in curvature of the spine or stunted growth. Excessive amounts of some amino acids are also unhealthy.

When protein intake is too low, growth and tissue replacement slows or stops. Overfeeding of protein can result in water-quality problems. Herbivores gain much of their needed protein from the vegetable matter they consume, whereas carnivores and omnivores get their protein mostly from meaty foods. Each has internal enzymes that break down the consumed matter and extract the required protein for growth and tissue repair. About 35 percent of a growing marine fish's diet should be digestible protein; fully-grown fish require somewhat less, about 30 percent.

CARBOHYDRATES Carbohydrates, including sugars, starches, and fibers, provide energy and aid in digestion, supporting the role of protein in growth and tissue repair. Most are found in plant material, which carnivores have problems digesting but herbivorous fish utilize easily. Other sources include chitin ingested in crustacean exoskeletons and glycogen in animal flesh. Actually, there is little need for special attention to carbohydrates in the diets of most marine aquarium fishes, as long as the appropriate types of food for each species are being provided.

LIPIDS Lipids, in either solid or oil form, are needed for energy and building or repairing tissue, and they are found in both plant and animal tissue. However, as we discussed earlier, excessive amounts of fats, particularly those associated with the feeding of freshwater feeder fish such as goldfish, can cause abnormal fat buildup in internal organs. Because of that, we do not recommend that marine fish be fed on freshwater fish or their derivatives as this practice can lead to fatty liver degeneration and, ultimately, a premature death.

The most common example of this is the lionfishes, which put on an amazing display of predatory behavior when offered live goldfish or freshwater feeder minnows.

Hobbyists who make a habit of showing off their prized lionfish in this manner all too often end up with a dead specimen that seems to have met a mysterious end.

Saturated fats from land animals are basically indigestible by fishes, whereas fats found in marine creatures are

Modern marine rations, both dried and frozen, allow the aquarist to feed a varied diet of meaty items of saltwater origin as well as vegetable matter, including *Spirulina* and other nutritious algal ingredients.

unsaturated and more easily digested. If you enrich fish foods with commercial supplements, look for products having highly unsaturated fatty acids (HUFA) containing omega-3 fatty acids—eicosapentaenoic (EPA), docosahexaenoic (DHA) and alpha linolenic acid (ALA).

Lipids should make up about 10 percent of the diet. A

lipid deficiency usually results in loss of color and poor growth, especially in older fish, and the afflicted fish may exhibit a listless disposition. Foods held too long or at the improper temperature will become rancid and lose the value of their fatty acids. Rancid fish foods can cause health problems or even death in some fishes.

VITAMINS   Vitamins are organic substances necessary for normal health and growth, and there are two forms, water-soluble and fat-soluble. Vitamins are needed as catalysts in many biochemical functions, and a deficiency can cause

Voracious predators such as lionfishes, large wrasses, groupers, and moray eels can easily be fed to excess, resulting in rapid growth and generation of copious amounts of nitrogenous wastes that can overwhelm some systems.

slow growth, anemia, weight loss, exophthalmia, scoliosis (spinal deformities), fading colors, and other problems.

Fat-soluble vitamins include vitamin A, which affects the quality of vision and growth; vitamin D, which gives bones integrity; vitamin E, which acts as an antioxidant,

❗ ▶ **Preventive Poaching:**

Raw seafood can transmit diseases and parasites to aquarium fishes. Steam or microwave gently for safer feeding.

and vitamin K, which enhances blood clotting and skin integrity. These essential vitamins come from fish flesh and fish oils, such as cod-liver oil and krill oil.

As for water-soluble vitamins, both B and C are very important. The various B vitamins, B1 (thiamine), B2 (riboflavin), B3 (niacin), B5 (pantothenic acid), B6 (pyridoxine), and B12 (cyanocobalamin), provide nutrients for the following functions:

- Growth
- Digestion
- Lipid, protein, and amino acid metabolism
- Adrenal functions
- Cholesterol metabolism
- Vision, other vital functions

Deficiencies can cause numerous conditions: poor growth, loss of appetite, cloudy eyes, loss of equilibrium, rapid breathing, and muscle atrophy, to mention a few.

Vitamin C (ascorbic acid) is a powerful antioxidant that enhances the immune system and aids in normal tissue repair. A deficiency in vitamin C in fish can cause spinal abnormalities (scoliosis) and hemorrhaging of the skin, liver, muscles, and kidneys.

As mentioned above, your fish should not receive a steady diet of uncooked fish and/or shellfish flesh. The value of vitamin B1, which is important for maintaining certain biological activities—appetite, growth, normal digestion, and brain activity—can be neutralized by the enzyme thiaminase, which some uncooked fresh fish and shellfish flesh contains. To stop the action of this enzyme, first briefly steam or microwave the flesh to be fed. In fact, gentle, greaseless cooking does not degrade the nutritional value of the flesh; energy content per gram actually increases because tissue water content is lowered. Cooking will also help limit the transmission of certain parasites and infectious diseases.

Vitamins B and C can be absorbed directly from aquarium water to some degree, as marine fish ingest the wa-

Cuban or Spotfin Hogfish (*Bodianus pulchellus*) with a mouthful of live grass shrimp. Most fish respond enthusiastically to occasional feedings of live foods.

ter. Therefore, these vitamins can (if needed), be added directly to the aquarium water.

Besides commercial fish vitamin additives and supplements, there are all-natural (without preservatives) vitamin B complexes and/or vitamin C liquids available in health food stores that can be used directly in the aquarium water or on various foodstuffs. If there are no dates on the bottles, do not use them.

Though this is a fairly easy method to assure the uptake of these vitamins, in our opinion, the best way to provide your fish with essential vitamins is to directly apply them to the foodstuffs before feeding several times a week.

Vitamin Sources

Vitamin A is found in crustaceans (krill), algae, lettuce (especially Romaine and leafy lettuces), spinach, broccoli, green peas, sweet corn, cod-liver oil, seaweed (*Porphyra yezoensis*, *Palmaria palmata*, and *Porphyra umbilicalis*), and fish livers.

Vitamin B1 is found in algae, Romaine lettuce, broccoli, green peas, spinach, seaweed (*Palmaria palmata*, *Porphyra yezoensis*, and *Porphyra umbilicalis*), yeast, bivalves, beef heart, *Spirulina*, and fish flesh.

Vitamin B2 is found in Romaine lettuce, spinach, broccoli, green peas, seaweed (*Palmaria palmata, Porphyra yezoensis,* and *Porphyra umbilicalis*), and fish flesh.

Vitamin B3 is found in brewer's yeast, broccoli, Romaine lettuce, spinach, green peas, fish/crustacean flesh, and seaweed (*Palmaria palmata, Porphyra yezoensis,* and *Porphyra umbilicalis*).

Vitamin B5 is found in liver and other organ meats, fish flesh, and broccoli.

Vitamin B6 is found in green peas, broccoli, spinach, Romaine lettuce, fish flesh, and seaweed (*Palmaria palmata, Porphyra yezoensis,* and *Porphyra umbilicalis*).

Vitamin B12 is found in green algae, lettuce (especially Romaine), seaweed (*Palmaria palmata, Porphyra yezoensis,* and *Porphyra umbilicalis*), spinach, bivalves (clams & oysters), shrimp flesh, and tubifex worms.

Vitamin C is found in seaweed (*Porphyra yezoensis, Palmaria palmata,* and *Porphyra umbilicalis*), green peas, lettuce (especially Romaine and leaf lettuces), broccoli, spinach, and some other dark green leafy vegetables.

Vitamin D is found in earthworms, mealworms, tubifex worms, fatty fish such as salmon and mackerel, fish liver, cod-liver oil, and crustacean flesh.

Vitamin E is found in green algae, lettuce, spinach, seaweed (*Palmaria palmata, Porphyra umbilicalis*), and broccoli.

A mere youngster, this Queensland or Giant Grouper (*Epinephelus lanceolatus*) will take all manner of marine meaty foods, but will present a feeding challenge to its owner as it grows toward its adult maximum size of 9.8 feet (300 cm) and over 880 pounds (400 kg). It is a threatened species in the wild.

Vitamin K is found in fish meal, green peas, broccoli, spinach, and some other green leafy vegetables.

There are many prepared vitamin additives on the market that can be added to the foods we feed our fish, and if they are used diligently and correctly, the chances of vitamin deficiencies are slim, especially if a variety of foods are offered throughout the week, including occasional meals of live foods that all fishes relish.

Minerals

Minerals, such as calcium, phosphorus, potassium, magnesium, iron, copper, manganese, iodine, selenium, zinc, and others, are absorbed by marine fish from the surrounding water. Mineral supplementation is not routinely required. However, iodine deficiency can result from poor diet. Small weekly additions of iodine to the aquarium water can be useful, but monitor iodine levels closely so as not to overdose. Sharks and other elasmobranchs are susceptible to goiter if they don't get enough iodine.

Feeding Frequency

Poor diet, like poor water quality, can be a factor contributing to the cause of many diseases. The remark, "I only feed every other day," from someone who has a variety of plankton or algae grazers in his system shows poor animal husbandry. In the wild, most coral reef fishes popular with aquarists eat throughout the day, most actively at sunrise and sunset. Two feedings a day is a reasonable minimum if you want to be successful at keeping marine fishes. The exceptions to this rule are the bigger predators, such as moray eels and groupers, which can get by nicely on a meaty meal every few days. Feeding them daily is neither necessary nor advised. Captive marines can become overweight, sluggish, and unhealthy.

Always pay attention to your fish, particularly at feeding time. This is the most opportune time to assess each fish's overall health by looking for aberrant behaviors and other symptoms of disease or malnutrition. Be sure all inhabitants of the community are getting enough food, but

Red & Black Clownfish (*Amphiprion melanopus*) shows pinched dorsal musculature (1) that is an unmistakable sign of malnourishment. Not all such fish can be nurtured back to good health.

never offer more food than can be cleaned up completely within five minutes or so. Overfeeding is a definite problem, leading to unhealthy fishes and poor water quality.

If water quality is a concern, there are ways to correct that without starving the fish. Effective approaches include water changes of 10–20 percent weekly; adding more filtration capacity, including a more efficient protein skimmer; using activated carbon properly; and boosting water circulation and turbulence within the display tank to be sure wastes are carried out and into the filter.

Unfortunately, the signs of malnutrition take a long time to become evident, and once fish become weakened with nutritional deficiencies they may never recover, no matter what changes are made to their diet. Above all, verify that all fish are eating properly, whatever their needs.

TANK NAME HEB-1
SPECIES
SPECIAL INFO:
Am Feed 3 cubes
Om Feed 2 cubes
1.3.0

Marine biology researcher
Ashley Romero feeds mysid
shrimp to a breeding pair of
seahorses at Florida Tech.

Fish Foods & Feeding

Building a menu suited to your marine charges

In the wild, live food makes up most of the diet that provides coral reef fishes their essential nutrients, vitamins, and minerals. In captivity, dry and frozen foods are the primary staples for most home aquarists. Fresh seafoods and live foods can also form an important part of a balanced, healthy diet.

Don't be surprised if a new fish is a reluctant eater at first. Some fish are fussy feeders but adapt within a few days to a week, and then there are those that truly require a special diet. Nevertheless, when hungry, the most popular, hardy and adaptable aquarium species will eat almost anything offered. We are fortunate to have many choices when it comes to fish foods.

Perhaps as a spillover from human nutrition and labeling laws, as well as the rising level of sophistication of the marine aquarium hobby, many manufacturers of fish foods are becoming very good at labeling their products, allowing us to make more informed choices about fish nutrition.

For newcomers to marine fishkeeping, all the menu choices can be daunting, but you can avoid most nutrition problems by following two simple rules: (1) Feed a variety of foods. (2) Be sure that each particular species or fish in your tank is getting enough of the proper food.

As pointed out in the previous chapter, a poor diet can result in loss of color, diminished vigor, general ill health, and a greater susceptibility to pathogens and diseases. A fish that is persistently underfed or is not getting the right types of foods may perish (or just disappear into the aquascape). Some hobbyists find these deaths and disappearances mysterious, but in an unfortunate number of cases they can be traced to simple starvation or lack of proper nutrients.

Due to the processes involved in producing dried and freeze-dried foods, their nutritional value, and very possibly their palatability, are not always as good as those of fresh, live, or frozen foods. This can be easily corrected by enhancing the dry ration with a vitamin/mineral additive. Adding either an all-B vitamin solution (about three drops mixed in a teaspoon of water) or a similar vitamin C solution to any of the dried or freeze-dried products is a good way to bolster fish health. Many vitamin and mineral supplements can be used to fortify dry foods. Dry foods should be kept in airtight containers or packaging and protected from heat and light. In fact, the best place to store them is in the refrigerator in sealed packages to exclude moisture and odors.

FLAKE/GRANULE/PELLET The most commonly offered prepared foods are flake products, which contain a variety of ingredients, including shrimp meal, fishmeal, algae, *Spirulina*, yeast, tubifex worms, and beef heart, to mention just a few. The color of the flakes is sometimes a nutritional indicator. Green flakes provide vegetable matter and enhance colors. Red and brown flakes are often high in protein from meaty sources and may contain color enhancers. Yellow and orange flakes tend to be high in carotenoids and other pigments that are needed for bright coloration.

We recommend not feeding marine fish flakes made for freshwater fish, as they may contain too much fat, not enough protein, and too many ingredients of freshwater or terrestrial origin.

Granule products are fine for many fish, but they often sink quite quickly and may get lost in the substrate. Float-

Newly purchased fishes are often in need of a restorative diet to make up for lack of food or less-than-ideal feeding during their transition from the wild to the home aquarium. A quarantine tank facilitates targeted feeding.

Dry Foods

A visit to any well-supplied local aquarium shop will reveal a large array of dry foods in myriad forms: flake, tablet, granule, pellet, ground meal, sheets, freeze-dried whole organisms, and feeding blocks.

Flake foods for marine fishes have improved by leaps and bounds in recent years, with more appropriate ingredients and better labelling. When used to augment a diet of frozen rations, dried flakes can provide needed variety. Colors sometimes provide some clues to nutrition: Green flakes are often rich in vegetable matter, multicolored flakes for omnivores can deliver a variety of nutrients and pigments, while red or brown flakes are typically high in protein.

ing pellets are fine for many surface feeders, and do not disintegrate as quickly as sinking pellets. Sinking pellets are acceptable if bottom feeders, such as goatfish, are present. Their density allows such fishes to quickly get a greater quantity of nutrients than if it were flake food.

SPIRULINA The blue-green microalgae *Spirulina* is one of the more important flake foods, especially for herbivores. Even though it's especially grown for human consumption, its high protein and beta-carotene content also make it an excellent foodstuff for many marine fish. And besides helping to maintain fish coloration, it provides many important vitamins and minerals. It's also a natural antibiotic and helps to promote general good health. It is an excellent food for surgeonfish, angelfish, rabbitfish, and others that require vegetable matter in their diets. Another plus is that its cell wall is a saccharate, a sugar-like product that will provide some energy, rather than a celluloid-like material, as in lettuce, which may cause binding in the digestive tract.

KELP/NORI Dried sushi/nori seaweeds, such as *Porphyra yezoensis, Porphyra umbilicalis,* and *Palmaria*

Scrawled Filefish (*Aluterus scriptus*) displays an elongated snout and specialized mouth for bottom feeding on an omnivorous mix of algae, seagrasses, and various sessile invertebrates.

A complex, beautiful community of reef fishes populates David Saxby's 2,900-gallon (11,000 L) London reef aquarium and requires foods to suit numerous herbivorous tangs and surgeonfishes, carnivorous planktivores such as anthias and wrasses, as well as many omnivorous damsels, clownfishes, and others.

palmata, are an excellent source of protein and contain various vitamins, minerals, and lipids. Also known as Japanese sea vegetables, these seaweeds can be purchased in Oriental food stores, most local aquarium shops, or from mail-order companies. They come packaged in sheets as thin as newspaper or already cut into useable strips or flakes. There are generally three choices, green, brown, and red, or a mixed bag containing pieces of each. Our experience has shown the green to be the most popular with fishes, and it is an excellent foodstuff. Be sure to buy nori without additives or preservatives and feed using a seaweed clip. (We have seen watersoaked pieces of nori break off and float into overflows, blocking water egress and causing the aquarium to overflow.)

FEEDING BLOCKS Commercially prepared feeding blocks for herbivorous fish consist of different green foods encapsulated into a plaster of Paris base. These are perfect for surgeonfish and rabbitfish, who like to graze on veg-etable matter. Public aquariums often make their own feeding blocks, but for the home aquarist, the commercially available blocks will suffice. And, as for the plaster of Paris base, it's nothing more than calcium and will not harm the aquarium environment. In fact, it may even help boost the calcium content somewhat in the system water.

FREEZE-DRIED Freeze-dried or lypholized foods are convenient and quite popular. Krill is among the most nutritious, then bloodworms, tubifex worms, and brine shrimp, in that order. Their moisture is quickly removed under high pressure in a vacuum, yet they retain much of their fatty-acid content. Freeze-dried foods, on the whole, are somewhat better than frozen foods and usually more expensive. These products are very good at absorbing fortifying additives containing omega-3 fatty acids and vitamins. (One note: As with freezing, the lypholization process does not necessary kill all pathogens, which may survive in a dormant state.)

Freeze-dried copepods, such as Cyclop-eeze™ (Argent Laboratories), are not only high in protein (about 50 percent by dry weight), but the lipid content is also quite high at about 35 percent. Furthermore, the carotenoid pigments, astaxanthin (a pink pigment) and canthaxanthin (a red pigment), help maintain fish coloration. Other health benefits include enhancing growth, increasing stress tolerance, protection from UV, and boosting the immune system. Cyclop-eeze™ has a carbohydrate content of about 12 percent, making this foodstuff and other brands using this copepod, or similar ones, such as *Apocyclops royi*, among the best all-around nutritionally balanced foods available to marine fish hobbyists.

KRILL The most common freeze-dried food is krill, which is high in protein, carotenoid pigments, fatty acids, and vitamin A. In fact, it is the world's richest natural source of animal protein. It comes in many forms, sizes, and shapes: pellets, flakes, meal, and the whole dried crustacean, ranging from tiny to quite large.

Soaked in Supplements:

Liquid vitamins and fatty acids can be delivered to fishes easily by soaking dry or freeze-dried foods before feeding.

Besides being an excellent fish food, it is also fed to many land-based animals, such as cattle and poultry. There are some 85 species that may be labeled as "krill," but it's *Euphausia superba* (the Antarctic species) that whales feed upon, and this is the most commonly known and utilized species. It is available both freeze-dried and frozen.

Krill are small, basically translucent 2.5-inch- (6 cm-) long crustaceans that have a life span of about seven years. They go through five stages of change during the three to four years it takes to reach adulthood. They can go 200 days without food and must continually swim or they will sink to the bottom. Swimming in dense clouds, they can sometimes number a half million in one cubic meter! It is estimated there are

Freeze-dried foods, such as tubifex worms, below left, and krill, below right, can provide convenient, nutritionally rich options for the aquarist trying to offer a variety of choices. These foods are especially useful in soaking up liquid supplements, such as Selcon®, above, to deliver essential fatty acids and vitamins.

Brine shrimp (*Artemia* sp.) lifecycle, clockwise from bottom left: (1) Eggs rehydrated from dried cysts. (2) Nauplius, six hours after hatching. (3) Nauplius 24 hours post-hatch. (4) Nauplius 48 hours post-hatch. (5) Nauplius three days post-hatch. (6) Adult female. Newly hatched brine shrimp nauplii are a highly nutritious food, rich in essential fatty acids and energy. Adult brine shrimp can be a relatively poor choice of food, unless enriched before being fed to fish. Enriching calls for adding a supplement such as Selcon® to their tank water for 8 to 12 hours before feeding to allow them to pack themselves with nutrients.

Decapsulation process for brine shrimp eggs: Dessicated cysts right out of the can, left. Hydrated with water to smooth the capsules, middle. Eggs after bleaching with leathery chorion removed, middle. Removing the shells prevents fish from eating them and having the husks collect in their digestive tracts.

hundreds of millions of metric tons of krill in the Antarctic. Krill is highly sought after by many nations since it represents one of the most perfect animal food sources known.

One warning from Kelly Jedlicki, who moderates a popular online fish health forum: "Feeding a diet solely or mostly of krill can lead to an irreversible condition known as lockjaw. Be sure to vary the diet of all marine fishes."

BLOODWORMS These are not really worms, but actually the larvae of midges in the genus *Chironomus*, a freshwater insect. Whether freeze-dried or frozen, this commonly available foodstuff is high in protein and suitable for carnivores. Yet, since it's not of marine origin, it should only be fed as an occasional treat. And if overfed, it can cause system water nitrate levels to increase, possibly leading to diminished water quality.

Live/Fresh Foods

Live foods in good condition can be superior to all other types of foodstuffs as they contain fresh, active ingredients, which aid digestion. Additionally, live foods tend to stimulate the innate feeding responses of fishes, a fascinating thing to watch, and they sometimes trigger breeding behaviors. However, they must be chosen with care, as overuse of certain live foodstuffs can cause needless problems like poor water quality, unbalanced diets, and even certain

Live male brine shrimp: note nutrient-packed digestive tract

Frozen male brine shrimp: note nearly empty digestive tract

Feeding live grass shrimp to an eager spawning harem of Shortfin Lionfish (*Dendrochirus brachypterus*). In addition to delivering important nutrients, high-protein live foods can stimulate reproductive behaviors.

serious health problems. Cultivating some live foodstuffs is a very feasible approach and something the serious hobbyist may want to explore further. As a starting point, here are some interesting ones that are fairly simple to raise.

BRINE SHRIMP Brine shrimp, *Artemia* spp., is probably the most popular live food, although it can also be purchased frozen, freeze-dried, mixed with other foods, or in cyst form. Brine shrimp are small crustaceans, sometimes sold as "Sea Monkeys," and are raised in seawater. Newly hatched brine shrimp are very nutritious for the first 24 to 48 hours. As they grow to adulthood over the following few weeks their nutritional value diminishes greatly. Most adult brine

shrimp, unless specifically nourished, are a relatively poor foodstuff for our marine fish. Therefore, adults should be enriched with a commercial additive, such as Selcon® or another supplement brand containing omega-3 fatty oils, prior to feeding. Live brine shrimp can also be enriched by feeding them Cyclop-eeze™.

To enrich, first place live adult brine shrimp, place them into a container of saltwater (preferably aquarium water) to which a small amount of the fortifying/enriching product has been added. Allow the shrimp to feed for at least 8–10 hours before placing them in the aquarium, and your fish will have a more nutritious foodstuff.

Live brine shrimp should not become an everyday food, as nutritional imbalances can result, but are useful in getting stubborn fish to eat or to stimulate breeding instincts. Some cautions: Do not allow any brine shrimp hatching water into the aquarium. The possibility of introducing pathogenic bacteria is very real. Always rinse the shrimp in clean water before feeding to your animals.

DECAPSULATION OF *ARTEMIA* CYSTS There is a large price difference between regular and decapsulated, or shell-less, brine shrimp eggs. Shell-less eggs are great for use directly in the marine aquarium, but the regular eggs are not, as their shells will float, causing an unsightly mess. To separate eggs from their shells, simply place a few ounces of cold freshwater and one teaspoon of eggs in a glass container. Aerate for one hour to rehydrate the eggs, then add two ounces of regular household bleach. Continue to aerate and within the next few minutes the eggs' shells will melt away, changing egg color from brown to pink. Foam will build up because of the dissolving eggshells.

When the eggs are shell-less, usually within three to five minutes, pour the contents into a fine mesh net or coffee filter and rinse under cold freshwater until the smell of the bleach is gone. To make sure there is no remaining bleach, place one tablespoon of white vinegar in eight ounces of cold freshwater and soak the net or coffee filter

Grass shrimps (*Palaemonetes* spp.) come in various colors and sizes and make an excellent live food to entice reluctant feeders to start eating. Aquarists living near a seashore can harvest their own with nets.

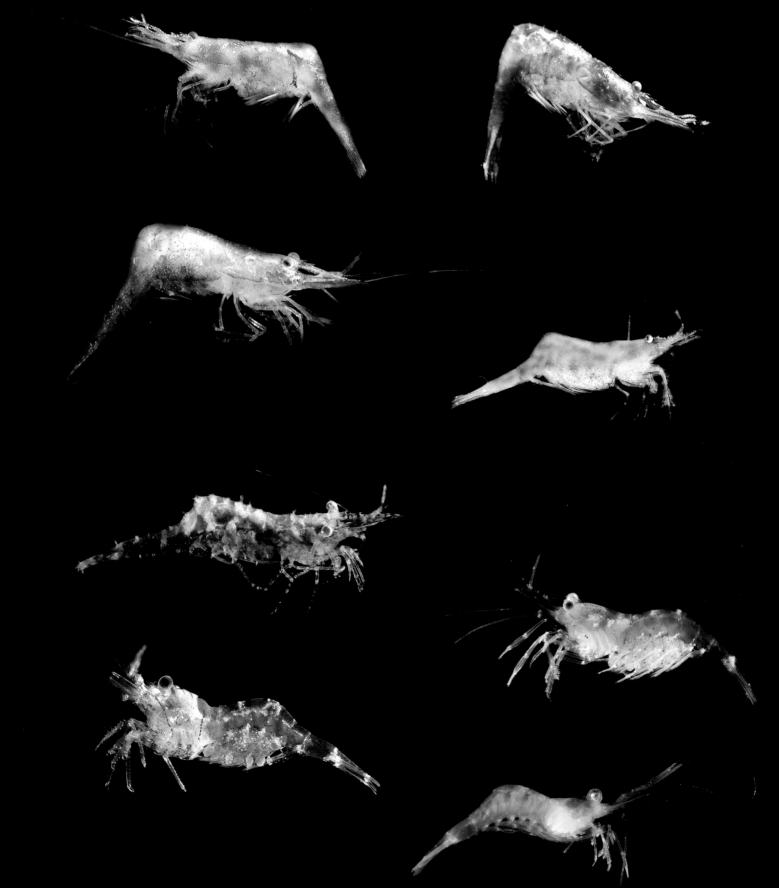

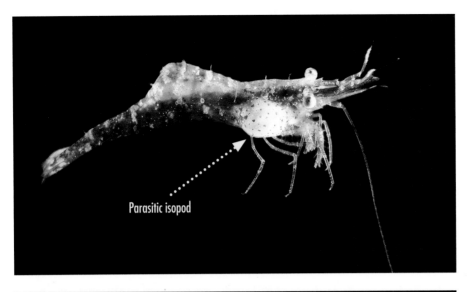

Parasitic isopod

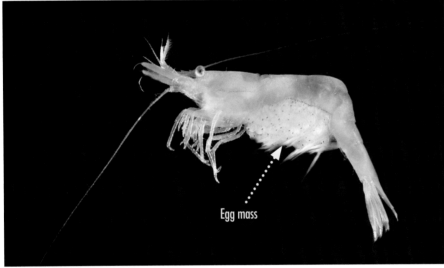

Egg mass

Grass shrimps, upon closer inspection, can provide biological interest to the curious aquarist. Left, top: shrimp with parasitic isopod attached and intent on devouring its gonads. This parasite does not attack fishes. Left, bottom: green grass shrimp with a mass of eggs carried in its pleopods or swimmeretes. Note eyespots in developing eggs.

GHOST/GRASS/GLASS SHRIMP

Many fish find live shrimp, such as ghost shrimp or grass shrimp, quite irresistible and appetizing. Some people refer to these animals as glass shrimp because of their translucent bodies. There are many species of shrimp lumped into this group, but most of them belong to the family *Palaemonidae* and the subfamily *Palaemoninae*, such as *Palaemon debilis* and *P. pacificus*. *P. debilis* (also known as the Feeble Shrimp) can reach about 1.25 inches (3 cm), and *P. pacificus* (also known as the Tiger Shrimp) may attain about 2 inches (5 cm) in length. They are usually found close to shore along protected, rocky stretches, although *P. pacificus* prefers slightly deeper waters.

full of shell-less eggs for one minute. This will neutralize any remaining bleach. Remove and wash the net of eggs under tapwater. The shell-less eggs are now ready for hatching or use directly as a foodstuff for the fish and/or some corals in your aquarium.

Newly hatched brine shrimp are one of the most nutritional foodstuffs available to small fish and are very important food in rearing aquacultured fishes and invertebrates. Their protein content is about 70 percent and their lipid content about 18 percent, along with small amounts of fatty acids and the pink pigment, canthaxanthin.

These shrimp are primarily herbivores, and may be living in great numbers in areas where algae (particularly filamentous) are prolific. Since they can tolerate (some even prefer) brackish waters, these shrimp are also found in ponds and estuaries. They can even be collected in rivers that feed the estuaries quite a distance from the ocean. The so-called ghost shrimp is clear, but some are tinted pink to red or even green, and others may have stripes or bands. Often available in local aquarium shops, they are an excellent live food for many fish, although their cost can be somewhat prohibitive over the long term. Aquarists

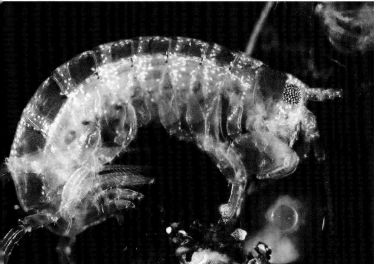

Amphipods, greatly enlarged (both images above): These tiny crustaceans are ubiquitous in established reef aquariums, where they graze on live rock and in the substrate and provide an excellent source of live food for mandarinfishes, pygmy angels, and other small bottom hunters.

living near the shore can catch their own. Live shrimp can be "gutloaded" with enriching nutrients by offering them Cyclop-eeze™ or pulverized flakes of *Spirulina* 8 to 10 hours before feeding to your fishes.

COPEPODS A huge part of the world's marine plankton, copepods are crustaceans and, when available in the cor-

rect sizes, excellent fare for a variety of fishes, from very tiny to reasonably large.

Live copepods can be cultivated in refugiums or dedicated culture tanks, and various commercially preserved forms are now available in the aquarium trade. They are variously sold as "Arcti-Pods" (*Calanus finmarchicus*), "Reef Plankton" (Red *Calanus* spp.), and "Tigger-Pods" (*Tigriopus califoricus*), and are all eaten with relish by reef fishes.

AMPHIPODS Small, shrimp-like crustaceans that often proliferate in established reef aquariums, amphipods in the genus *Gammarus* are especially appropriate live foods for many smaller reef fishes. Gobies, mandarinfishes, pygmy angelfishes, and many wrasses that are otherwise challenging to keep will do much better in a system with a constant supply of live amphipods.

Amphipods thrive in tangles of the macroalgae *Chaetomorpha linum* and *Ulva*, and a new refugium can be inocu-

"Rosy Reds," domesticated fathead minnows (*Pimephales promelas*), are sold as "feeder fish" but, like goldfish, are never recommended for feeding to marine fishes.

lated with amphipods merely by acquiring a large portion of one of these green algae species. Amphipods graze on detritus, diatoms, and hair algae. Look closely in any refugium or near the substrate in an older reef tank and you will likely find amphipods grazing.

FEEDER FISH For certain marine fish (lionfish, groupers, rockfish, moray eels, and triggerfish), occasional offerings of live mollies, guppies, goldfish, and/or *Gambusia* provide for that natural feeding excitement found in the wild.

These small, live freshwater fish should be considered only an occasional treat and should not become a steady diet, as they lack the fatty acids that marine fish need to stay healthy. All of the fishes mentioned above should be trained to accept frozen or freshly prepared marine shrimp

❗ Feeder Foibles:

"Feeder goldfish" and other freshwater species should not be fed to marine predators, which may relish the live prey but can develop fatal liver problems over time.
••

and fish flesh of various kinds. These foodstuffs should also be treated or fortified just before feeding with one of the better vitamin/mineral additives on the market.

For those of you who live near marine coastal areas, the small, live marine baitfish and/or shrimp that some bait shops provide their local fishermen are an excellent source of live food. And if the hobbyist utilizes a sump or refugium, the practice of temporarily holding a few baitfish or live shrimp in those systems as a ready live food source should be considered. (Don't be tempted to overstock, however, or your water quality will suffer.)

As an occasional treat for both the fish and the aquarist, consider feeding live mollies, especially those raised in seawater. They are often raised under much better condi-

Aquarist uses a feeder stick to wiggle a silverside to entice a feeding response. Silversides are of marine origin and have the correct amino acid and fatty acid profiles to meet the needs of saltwater predators.

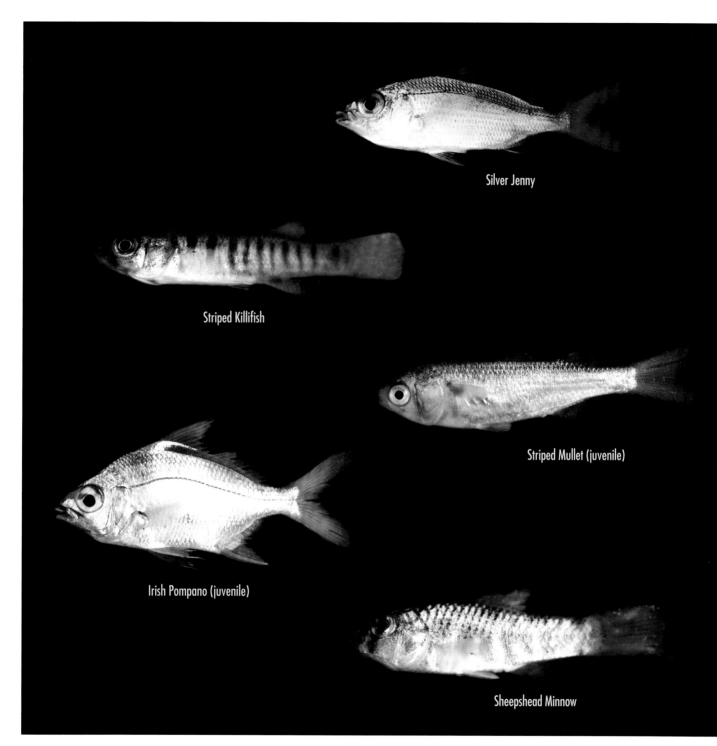

Silver Jenny

Striped Killifish

Striped Mullet (juvenile)

Irish Pompano (juvenile)

Sheepshead Minnow

Saltwater minnows, baitfish, and various juveniles of marine species are an excellent live food option for aquarists who have access to netting areas or dealers who stock them. If necessary, they can be held in a barebottom quarantine tank and observed for signs of disease before releasing into a display aquarium.

Striped Anchovies (*Anchoa hepsetus*), an excellent feeder species, are available fresh in some coastal areas. Most inland aquarists can substitute frozen Atlantic Silversides (*Menidia menidia*), which, when thawed, will be readily accepted by most carnivores, such as lionfishes, groupers, moray eels, and large wrasses.

tions than feeder goldfish and can survive in the marine aquarium, even if not originally raised in seawater, until your fish are ready to feed. Mollies raised in seawater and fed marine fish foods make for a much better choice than other live freshwater fish.

Among the other goldfish substitutes, we have found frozen, minnow-like, saltwater silversides, first defrosted, to be excellent for lionfish and moray eels, which will take them greedily. Keep in mind that these must be kept in an airtight container to prevent them from drying out. Large, freeze-dried, whole krill, soaked in a vitamin supplement to plump them up, are also eaten with relish.

EARTHWORMS As an occasional treat that is high in protein, calcium, and various vitamins, these worms, *Lumbricus terrestris*, are good for large fish like stingrays, squirrelfish, hawkfish, and snappers. When chopped or shredded, they are also excellent for smaller carnivorous fishes. These dark red worms reach about 6–8 inches (20 cm) in length and can be purchased at bait stores or even dug up in your own backyard. They can be kept in a Styrofoam® box in a medium such as peat moss. If kept slightly damp and in a cool, dark place and fed baby oatmeal, they may breed and provide a never-ending supply. They can be maintained for months in the refrigerator if kept slightly moist (and discretely tucked out of the view of other family members.)

Caution is advised if the worms are acquired from an agricultural site where fertilizers and pesticides have been used. Because they eat dirt, they can contain a large amount of it. It is wise to stretch the worm out on a firm surface and roll a pencil over it lengthwise to force out its gut contents before using it as a food source for your fish.

WHITE WORMS These are closely related to the common earthworm and range from 0.5 to 1.5 inch (2 cm). They live in moist soil and feed on decaying vegetation and cellulose matter. You can purchase them at many pet shops or mail-order a starter culture and raise them yourself. Use a container filled with damp potting soil, preferably with a tight-fitting cover to keep out ants. Occasionally dust the top surface of the soil with baking soda to keep it alkaline. Bread or crackers soaked in milk, baby food, mashed potatoes, cottage cheese, yogurt, and cornmeal are good foodstuffs. Add fresh food as old food disappears. A crushed multi-vitamin tablet or enriched yeast and cod-liver oil can also be added to their diet if desired. White worms represent a good occasional treat, and may be used during breeding. As these worms are quite fatty, be careful not to overfeed and be sure to wash them well before using.

TUBIFICID WORMS Blackworms (*Lumbriculus variegatus*) or red worms (*Tubifex* spp.) are small, hair-like worms, about 1.5 inches (2.0 cm) in length. Although they are very high in protein, red worms are usually collected from areas very high in nutrients, sometimes where sewage is discharged. Therefore they may be contaminated with bacteria or heavy metals. Blackworms make a much better choice, as they are usually deliberately cultured and therefore less apt to contain harmful contaminants.

The worms generally anchor themselves in the substrate, and when lacking substrate they form a ball anchoring themselves to each other. They die almost immediately upon contact with saltwater. One good trick is to place a small number of worms in a clear plastic butter dish and slowly allow aquarium water to fill the dish as it is placed on the aquarium bottom. Fish then swim into the dish to feed, selecting the worms as needed and preventing dead worms from getting swept around the aquarium where they would disintegrate and add unwanted pollutants.

These worms can be stored in the refrigerator in a small dish containing just enough freshwater to cover them. The water they are kept in must be changed at least once daily. This is another live foodstuff that can be utilized as an occasional meal or treat.

MEALWORMS An insect larva, usually of the small beetle *Tenebrio molitor*, mealworms, sometimes available at pet shops and also easy to culture, are another occasional treat option. The younger larvae are the most suitable because they are

the softest. They can be cultured in any type of container other than cardboard, as they would eat their way through it. Crumpled newspaper is a good substrate. Provide some ventilation and feed potatoes, bread soaked in milk or beer, powdered rice, chicken feed, oatmeal, bran, flour, dog biscuits, graham crackers, cornmeal, apples, breadcrumbs, or lettuce. Place the grain food in the bottom, then some

Bloodworms, available freeze-dried or in frozen form from aquarium shops, are midge larvae and are very enticing to many fish. They can be used as an occasional very rich treat as well as a conditioning food.

rolled oats or sliced potatoes, then crumpled newspapers. Add about 100 mealworms in a shoebox-size container and keep at about 80°F (27°C). About three weeks later harvesting can begin. Mealworms are a good food source that can sometimes get fussy butterflyfish and eels to feed.

FRUIT FLIES Yet another food source that can be utilized as an occasional treat is wingless (*Drosophila melanogaster*) or the larger flightless fruit flies (*Drosophila hydei*). Cultures and culture media are available from various sources. They

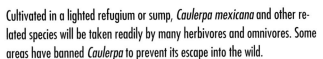

Cultivated in a lighted refugium or sump, *Caulerpa mexicana* and other related species will be taken readily by many herbivores and omnivores. Some areas have banned *Caulerpa* to prevent its escape into the wild.

are an especially good food source for fish that will take food from the surface. A jar capped with cheesecloth will prevent wild flies from entering the culture. To make your own media, use equal parts water and baby food with a slight bit of yeast, or use overripe fruit mixed with bran, then sprinkle with some yeast. Place an ice-cream stick or piece of chopstick in the jar, almost reaching the top, so that some flies can easily be moved to a new culture, which should be started every three to four weeks. Because the flies are flightless, simply remove the ice-cream stick,

which is usually covered with flies, and shake over the water's surface. They will remain alive on the water where interested fish can get them.

Herbivore Foods

LIVE MACROALGAE Many of the species of leafy marine algae are an excellent source of live food for herbivorous fishes. They are also a good source of EPA (eicosapentaenoic acid, an omega-3 fatty acid). In fact, we have found two species of *Caulerpa*, *C. mexicana* and *C. prolifera*, to be favorites of many herbivores, especially surgeonfish. Others report good success with *C. sertularoides*.

One warning: All species of *Caulerpa* are now banned in California and aquarists everywhere are encouraged to use extreme caution in keeping them from escaping into the wild. Huge areas of the Mediterranean Sea are overrun by *Caulerpa taxifolia* that was inadvertently released from a public aquarium. This is considered a noxious, invasive weed and must be used only with care or not at all. When disposing of any type of marine algae, freeze it for at least 24 hours and put it in the garbage or compost heap. A responsible aquarist will never flush any live aquarium material down the drain.

There are many other large-bodied algae species, whether brown, green, or red, that various fish find tasty and that do not have the stigma that is attached to *Caulerpa*. Among those especially liked by tangs or surgeonfishes are the red or yellow, stringy *Gracilaria parvispora*, the green lettucelike *Ulva* spp., and the golden *Sargassum spp*. Matching a species of algae to a particular species of fish is a subject far beyond the scope of this book. Be assured, however, if you keep herbivorous fish, that these macroalgae species appear to provide many of the important trace nutrients, fatty acids, and vitamins these fish need to remain healthy.

TABLE FOODS/LETTUCES Human foodstuffs such as Romaine lettuce, iceberg lettuce, green peas, spinach, and broccoli do not deliver the same high level of nutrients that fresh macroalgae or dried nori seaweed do. Many of us have stopped using terrestrial plant matter, as marine algae has become more economical and much more readily available. However, these foods continue to be used by aquarists and at least can help provide for a variety of useable foodstuffs in the diet of some fish, especially herbivores.

If using garden greens, avoid iceberg lettuce, as it is very high in cellulose, which may clog the digestive tract if fed too often. Romaine and other leafy lettuces provide a much better source of Alpha Lipoic Acid (ALA), one of the vital omega-3 fatty acids.

Frozen peas, according to Kelly Jedlicki, have been known to cause bloating, bouyancy problems, and flatus (gas) in pufferfishes.

Spinach should be used with caution as well, as it contains oxalic acid, which can cause crystals to form in the kidneys. In fact, most of these green human foods are high in nitrate, which may sooner or later result in higher levels of nitrate in the aquarium water. But occasional feeding of these greens can add fiber and help keep fish digestive tracts clear, with "occasional" being the key word.

For those who wish to use lettuce, we recommend first blanching it in scalding water for about 30 seconds or freezing it prior to feeding. This will aid in the break-down of some of the cellulose content and may also aid in the digestion of other foods consumed. Some place it in a microwave for 15 seconds prior to feeding to break down the cellulose. Placing these leafy greens in a lettuce clip is a good way to manage this type of food. As in the case of nori, be careful not to allow the lettuce to block your overflow, causing water to rise over the rim of the tank. When feeding leafy things, it may be wise to remove any uneaten material before turning the lights out for the night.

Hold the iceberg: Sea Lettuce (*Ulva lactuca*) is one of a number of highly nutritious marine macroalgae species being aquacultured and becoming more widely available for the feeding of aquarium herbivores.

FISH/SHELLFISH FLESH The flesh of some marine animals is an excellent source of protein and fat and provides much energy potential. Additionally, some live shellfish are tempting for some very difficult feeders, especially Moorish Idols. This species, and many others, may enjoy picking at a just-opened clam or mussel half-shell containing a live, meaty morsel. If you can't get fresh shellfish in your area, try getting an empty clamshell and putting a similar frozen food on it, then placing it on the bottom of the aquarium. Keep in mind that mussels harvested and

Noxious Seaweed:

California has banned all *Caulerpa* macroalgae species and other areas may be ready to follow suit. Never allow any live aquarium plants or other matter to be flushed down the drain or released into local waters.

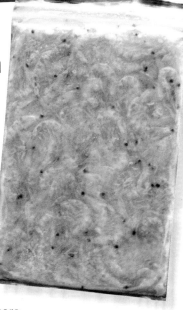

A virtual smorgåsbord of frozen foods can be found at most aquarium retail shops. These range from plankton, sponge-laced rations, bloodworms and herbivore formula foods, top, to krill, right.

fed live to fish may harbor parasites such as *Cryptocaryon*. In addition, many mollusks, including clams, mussels, and snails, harbor and release the infective cercaria stage of many species of digenetic trematodes. These types of foods should be frozen before use to kill potential parasites.

FROZEN FOODS You can either purchase a wide variety of already prepared frozen aquarium foods or prepare your own. Keep in mind that freezing alters amino acids and that vitamins C and E rapidly deteriorate. Adding a vitamin supplement prior to feeding most frozen foods is highly recommended.

Defrosting store-bought frozen fish foods in water prior to feeding is an ill-advised approach, nutritionally. Water-soluble vitamin B and antioxidant vitamins C and E are leached into the thawing water from the frozen product, mostly going to waste. Such a practice also causes some foods to break down into such fine particles that fish are no longer able to utilize the food source. We recommend simply allowing frozen food to naturally soften at room temperature for a short period of time and then placing the morsels into the aquarium. Thawing can also be done in the refrigerator, slowly and with the food covered by plastic to prevent drying or odor contamination .

HOMEMADE RATIONS To prepare your own frozen food, purchase a small quantity of various marine fish and seafood items, such as squid, shrimp, clams, scallops, mussels, crab, and fish flesh (halibut, perch, flounder, snapper, or haddock). Avoid oily flesh such as salmon, tuna, mackerel, herring, and sardines, as they create an oily film on the water's surface. Stay away from all freshwater choices, including tilapia, catfish, and trout.

The simplest method is this: Cut and clean each item and separate into small pieces. To make very small, bite-sized pieces, run the frozen piece over a cheese grater. Next, lay out a sheet of aluminum foil. Starting across the top of the sheet, place a variety of these pieces on the foil, separating them with a space about the width of your finger. About the same amount of space down, start another row, and repeat. After the sheet is filled, roll the sheet lengthwise and compress, so as to loosely seal the areas between pieces. Then place the whole roll in a large plastic freezer bag and store it in the freezer. Never allow bits of foil into the aquarium.

It's then only necessary to slightly unroll the sheet to have a variety of frozen foods so your fish have something different at each feeding.

Recipes for more ambitious homemade rations are included on page 111. These formulas are meant only as a starting point and are infinitely adaptable to suit your budget, the availability of different ingredients in your area, and your preferences regarding supplements and enriching agents. A general rule is to stick with ingredients of marine origin. Reading the labels of the better commercial marine food brands will provide additional ideas for customizing your particular recipes.

MYSIS SHRIMP Frozen *Mysis* shrimp are without doubt one of the best frozen foods available for your fish. These small crustaceans, *Mysis relicta*, are excellent for both freshwater and marine fish. In the wild, they make nightly verti-

Wild *Mysis* sp. shrimps in shallow area on the Norwegian coast: This is a fish food *par excellence* — much superior to the nutrition profile of adult brine shrimp and widely available as a frozen food. Mysid shrimp are a preferred food for seahorses, and some breeders are now keeping live cultures of this crustacean.

cal migrations from about 360 feet deep up to the surface to eat, then return to the depths at daybreak. These migrations require enormous amounts of energy, which is stored as animal fat, so they contain large quantities of naturally occurring fatty acids (omega-3 and omega-6), making them a highly nutritional food source. They are also very high in protein (about 70 percent) but low in carotenoids. If feeding a fairly steady diet of *Mysis*, which are harvested from freshwater, consider supplementing them with specialty foods known to contain color enhancers. However, we have performed necropsies on fish fed primarily on a *Mysis* diet and discovered fatty liver degeneration as a cause of death, so be sure to vary the diet with other foods.

Always look for a product that contains intact *Mysis* specimens when thawed. The reason for this is that pieces of *Mysis* shrimp leach their valuable fatty acids into surrounding water. Products that are made up of pieces are of less nutritional value to the animals consuming them.

There is also a preferred way to defrost *Mysis* shrimp so the whole specimens do not burst open and lose their very valuable fatty acids. Simply keep a small container of seawater in the refrigerator that is slightly above the salinity normally found in the wild (about 1.025). Place the piece of frozen *Mysis* to be fed in a small container and cover it with some of the refrigerated seawater. Allow it to thaw at room temperature and then pour it through a small net and feed. If you do pour the thawing water into your aquarium, keep an eye on your protein skimmer, as this may cause excessive foam production, possibly making your skimmer overflow.

Marine researcher Zan Didoha with a handful of fresh table shrimp destined to be minced into rations for marine aquarium fishes.

Do-It-Yourself Marine Rations

Make your own top-quality frozen foods

Aquarists with minimal kitchen skills, a food processor, a freezer, and a tolerant family can make very high quality, economical rations using ingredients from the seafood counter, drugstore, and supermarket or health food store.

Equipment
• Food Processor

Supplies
• Ziploc® freezer bags (pints or quarts)

Ingredients from seafood market
• Shrimp/prawns
• Squid
• Mussels
• Clams
• Octopus
• Marine fish fillet (white or non-oily flesh, such as Pacific cod, mahi-mahi, sole)
• Nori/kelp sheets for sushi

Ingredients from aquarium shop
• Silversides
• Dried seaweed sheets or flakes
• *Spirulina* flakes
• Marine vitamin mix
• Cyclop-eeze®
• *Mysis* shrimp

Ingredients from drugstore or health food store
• Fish oil, krill oil, cod-liver oil
• *Spirulina* powder
• Liquid multi-vitamins
• Dry seaweed (nori, dulse, kombu, wakame, sea palm)
• Spinach (frozen)
• Peas (frozen)
• Agar-agar (or unflavored gelatin)

Steps

1. Freeze seafood items for approximately 4 hours or overnight. (Optional: To kill any pathogens, you may opt to gently steam or microwave the raw fish, usually for no more than 5 minutes.)

2. Cut or break any dried seaweed sheets into smaller pieces.

3. Mix all ingredients and chop in a food processor (do not add water), stopping frequently to check the size of the chunks. Aim for bite-size pieces to suit your particular fishes. (You may want to remove some of the mix at a larger size for bigger fishes, then continue chopping for smaller species.)

4. Place a scoop of the finished mix in a plastic bag, place on a counter or cookie sheet, and press gently to make a uniform flat cake, no more than a quarter of an inch thick. (Thicker cakes will be hard to break into pieces at feeding time.) Expel as much air as possible from the plastic bag and seal. Place flat in freezer immediately.

5. To feed, break off chunks, return unused portion to the freezer, thaw chunks briefly, and add to the aquarium. Use within three months to avoid freezer-burn.

Basic Omnivore Formula

8 oz shrimp or krill
6 oz marine fish fillet
2 oz squid (calamari)
½ cup dry nori/seaweed or *Spirulina* flakes
1 tsp vitamin supplement
Optional: gelling agent (see below), 1 Tbsp Cyclop-eeze®

Herbivore Formula

8 oz *Mysis* shrimp or reef/ocean plankton (copepods/krill)
1 cup dry nori/seaweed or *Spirulina* flakes
½ cup frozen baby peas
½ cup frozen spinach or baby spinach leaves
1 tsp vitamin supplement (Selcon® or other)
Optional: gelling agent (see below), 1 Tbsp Cyclop-eeze®

Gelling Agents

Rations can be thickened with unflavored gelatin from any supermarket (follow package directions) or, more appropriately, with agar-agar, a clear, flavorless gel of seaweed origin (follow package instructions for gelling). Available in bakery sections and health food stores. Some fishkeepers feel that using a gel is not necessary, as the food is consumed so rapidly by their fishes.

Diseases & Conditions

The alert aquarist who observes his or her fishes daily can often catch problems before they get out of hand. Previous page: Large Maroon Clownfish female with onset of ectoparasite attack.

You're the Vet

How to react when problems arise

Sooner or later, the time will come when one of your fishes no longer appears to be acting normally. Chances are slim that you will be able to call a veterinarian, as relatively few small-animal practitioners are prepared to deal with sick aquarium fishes. You might be able to bring in a local aquarium shop owner, if you are on good terms with him or her and want to invest in a house call. In most cases, you are on your own and will have to treat the fish yourself.

This is the time to try to place the abnormal appearance or behaviors into some categories and apply the appropriate treatment. Symptoms are not always textbook perfect, but here is the starting point for defining a possible problem and charting a course of action.

Disease Symptoms

Various behaviors and external clues often indicate the presence of disease. These include:
- Increased respiration (gasping, pumping gills rapidly)
- Pale coloration
- Cloudy eyes
- Frayed fins
- Visible ulcers or open wounds
- Scratching against substrate
- Decreased swimming activity
- Odd swimming patterns

Researcher Melanie Rhodes at the Mote Marine Laboratory sets up to test samples of aquarium water, often the first diagnostic step to take when the sudden onset of certain symptoms is spotted.

- White or red spots on the body and fins
- Refusal to eat
- Clamped fins
- Unusual behavior

These observations can generally be fitted into two broad-ranging categories, depending on how quickly the onset occurred: Suddenly or over a period of time.

Short-Term Symptoms (Sudden Onset)

Short-term symptoms, appearing within a period of hours rather than days, and with no outward signs of disease, may include the following: All fish are swimming near the surface, some may use sudden darting movements or swim-

ming patterns that are not normal, many are sloughing their slime coats, some have torn fins and/or body wounds, and/or some appear to be hiding more than usual. If your fish are displaying any of these symptoms, an environmental or water-quality problem may very well be the cause.

TO DO: CHECK WATER PARAMETERS To begin your diagnosis, first check the essential measures of water quality in your tank: temperature, specific gravity, ammonia, nitrite, nitrate, pH, and, if possible, dissolved oxygen level. Have there been any major water changes lately, and if so, what was the volume and quality of the water? There's no doubt that if the volume is too large or the water has not been adequately dechlorinated, the change can cause animal stress. What are the levels of those nitrogen-laden products mentioned above? We believe no ammonia or nitrite should be present, as this would indicate that the nitrification process is either out of balance or, worse, overwhelmed and the biological system is stressed. Check that there is not a dead animal or an equipment malfunction in the system. Additional filtration and housekeeping are in order, and very possibly the sand bed needs vacuuming.

Has aquarium maintenance fallen way behind, or is the system so overcrowded that fish are staying near the surface and breathing rapidly? If so, lack of oxygen may be the cause, and this can usually be corrected quickly with an increase in aeration and/or water circulation and a good cleaning of the aquarium. However, there could be a *Vibrio* infection caused by poor maintenance. Check its symptoms, therapy, and control on pages 176-177.

Preventive measures include monthly water changes of about 15 percent to dilute the by-products of metabolism and replenish some of the more important trace elements that fish ingest daily.

As for temperature, a fairly steady level between 75 and 80° F suits most marine fish. Temperature sensitivity is species-dependent, but fluctuations of more than 2–3 degrees in a day can cause stress to any fish, possibly leading to disease. Fish thrive on stability. Be sure that your heating and chilling equipment are adequate for the size of the system and working properly.

The possibility of airborne chemicals should also be

Suspect water conditions, often accompanied by telltale signs of nuisance algae and accumulated wastes in tank and filter system, can set the stage for disease.

given some thought. Have paints, glues, or varnishes been used recently in the home? Have insect sprays been applied to areas inside the home? Have aerosols containing cleaning fluids, such as free ammonia, been used to clean nearby surfaces such as windows or countertops?

If so, changing the water and filtering it through fresh activated carbon or a contaminant-absorbant Poly-Filter® may be necessary.

Aquarium Environment

If there are injured inhabitants, odd swimming patterns, or sudden deaths in the aquarium, several initial questions must be asked. Are the species in the tank compatible? If not, the aggressors (or victims) should be moved to other suitable quarters. Is the system overcrowded? This causes territorial disputes and leads to the strongest of the occupants becoming aggressive, resulting in stressed, injured, or dead tankmates. Overcrowding a system can also tax water quality, compounding the problem. Are there sufficient hiding places in the aquarium for all its fish? Does the aquarium look to be maintained properly, or is there detritus collecting in huge amounts? Does the system appear to have adequate filtration and water movement for its size and number of inhabitants? The resolution of such issues is self-explanatory.

Postmortem & Euthanasia Protocols

It is far better to perform an "antemortem" (before death) examination on a live fish and successfully diagnose and treat it, saving it and its tankmates, than to perform a postmortem examination, or necropsy, on a dead fish. Unfortunately, there are times when fish die without any clear outward signs that would adequately reveal the nature of the problem. To get an expert opinion on what killed a fish, it will be necessary to preserve the specimen properly and in a timely fashion.

Moving swiftly is the key, as a fish that has been dead for over 30 minutes begins to deteriorate and lose its postmortem value, and any parasites that may have been present begin to leave the host.

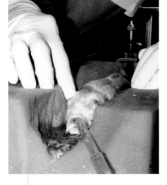
Examination of a live fish calls for anesthesia with MS-222 or clove oil.

Chemical Preservation

Biological specimens can best be preserved in a formalin fixitive. Prepare this solution by adding nine parts water to one part formaldehyde (37 percent). Each fish to be preserved should be submerged in fixative that is about 10 times the volume of the specimen. Fish under one inch (2.5 cm) can be preserved whole, without any further openings made on the body. With larger fish, the belly should be slit open so the fixative can penetrate the organs. The containers holding these specimens should be unbreakable, with tight fitting lids, and should be clearly labeled.

Deep Freezing

Unfortunately, preserving a fish by freezing may yield inconclusive results. Freezing causes tissues to expand and burst, making the identification of any parasites almost impossible. If you have no other choice, simply place the specimen in a Ziploc® plastic freezer bag and seal. Then place it in a second bag, seal, label with date and place it in the freezer.

Outside Laboratories

Some veterinarians and colleges will take properly prepared specimens can be taken for examination—for a fee or in exchange for a small donation. If it is necessary to ship specimens to an examining laboratory, those that have been chemically prepared must have been in a fixative solution for at least two days. They can then be removed, wrapped in a cloth made damp with the fixative, and double-bagged sealed Ziploc® plastic bags.

Euthanasia

The best path to take when a fish is clearly suffering or obviously dying is humane euthanasia. Freezing the still-living fish, flushing it down the drain, or asphixiating with club soda or Alka-Seltzer® (CO_2) are not considered appropriate or humane. A much better choice involves overdosing with such anesthetics as MS-222 (tricaine methanesulfonate), quinaldine or clove oil (eugenol), the latter being both very effective and easily available at health-food stores.

Marine researcher Matt Wittenrich offers this protocol: "Clove oil is insoluble in cold water, so a solution of clove oil and ethanol (ethyl alcohol, 70-90%) should be prepared

> ### ! Humane Euthanasia:
> Never use freezing or flushing down the drain to end a dying fish's life. More humane methods, including anesthesia with clove oil, are readily available.

(9 parts ethanol to 1 part clove oil). (Some hobbyists simply add clove oil to warm aquarium water in a plastic bag and shake vigorously.) This is about 2 ml of the solution per 5 liters of water for anesthesia. Fish should be immobilized within three minutes. Euthanasia is either an overdose of clove oil, a longer bath, or, after anesthesia, fixation in formalin, alcohol or freezing. The solution should be freshly mixed and not be stored for later use. A bath with a concentration of 40 mg/L is a good starting point."

A microscope is a great tool for the serious aquarist and a must-have for any aquarium retail shop. Even an inexpensive beginner or student model in the 40X-100x magnification range will prove very helpful in examining suspected parasites, foods, or unexpected items that appear in every ecosystem.

If a dead fish is seen and does not appear to have been killed by its tankmates, its age should be questioned, as some species are short-lived and it may just have come to the end of its natural life. On the other hand, if the dead fish was recently quarantined and treated with a medication, its immune system or other biological processes might have been compromised.

Large Sudden Fish Loss

If there has been a large die-off of fish (commonly known as a wipeout), was a toxin released into the water? Possible sources include cleaning fluids, pesticides, or even natural toxins released by a fish, such as a soapfish, or an invertebrate, such as a sea apple. Has an overload of food been spilled into the tank? Another possibility is mechanical failure: Did an automatic water-level valve allow the tank to be filled with freshwater? Did a heater or chiller malfunction and cause a dramatic temperature shift? Before suspecting disease, ensure that all filtration, circulation, and temperature control systems are functioning properly.

If a toxin is suspected, a series of major water changes (25 percent every four hours, if possible) should be started, using properly mixed and temperature-corrected water.

Activated carbon and/or Poly Filters should be employed to help pull any toxins out of the water, preferably with a canister or power filter or in the sump where all system water is forced through the carbon or filter pad. If the dead fish have been in the water for very long, it will take some drastic measures to get your water parameters back to normal.

Alternatively, did a virulent disease bloom to epidemic proportions? We have seen cases where diseases such as *Brooklynella* and *Amyloodinium* have caused an entire population of fish to be wiped out within 48 hours of identification of the disease.

Long-Term Symptoms (Slow Onset)

Symptoms or warning signs that develop over a number of days or weeks can include unexplained losses, scratching and irritations, tumors, loss of balance, and/or wasting away. Such long-term symptoms may also be considered chronic. Do not medicate until you're sure of the source of the problem or the offending disease has been identified, or at least you've narrowed down the possibilities to a few strong ones.

Scratching, along with white pinhead spots on the body and fins, could well be a case of *Cryptocaryon irritans* (marine ich). What may appear as a fine dusting of white powder could be the deadly *Amyloodinium* (marine velvet). Cauliflower-like growths on fins and/or skin may be lymphocystis. Hemorrhages or ulcerations may be caused by a bacterial infection or disease. Loss of weight (emaciation) may be the result of incorrect diet or an internal disease, including bacteria, or parasites. A distended eye (popeye) may simply be an injury, but it could signify an internal bacterial infection or, worse, an incurable internal fungus. Erosions on the face and along the lateral line may be HLLE (head and lateral line erosion). Small black dots seen on the sides of brightly colored fish, such as Yellow Tangs, may be turbellarian worms. All of these maladies are examined in detail in the next chapters. Difficult diagnoses may require that you get a sick fish to an expert for examination before it dies.

NUTRITIONAL NEEDS Should fish appear weak or wasting away, it may be from improper nutrition. Are the fish being offered a nutritionally sound and balanced food supply? Are they being fed frequently and regularly? Feeding a big meal once a day (or, worse, less frequently) is usually not in the best interest of many fishes in a mixed environ-

Calculating Water Volume

The dosage levels of the medications used most often in the aquarium hobby are often noted as parts per million (ppm) or the ratio of grams to a given number of gallons or liters of water. Therefore, it is important to make a fairly accurate calculation of the volume of water in the container to be treated. There are three measuring systems: U.S. customary, Imperial, and metric.

If the container is square or rectangular, measure (in inches) its inside dimensions, as they will yield the true volume. (If there is a sand bed in the container or aquarium, measure the height from halfway up the bed to the top of the water.) Then multiply length x width x height and divide the result by 231, which results in the number of U.S. gallons in the container. Should the container hold other substrate, such as rock, depending upon the space it occupies it would be advisable to deduct a minimum of 5–15 percent from the total to get a fairly accurate water volume.

If the metric system is to be used, take the same inside measurements in centimeters (1 inch = 2.5 cm), mulitply length x width x height, and divide the result by 1,000 to find the number of liters in the container.

That was easy, but what if the container is round?

First measure the inside diameter of the base in inches and divide that number by 2 to get the radius. Next, measure the height of the water in the container. Then square the resulting radius number and multiply it by 3.14 and by the water height, which tells you the number of cubic inches. Divide that figure by 231, resulting in the number of U.S. gallons of water.

If using metric, simply use centimeters instead of inches, proceed as above, and divide the result by 1,000 to get liters.

ment. Nor is the feeding of only one type of food, as a community of captive fishes needs a variety of different foodstuffs to remain healthy.

All foods being fed should be fresh. Avoid foods that have been improperly stored for a long time. Rancid dry foods are a threat to health, and spoiled or freezer-burned frozen foods are unfit for consumption, although a very hungry fish may take almost anything. Keep in mind that some fish are shy feeders and may not be getting their share of available foodstuffs. Take a look at the mix of species in the aquarium and be sure all have access to the foods they need at feeding time. If one fish is dominating the tank and driving others away from their food, it may be time to remove the bad actor.

Through a lens: magnified view of parasitic copepods on a marine fish. All three specimens are females with tubular egg sacs filled with white eggs.

Disposal of Dead Fish

It is neither humane nor responsible to flush dead or dying fish down a toilet. The potential for plumbing problems aside, those disease organisms could infect other animals if the waste eventually ended up in natural waters. A much better method is to wrap the dead fish in paper and wet the paper with a disinfectant or bleach, then seal it inside a plastic Ziploc® bag. Dispose of it in the trash container.

Do-It-Yourself Antemortem and Postmortem

We highly recommend that most shop owners and serious aquarists, especially those with large investments in their aquariums, have a small, well-equipped, sanitary area where antemortem and postmortem procedures can be carried out. We offer here a simplified overview, not a detailed

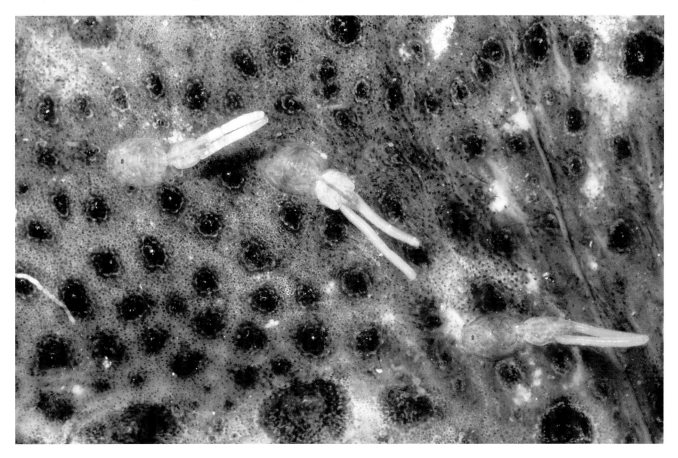

A male Shortfin Lionfish (*Dendrochirus brachypterus*) badly beaten by a male conspecific. Quickly isolated in a hospital tank, this fish was able to recover.

set of how-to instructions. For that, we recommend taking classes at disease workshops offered by many universities and organizations with interest in the fields of fish care and aquatic veterinary medicine. Obviously, the hobbyist will generally be involved in all of this as an observer and will need an expert to do the actual hands-on work or receive training before attempting it himself or herself.

Most fish health experts segregate problems into three categories: quickly developing, gradually occurring, and affecting a particular species.

When symptoms quickly affect most fish in a system, including a range of species, environmental causes must be considered—first check all water quality parameters and take immediate corrective action. For those symptoms devel-

oping over a period of days and intensifying as time passes, whether affecting one or more species, an infectious disease is a good possibility and more in-depth analysis is required. Should the disease be limited to a small number of fish or a particular species and show no signs of spreading, placing the affected fish in a quarantine/hospital tank until an antemortem procedure can be done may be the best way to proceed. Very slow development of a problem can be related to nutrition, environment, or certain internal parasites.

ANTEMORTEM These examinations are done on afflicted but still living specimens. Fish tissue deteriorates very rapidly after death, and fish disease experts usually much prefer to work with a live fish.

To accomplish some of the more common tests, such as

cultures and biopsies, some general equipment and supplies are required. A microscope with multiple magnifications, e.g., 4x, 10x, 20x, 40x, and even up to 100x, would be more than adequate for most needs. Other items include, but are not limited to, microscope glass slides and coverslips; a dissection kit containing scissors and forceps of the proper sizes and lengths; a sharp scalpel and tweezers; hypodermic needles (25–28 gauge); syringes (1 and 3 ml); culture dishes; and, to define bacterial infections, gram stains.

Tests can be done on alert/awake animals, but anesthetizing them first may prevent or at least lessen damage to the individual. MS-222 is the preferred anesthetic. Once the fish is removed from the aquarium, it should be placed on a damp towel, which has been wetted with aquarium water. The fish is held with a plastic-gloved hand, and the damp towel should cover most of the fish, with a small opening to give access to the necessary area, depending upon what test(s) will be conducted.

Fish that are not eating or are wasting away may have an internal disease, and a bacteria culture may be the best way to proceed. A gill biopsy might be the correct approach for a fish experiencing breathing difficulty. A skin scraping, or the removal of a section of fin, may be the correct approach for lesions on the skin or fins. A fecal specimen can also be obtained to test for internal parasites. Cultures can help determine the correct treatment procedure, especially where bacterial infections are concerned. Once the cause is clear, a treatment path can be charted.

POSTMORTEM This procedure must occur on a specimen that has died within the past 30 minutes. Keep in mind that a specimen found dead in the aquarium may have died hours earlier, and in that case a postmortem would have limited value in evaluating the cause of death. Nevertheless, a postmortem procedure should still be considered as a learning tool for future similar procedures.

The postmortem involves external and internal examination. It's wise to wear rubber gloves, as some animal diseases are transmittable to humans and can easily enter our bodies through an open wound, or by rubbing our eyes. As for an external examination, it is pretty straightforward: Look for a thinner-than-normal appearance for the species, damaged fins, lesions, visible parasites, and other outward irregularities. Appropriate treatment can then be made available to the tankmates.

If no obvious cause is seen, then an internal examination should be performed. Again, this is far beyond the

Sudden Onset Alert:

If all fish in a community tank suddenly show signs of distress, immediately check all water parameters, pumps, and temperature-control and filtration equipment. Look for the possibility of poisoning. See Non-pathogenic diseases, page 181.

scope of this book, but the postmortem is a powerful tool in fish husbandry, as the information gathered can save other fishes by making sure we treat the specific ailment with the correct medication or environmental change.

Calculating Drug Dosages

Generally, dosage terminology is in parts per million (ppm), milligrams per liter (mg/L), or grams/milliliters (g/ml) per volume of treated water. One ppm equals 1 mg/L or 1 milligram (mg) of the chemical in 1000 milliliters (1 liter) of water. Another way to put it is 3.8 milligrams in 1 U.S. gallon of water. The conversion factor, therefore, is 0.0038, as there are 38 milligrams per gallon, resulting in 1 ppm. (1.0 gram equals 1000 milligrams, 0.1 gram equals 100 milligrams, and 0.01 gram equals 10 milligrams.)

There may be times when the drug to be used is not in its pure form (100% pure) and is mixed with a carrier, which reduces the potency. If so, it should be indicated on the label. If the treatment calls for a specific amount of a drug to be added to a specific amount of water, and the product to be used contains a "purity factor," the following method can be used to determine the amount of the product needed to meet the dosage recommendation: Multiply the number of U.S. gallons by the recommended dosage in ppm, and multiply that result by 0.0038. Then, to find the dosage in grams, multiply that result by the purity factor. For example, you have a product that is only 50 percent pure and have 100 gallons requiring a 0.5 ppm application. The following formula then applies: 100 gallons x .5 ppm x 0.0038 = 0.19 grams; then divide by the purity factor (.19 grams/.5 = .38 grams).

Should the metric system be used, apply the same formula but do not apply the conversion factor (0.0038). Many people find it simplest to work with metric only, rather than mixing units of measure. This usually means nothing more than converting the volume of water in the treatment tank from gallons to liters.

Treatment Protocols

In general, it is a good practice to treat all the fishes in an infected aquarium whenever any one of them shows signs of infectious disease. Once a disease is introduced into an aquarium, all of the fish are exposed and susceptible.

The exception to this is in the case of reef systems, where treatment must be conducted in a separate hospital

Moribund Clark's Clownfish (*Amphiprion clarkii*) suffering from *Brooklynella hostilis* infestation. When treatment fails, humane euthanisia is called for.

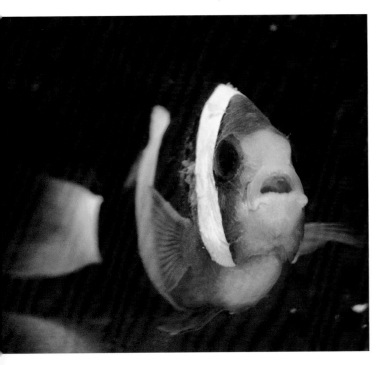

tank, since many of the recognized remedies are toxic to invertebrates. In this case, treating your fish will only be part of the solution. After you have separated your vertebrates from your invertebrates, a fish pathogen could continue to lurk in your aquarium for some time, only to again afflict your previously treated fish when they are reintroduced.

For example, most of the parasites of concern to aquarists are obligate, meaning that they require a fish as a host in order to complete their life cycle. In order to break the parasite's life cycle, you must keep the potential hosts out of the show aquarium for a period no shorter than the life cycle of the parasite in question. Life cycles of some specific parasites can be found in the chapter on parasitic diseases (pages 142–171).

Diagnosing Disease

Fish diseases and conditions are many, but the following chapters will cover most of the problems encountered by the majority of marine aquarists. In each case we will offer insight into how to recognize a disease or health condition, how to treat it, and how to prevent its occurrence.

Using reference photographs to identify diseases and health problems is a starting point, but it has its limitations. Because many fish diseases exhibit similar outward symptoms, it is difficult or impossible to diagnose some of them from outward appearance alone. Positive diagnosis of many fish diseases requires microscopic examination of biopsy material. There is some skill involved in taking specimens and preparing slides to view under the microscope. For those fishkeepers who have these skills, we have included photos of the pathogens that cause many of the diseases discussed.

A good local aquarium store can be your best friend at the time of a disease outbreak—the staff may be able to help with the diagnosis or direct you to a local veterinarian or marine biologist. Similarly, an aquarium society may be able to direct you to someone willing and able to help.

In seeking outside advice, you should be prepared to reveal all your water parameters and environmental conditions: volume of system, stocking details, temperature, pH,

Young Clown Triggers (*Balistoides conspicillum*) on display in a local fish store: Any white spots call for quick quarantine and treatment.

specific gravity, ammonia/ammonium level, nitrite level, nitrate level, and any other readings you may have. What is your water change schedule? Have you recently added a new animal? Was it quarantined first? Chances are there will be clues to what triggered the problem when water quality, husbandry, and stocking history are evaluated.

Medication Cautions

While many aquarium medications can be bought without a prescription, they must be handled with respect.

Because many medications are toxic to humans, safety is of the utmost importance. Many of these compounds are considered carcinogenic and can be exceptionally dangerous. It has been demonstrated, for instance, that formalin is harmful to fetuses, so women who are pregnant should never handle it or any compound containing it.

It is absolutely essential to practice proper techniques when handling any medications or chemicals used in the treatment of fish diseases or the sanitizing of equipment. We recommend the use of eye protection and latex gloves when handling liquids such as formalin, malachite green, and copper sulfate. In addition, wear a dust particle mask (available at hardware stores) when handling powders, antibiotics, and the like. And, of course, always keep all medications out of the reach of children and pets.

Furthermore, many chemicals can have deleterious effects on the environment and can kill other organisms in the waterways. They can pollute our municipal water systems, or cause undesirable algal and vascular plant blooms or die-offs. Although organophosphates are used extensively in small quantities as a treatment for monogeneans,

Environmental watchdogs have great concerns about aquarium chemicals and contaminants being flushed into local watersheds. Always dispose of aquarium drugs and wastes in a responsible manner.

they can kill sharks and rays, as well as waterfowl and invertebrates, if allowed to enter the waterways. This is of special concern if such chemicals accumulate above normal tolerance levels in natural habitats.

Many other chemicals can cause fish die-off when dumped down the storm gutters. Chlorine will oxidize everything it comes in contact with. Always think of the

> *"Many aquarium chemicals, if not properly disposed of, can have deleterious effects on the environment and can kill other organisms in the waterways. They can pollute our municipal water systems, or cause undesirable algal and vascular plant blooms or die-offs."*

water table and where the medication or chemical will ultimately end up before you use it, and dispose of it responsibly. Be sure to read and fully understand all of the use and precautionary instructions provided by the manufacturer. There is nothing more important than your safety and the preservation of the world in which we live.

Many communities now have toxic waste drop-off locations, where people are encouraged to bring paint, solvents, pesticides, and the like. If you have aquarium medications that need to be disposed of, this may be the best solution.

Finally, the mention of any chemical or drug in this book in no way represents an endorsement or a recommendation for its use; nor does it imply that it is approved for use by the Environmental Protection Agency or the Food and Drug Administration. The inclusion of a drug or product here does not guarantee successful treatment, but does indicate that the authors and other aquarists have experienced positive results from its use.

In most cases, the outcome you experience will depend on how quickly you spotted the problem and how quickly you moved to correct it. For many of us, a disease outbreak or incident is a wake-up call, letting us know that we need to make some changes in our fishkeeping methods or in the way we introduce new specimens into our aquariums.

Remedies abound at most local aquarium shops. Many aquarists like to have a simple first-aid kit on hand for emergencies.

First Lines of Defense

A basic drug kit and traditional therapeutic methods for treating common diseases, conditions, and maladies

When disease appears in one of your fishes, a quick response is essential. A marine fish can go downhill rapidly and can infect others in a community setting. The first decision to be made is where treatment will take place.

Ideally, a sick fish should be removed from the display aquarium and treated in a small hospital tank or quarantine tank. Most medications are deadly to invertebrates, so if your aquarium houses any corals, ornamental shrimp, crabs, clams, snails, or plants, it cannot serve as a treatment center. Additionally, gravel and rock absorb medications, making it very difficult to maintain therapeutic levels. Porous materials, including live rock and coral gravel, absorb medications that may be released back into the tank at a later time, with unwanted consequences.

Many drugs will negatively impact the beneficial bacteria in an established aquarium and its filtration system, leading to water quality problems that can compound a disease outbreak. This is yet another reason to have a simple, bare-tank quarantine system running at all times and ready to act as an isolation ward for a fish with signs of disease or other problems that need attention.

There are quite a few non-prescription, easily obtainable products or applications used by amateur and professional aquarists that can have therapeutic value. Some hobbyists like to have a selection of them on hand to treat fish in quarantine or in a hospital tank. Success, of course, lies in using them properly and starting treatment in a timely fashion. Careful consideration should be given to these products before using them, and they should be employed according to the manufacturers' recommendations for dosage, duration of treatment, and disposal.

Juvenile High-hat (*Equetus acuminatus*) with fin rot. A species that is a notorious pathogen carrier, it routinely requires quarantine and treatment on arrival.

Formalin

A solution of formaldehyde gas in water, formalin has a long history of use against ectoparasites and monogeneans in fish. It is often dosed along with malachite green to kill the organisms that cause marine ich and velvet and may be used in freshwater dips. According to Dr. Edward Noga, for brief baths it is used at 0.125–0.25 of formalin per liter of treatment water, with dip sessions lasting up to an hour.

It will kill plants and invertebrates and should not be used in a display aquarium. Do not use if the fish have just been subjected to shipping stress or have been kept at temperatures above 80° F (27° C. (See Chapter 8 for details.) Formalin must be handled with great care, as it is carcinogenic and the fumes can damage human lungs. Keep it stored in a dark, cool place, well sealed, and out of the reach of children, a good practice with all aquarium drugs and chemicals. (Formalin is now banned in some states.)

Hydrogen Peroxide

This common household product is a strong oxidizing agent with good disinfecting properties for cleaning empty tanks and all manner of aquarium equipment. It leaves no traces of contaminants and is thus safer to use than chlorine bleach. It is very cheap and a good thing to have in your basic aquarium maintenance and treatment kit.

Peroxide can also be used to solve an acute oxygen deficiency. During power outages, the common 3 percent solution (available in your neighborhood pharmacy) at a rate of 1 teaspoon (5 ml) per 50 gallons (1 ml per 10 gallons), dosed every six to eight hours, can help keep oxygen at good levels. Even though the product is not a poison and its dissociated products are water and oxygen, if overdosed it can act as an antibacterial agent and destroy nitrifying bacteria, and even burn sensitive tissue, causing fish death. Angelfish are particularly sensitive. Therefore, caution is recommended if used in established aquariums.

For the purpose of disinfecting damaged fins and tissue, particularly in cases of territorial aggression and bacterial infection, add 30.5 ml of the 3 percent solution (1.03 oz or 2.03 Tbsp or 610 drops) to a 100-gallon aquarium that has been newly set up or to a 10-gallon aquarium that is well established and has a considerable amount of organic detritus in the substrate.

According to Nelson Herwig, "...this is the lowest common denominator that should be harmless to fish cell structure while being lethal to microbial organisms. This is an oxidizing agent and burns up everything it comes in contact with, including old food particles in the gravel, mulm, microorganisms (both good and bad) and any cell tissue (living or dead) that is susceptible to its action and is unprotected by slime such as is found on the integument of fish and most higher invertebrates. Its action and use depends on the suppression of lower life forms and the oxidizing of dead and decaying tissue, thus allowing the normal healing process to continue unhindered at a much more rapid rate."

For a prolonged immersion in a separate hospital tank, Dr. Edward Noga recommends that a more precise treatment can be prepared with 0.25 ml of the 3 percent hydrogen peroxide solution added to 1 liter of water or 1.0 ml per gallon, which results in a 7.5 ppm solution. In cases when the need is not extreme, the treatment can be reduced to 0.10 ml of 3 percent solution per liter, which equals approximately 3 ppm.

Hydrogen peroxide can also be used as a protozoacide for skin parasites, but many fish do not tolerate this treatment. Noga suggests two short-term treatment possibilities—add 10 ml of 3 percent solution per liter, equaling 300 ppm, and treat for 10–15 minutes, or add 19 ml of 3 percent solution per liter, equaling 570 ppm, and treat for 4 minutes.

This utilitarian product may also be placed directly on a skin wound as a topical sterilizing agent while the animal is out of the water. (Hydrogen peroxide is no longer recommended for such use on human wounds, as it can cause scarring.) It can also be used at fish auctions where bagged

> **Peroxide to the Rescue:**
> Hydrogen peroxide (3% solution) can be used to elevate oxygen levels in water during power outages at a dosage of 1 teaspoon per 50 gallons, repeated every six to eight hours.

fish may have low oxysgen content. One drop to a bag is all that's needed to rejuvenate the animal. Do not repeat the dosage.

Also, although still on an anecdotal basis, we have been experimenting with a 35 percent food-grade hydrogen peroxide solution to control undesirable algae. Although far more potential for danger exists when using such strong concentrations, we have been very pleased with the results using a dosage of .35 oz per 100 gallons. Interestingly (as a side benefit), we witnessed what appeared to be the "cure" of an Emperor Angel that had been severely infested with a sporozoan, most likely a *Myxosporidian* sp. We have also been impressed with the apparent cure of a Koran Angel that was affected by lymphocystis. As both diseases remain incurable at this writing, further research will continue on our part; these instances of apparent cures are tantalizing.

Malachite Green

Malachite green is often used in the freshwater hobby as an external fungicide and is especially useful on saprolegnia, a freshwater fungus. However, in the marine side of the hobby it's generally combined with formalin products and/or mixed with quinine hydrochloride. These combination treatments are quite effective on *Brooklynella*, which may be resistant to copper treatments. There are reports that malachite green interrupts *Amyloodinium ocellatum* tomont division at 2 mg/L, but the protocol for its application is unknown. Furthermore, be aware that malachite green "is a respiratory poison, teratogen, and suspected carcinogen," according to Noga, and it must be handled with care. It can be removed from treatment water by filtration through activated carbon and should never be flushed down the drain.

Methylene Blue

Methylene blue is a classic old aquarium remedy. It has antiseptic properties, mostly as a fungicide, and has been used in the freshwater hobby to prevent fungal infections, particularly for eggs. However, it can be used in freshwater dips and in the aquarium itself, where, as an oxygen carrier, it eases fish stress, particularly in animals with dam-

❗ Handle with Extreme Care:
Malachite green, formalin, and other aquarium chemicals can be very harmful to humans. Read and heed warnings.

aged gills. Methylene blue acts like an oxygen donor and can be absorbed directly through the skin, decreasing fish hypoxemia.

Should fish become severely stressed, methylene blue can be added to the water, where there is good flow, at the rate of two drops per gallon. It can be repeated, if absolutely necessary, when the blue color dissipates.

Much caution is advised if this product is used in established show tanks, since it has been known to interrupt nitrifying bacteria to the point where it has been described

as toxic to nitrifying bacteria and could destroy biological filters. It can be removed by filtering the water through activated carbon. (Note: It will stain anything it touches.)

Potassium Permanganate

This is a strong oxidizing agent and has been mainly used in freshwater aquaculture as a clarifying agent and/or for algae control. It is occasionally seen as a treatment for reducing excessive organic loads in marine aquariums and is also available as an over-the-counter product at pharmacies. Small additions of this product will reduce/oxidize system organic content and quickly improve redox potential in marine aquariums. It will also kill external parasites.

A warning: Because potassium permanganate may burn sensitive gill areas if overdosed, it is a dangerous product if used incorrectly. It should be slowly dripped in where the current is quite swift. The treated tank should be equipped with a redox meter, and redox should not be allowed to rise too quickly or exceed an increase of more than 50 units per day. Additionally, redox should be not allowed to exceed 450 mV.

Garlic

Presently it is thought that garlic-supplemented foods act somewhat like an immunostimulant that fends off parasites. It is also thought it may help kill internal worms such as nematodes. Though current evidence of its effectiveness is mostly anecdotal, especially in the treatment of ongoing or severe marine ich (*Cryptocaryon irritans*), some hobbyists have reported success with garlic. And fish in a reef aquarium can be treated without removing them or endangering invertebrates. Allicin, a chemical found in garlic, is thought to be the active ingredient.

Besides several liquid products commercially available in the aquarium trade, liquid garlic extracts can be purchased from health food stores. Other forms of garlic generate much surface film, along with strong odors. Various types of food—flake, frozen foods, and kelp—are good absorbers. Feeding the liquid garlic product to live brine

Short dips in freshwater or water treated with formalin and/or malachite green can be used for recent arrivals or fish showing signs of ectoparasitic infection.

shrimp a few hours before they are fed to fish is also a very good way of getting the product to all fish, as most cannot turn down live food.

Treated foodstuffs should initially be offered daily or even more often if possible, for a period of three weeks. Thereafter, once-a-week feedings may be enough to keep the immune system reinforced. We consider this a promising prophylactic measure but recommend accompanying its use with additional water motion, efficient protein skimming to prevent possible surface films, and activated carbon to extract any residues. Kelly Jedlicki, a puffer and shark enthusiast, reports success feeding garlic oil caps to

newly acquired fish: "On many occasions, worms have been expelled in a garlic-oil blob or slick."

Freshwater Dip

A freshwater dip is a process where recently purchased fish or disease-infected fish can be placed briefly in freshwater to help dislodge attached parasites. The change in osmotic pressure causes large numbers of the parasites to swell with water and burst, or at least detach from their host.

The water should have the same pH and temperature as the home aquarium, and the dip should be limited to five

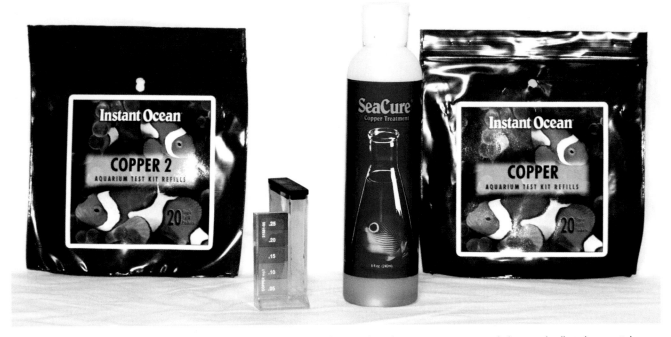

Ionic copper or non-chelated copper sulphate is the classic treatment of choice for a number of marine ectoparasites, including two deadly "white spot" diseases, marine ich (*Cryptocaryon irritans*) and marine velvet (*Amyloodinium ocellatum*). A test kit must be used to ensure that the proper dosage is kept up.

minutes. Remove the fish sooner if there are obvious signs of stress. Tapwater pH will usually be lower than marine aquarium water, and a commercial buffer or baking soda can be used to raise its pH if necessary. In rare cases, you may need to make tapwater more acidic, and swimming pool acid (muriatic acid) or sodium bisulfate can be used to lower pH. Take all the steps necessary to protect yourself and the surrounding area from any spillage or splash if using these chemicals.

Note that most water supply companies and municipalities are now using chloramine rather than chlorine to treat the water that flows through their distribution networks. It is therefore prudent to use commercially available ammonia neutralizers, available through your local aquarium dealer, before using tapwater as a freshwater dip. We prefer using purified (RO/DI) water for freshwater baths.

We do not usually recommend a freshwater dip for newly purchased fish, and rarely, if ever, for invertebrates. Fish are already stressed when you bring them home and

a freshwater dip can add to this. Diseased fish are even further stressed, but depending upon the severity of the problem, a freshwater dip may be beneficial. Remember, do not dip a fish with any lesions or open wounds in freshwater or formalin (although antibiotic saltwater dips or baths can be performed), as this could severely affect its osmotic balance and further stress or kill the fish, perhaps due to dehydration.

This same mechanism works on parasites. The lower concentration of salt in freshwater will cause an extreme osmotic imbalance, especially if it is below 11 ppt (1.008 SG) at 78°F/26°C, which is their internal salinity. As fluids move across a membrane, such as the protozoan cell wall, flow from areas of lower electrolyte levels in fresh water to areas of higher electrolyte levels in the protozoan cell body literally causes the parasite body to explode and fall off. Deeply embedded parasites will need to be treated by chemical means because they are usually coated with fish slime and quite well protected.

The freshwater dip has also proved to be beneficial for removing flatworms (turbellarians) on some soft corals. Using freshwater at the same temperature and pH of the aquarium water, the affected soft coral, usually mushroom polyps (*Discosoma* spp.), can be submerged fully for a period of up to one minute. After removing the specimen from the treatment vessel, any flatworms remaining can usually be brushed off. If possible, the treated specimen should then be kept in a small quarantine tank for about a week so as to allow healing of the affected areas. This freshwater bath is only recommended for severely infected corals or where there appears to be no other method of treatment.

Freshwater baths are also very effective in treating fish turbellarians (such as those that cause black spot disease) as well as some monogeneans, although trematodes that are mainly internal will not be affected. As for *Amyloodinium*, freshwater baths are often ineffective.

Hyposalinity

This form of therapy, in which the salinity of aquarium water is reduced to kill or weaken parasites, has been around for a long time. It has not gained popularity for several reasons. One is the fact that *Cryptocaryon* parasites can continue their life cycle at treatment levels of 1.015 SG or above, which is not dangerous to most invertebrates. Levels any lower than this (which is therapeutic against parasites) will require the removal of all invertebrates, live sand, and live rock (or all of the fish). Obviously, this is a very difficult proposition, and parasites may still survive without any fish present for some time. If the problem is in an established reef tank, the fish should be moved to a hospital tank if hyposalinity is to be implemented, to have a reasonable chance of success.

Take into account that salinity is the direct measurement of dissolved salts (measured in parts per thousand), and is therefore the most accurate measurement of salt content. It is the unit of measure used to quantify the salt content of natural seawater, typically measured with a refractometer. On the other hand, specific gravity is the measurement of density, which fluctuates with temperature and is usually measured with a hydrometer or, better yet, a combination refractometer. Due to dependencies, specific gravity is not always an accurate measurement, but either SG or salinity may be used if necessary.

Since most bony reef fish have an internal SG of about 1.008 (11 ppt), they can temporarily adapt to low salt content conditions for the treatment of ich. (Sharks and rays cannot be treated in this fashion since they have a different osmoregulatory system.)

We advise that the process be implemented immediately. Salinity can be reduced to 14–16 ppt (approximately 1.010 SG at 78–80°F (27°C) and the fish placed into the treatment facility on the same day without any ill effect. The treatment period is three to four weeks. At this level of salt content, *Cryptocaryon irritans* cannot hatch from the tomont stage.

Use hyposalinity with much caution, and check SG frequently. For anyone serious about using hyposalinity often, a refractometer is a great investment. Keep in mind that any increase in specific gravity above the recommended treatment level only prolongs the treatment period. Alkalinity and pH also must be monitored and, if necessary, a buffer added. Hyposalinity treatments for *Cryptocaryon* and black spot at 1.010 SG have produced good results, but maintaining this exact degree of salinity is difficult. (Daily monitoring of specific gravity and adjustments are essential, including replacing freshwater lost to evaporation.)

When raising the specific gravity at the end of treatment, one must proceed carefully. Do not raise it more than .002–.003 units per 24 hours (e.g., 1.013 up to 1.015–1.016 in a day). As a helpful rule of thumb, one cup of salt per 50 gallons will raise the SG approximately 0.002 units once the treatment period has ended.

Copper

Copper is an effective treatment for a variety of external skin and gill parasites, such as protozoan, crustacean, and dino-flagellate parasites like *Amyloodinium* and ciliates like *Cryptocaryon*. It does have one major drawback, however: It is very toxic to invertebrates and, at high levels, to all marine life.

When used correctly, especially in conjunction with other agents like formalin or methylene blue, it is extremely effective for most marine fish. Nevertheless, some angelfish, blennies, butterflyfish, cardinalfish, dragonets, and wrasses exhibit sensitivity to copper. Because copper increases the production of mucus in fish, dragonets may suffocate since they normally have a heavy coating of mucus.

Copper also inhibits biological filtration; therefore, it is best used in a separate hospital tank, and as a treatment of last resort in fish-only aquariums. Also, long-term copper treatments suppress immune systems, making fish more susceptible to other pathogens and perhaps head and lateral line erosion as well. Keep in mind that it's necessary to remove chemical filtering media such as activated carbon prior to adding copper, as these will remove the medication. Also, since copper disrupts biological filtration, keep a close watch for a rise in ammonia.

As for copper medications, there are basically two different types on the market, ionic and chelated, and it's important to understand the difference between them.

Ionic Copper (Copper Sulfate)

Ionic copper, or copper sulfate, is generally referred to as free ionic copper. In an aquarium that contains calcium carbonate substrate, the carbonate material will absorb about 50 percent of the copper in solution within the first two hours. Another 20 percent is absorbed over the next 24 hours. Therefore, 75 percent of the initial copper treatment solution is unavailable at the end of the first day of treatment, according to Cardeilhac and Whitaker (1988). Careful and frequent attention must be given to the therapeutic level of ionic copper if it is depositing or bonding itself to various substrates, especially carbonate based, as copper carbonate. A therapeutic dosage rate for most fish is between 0.15 and 0.20 mg/L.

In some lightly complexed forms, the copper sulfate is bound with chemical agents to help keep it in solution longer than a pure copper sulfate solution. However, they precipitate in various environments and must also be carefully monitored to maintain a therapeutic treatment level.

Chelated Copper

Chelation stops or slows copper from precipitating out of solution. The copper in chelated copper is bonded with various chelating compounds, which helps to solve the problem of having to closely monitor the copper level. Depending upon what brand is used, dosage level may either slightly or greatly exceed 0.2 mg/L.

▶ Copper's Downsides:
Copper treatments will kill corals and other invertebrates, along with beneficial bacteria in the biological filter. Overdoses can damage fishes and may render them infertile.

It appears that chelated copper products are easier to use, but we prefer using the ionic forms because even though ongoing attention and additional dosages are required, a more precise dosage level can be maintained. Not only that, but ionic copper is much easier to remove from solution and will not introduce undesirable chelating agents such as EDTA (ethylenediaminetetraacetic acid).

David Vaughan, Senior Quarantine Aquarist at uShaka Marine World, deals with very large displays with automated dosing systems, and he uses a photometer and high-end reagents. He notes the importance of working out the exact liquid volume of the tank so the correct dosage can be applied, which is something most general aquarists are unable to do. However, if one has the right tools and is able to accurately determine the liquid volume to be treated, chelated copper can be a viable option. If your choice is to use a chelated copper product, we highly recommend only using a test kit produced by the manufacturer of that copper medication to obtain a true and accurate reading.

Kelly Jedlicki has a preference for copper chelated with an amino acid (Cupramine®), which calls for a higher dosage of .5 mg/L, but may be used even with more copper-sensitive animals, such as sharks.

There are often complications when using copper in treatment tanks containing a substrate: At first the dosage seems to be adequate, then suddenly it is too high with-

Copper and formalin are an effective combination against a number of ectoparasites but are best used in bare hospital tanks without substrate. This basic 10-gallon quarantine unit is being used for two French Angelfish juveniles; a plastic eggcrate divider keeps them from fighting while under treatment.

out adding additional copper. First, copper is a transition metal—that is, it conducts since it is a positively charged ion looking for a negatively charged ion, such as oxygen. In fact, copper is more capable of oxygen attraction than iron, aluminum, magnesium, or calcium. Therefore, copper will bind oxygen and kill bacteria species, such as aerobic, autotrophic, and heterotrophic, that perform mineralization and nitrification.

Not fully understood is the fact that in aquariums with a substrate, facultative and obligate anaerobic heterotrophic bacteria living where little oxygen exists, deep in the sand bed or rock, actually take up the copper as a food source, possibly reducing the availability of an ionic copper product by as much as 80 percent. However, biochemist Dr.

Craig Jones suggests that when fish are fed carbohydrate- or sugar-based products, the anaerobes expel the copper in favor of this preferred food source, causing an increase in copper levels. Therefore, swings in bulk water copper levels can occur, especially when the treatment tank contains a fairly deep substrate or rock and the treated animals receive a diet containing sugar-like products. And if chelated copper products are used, those products used for chelation, such as heavy metals, can also be released into the bulk water when this oxidation process takes place. Therefore, as noted above, we prefer to use ionic copper forms in a bare-bottom hospital tank, handling the resulting ammonia problems via water changes.

When it comes to reef aquariums, the use of copper is

strictly taboo. In fact, the toxicity of copper need only be slightly higher than it is in natural seawater, i.e., 0.001–0.09 mg/L, to harm most invertebrates.

Finally, there are some potential long-term copper-treatment surprises. When copper is used in an aquarium, even a 100 percent water change will not remove all of the copper. Some of the copper remains on the inside surfaces and must be removed before the aquarium is put into service for copper-sensitive invertebrates.

According to aquarist and author George Blasiola, this residual copper is adsorbed onto the surface of the glass, and if there were to be a severe reduction in pH, into the range of 2.0, the copper could reenter into solution. The

a small tank include savings on medication and reduced use of saltwater. Substrate is usually not wanted or needed, nor is filtration essential, although using an established biological filter, as in a quarantine tank, is a good idea. Good aeration is extremely important, as are some inert plastic PVC fittings or other artificial caves to help keep the fish calm while treatment is in progress.

Having a spare small tank in the garage or basement is good insurance and might even cast a good spell that wards off the need to use it. One thing is for sure, a hospital tank is cheap and easy to set up."

The question of ammonia accumulation in hospital tanks often arises and should be considered, as ammonia is very

"Having a spare small tank in the garage or basement is good insurance and might even cast a good spell that wards off the need to use it. One thing is for sure, a hospital tank is cheap easy to set up."

trouble is that anemones secrete a glue-like slime substance at the base of their holdfast, and this substance has a pH of between 1.0 and 2.0. Since the toxicity of copper is inversely proportional to pH, and since the low pH zone around the base of anemones is formed due to its excretions, copper can be released at the basal holdfast of anemones and be absorbed at very toxic levels.

If you are concerned about reusing a glass aquarium which has been exposed to copper at some point in the past, first give it a cleaning with muriatic acid from a hardware or pool store. This should render it safe for use with corals and other invertebrates. Be sure to be safe when using the acid: Wear gloves and eye protection. As for acrylic tanks, there is no copper binding or adsorption that we are aware of, so cleaning with water or vinegar and a soft sponge removes any residual copper.

Hospital Tank

A hospital tank can be of any size, but usually a small, 10- or 20-gallon tank will do nicely as a short-term home for the animals, no longer than a month. The benefits of using

toxic to marine fish. Not only does it cause burns to fin, epithelial, and gill tissue, it prevents the excretion of waste, approximately 90 percent of which may occur through the gills. Using a viable biological filter, either a hang-on-the-back or sponge type filter, is highly recommended. It is always helpful to have some filter material (sponge, floss, or biomedia) available that has been pre-conditioned for at least two to four weeks, in case quarantining or hospitalization becomes necessary. A plastic salt or cleaned kitty litter bucket can be filled with aquarium water and used to hold one or more running air-driven sponge filters at the ready. Dose weekly with pure ammonia to keep the bacterial populations thriving. These filters are cheap, easy to sterilize in bleach after each use and can be amazingly useful when an emergency arises. Having several allows a rotation in the hospital tank if needed.

Again, water changes and controlling pH are the easiest and safest approaches to controlling ammonia in the hospital aquarium. Freshwater ammonia removers such as zeolite are ineffective in saltwater; a Poly-Filter® will absorb ammonia but will also remove most drugs from the water.

It is also prudent to feed a medicated flake food dur-

A basic marine fish first-aid kit may contain a broad-spectrum antibiotic (tetracycline, nitrofurans, or other), treatments for external parasites (formalin, methylene blue, malachite green, ionic copper, copper test kit), a dewormer (praziquantel), disinfectant (hydrogen peroxide), thermometer, nets, and test kits.

ing this stressful period and/or to use products designed to boost the animals' immune systems.

Bacterial Treatments

When it comes to bacterial infections, in an ideal world we would first identify the disease organism in order to treat it appropriately. However, culturing the bacteria takes equipment and techniques more sophisticated than most hobbyists possess, and such diagnostic procedures take a fair amount of time as well. Also, identifying species of bacteria and their sensitivities can be expensive. Beyond that, by the time a definitive diagnosis has been reached, the fish may be beyond saving.

A "shotgun" approach tends to be the best option available to most hobbyists. This regimen utilizes wide-spectrum antibiotics, and one must be willing to do water exchanges between doses because they also kill beneficial nitrifying bacteria. Typically, if no improvement is noticed within two to three days, switch to another wide-spectrum antibiotic until favorable results are achieved.

Over the course of time, inappropriate usage of antibiotics has created resistant strains of bacteria (especially in freshwater fishes aquacultured in Asia). This has presented researchers with many difficulties and created a constant demand for new antibiotics. Antibiotics normally have a specific dose rate for a specific length of time, and such instructions must be followed carefully once an effective drug has been identified. This will insure that additional resistances are not created inadvertently.

Since marine fish constantly take in water, a treatment bath created by placing the drug directly into the water will normally suffice. Most antibiotics will break down within a few hours of administration; therefore, daily dosing or saltwater antibiotic baths will be required in order to keep the concentration at a therapeutic level. Keeping antibiotics out of the aquarium will also spare the bacterial populations in your biological filter.

Typically, the duration of treatment for most antibiotics is 7–10 days, depending on the drug. While treating with any medication (and antibiotics in particular), monitor the ammonia and nitrite levels and perform a complete water exchange if they become elevated. (Most antibiotics kill beneficial bacteria as effectively as they dispatch the harmful organisms.) As a rule of thumb, a 50–75 percent water exchange should be performed at least every two to three days between doses, although some treatments require them daily. For best results, always refer to the manufacturer's instructions on dosage and disposal.

Among the broad-spectrum antibiotics marine aquarists rely on most are kanamycin sulphate, minocycline (Maracyn-2), neomycin sulfate, and the nitrofurans—nifurpurinol and nitrofurazone (Furacyn and Furanace). Many others are used as well.

The "Fish Market," a popular dive site in the northern Great Barrier Reef complex, Australia. Even with a profusion of fishes, disease is virtually never seen because water conditions are usually optimal and the animals are free of the sorts of stresses that can wear down their immunity.

Newly imported Coral Beauty Pygmy Angelfish (*Centropyge bispinosa*) with early signs of *Cryptocaryon irritans* infestation on its body and fins.

Parasitic Infestations

A rogue's gallery of pests that attack marine fish

Parasites are among the most common and most dreaded causes of fish disease and premature death in aquariums. Some of these parasites, most notably those classed informally as "ich" or "ick," are capable of reproducing quickly, sometimes quite explosively, in our aquariums.

Parasites disrupt the protective slime coating and epithelium (skin), can damage a fish's gills, and can lead to secondary bacterial infections. Our fishes are exposed to these same parasites in the wild, but in confined spaces the most deadly of these can achieve population concentrations that are able to overwhelm their victims.

Parasitic infestations associated with marine fish can be generalized into one of two main groups for our purposes: protozoan (single-celled) and metazoan (multi-celled) organisms.

PROTOZOANS

There are three main groups of protozoans, or single-celled organisms, that are worth mentioning: the flagellates, the ciliates, and the sporozoans.

Flagellated protozoans are motile, and they move, feed, and attach to their hosts using flagella—long, whip-like appendages. The flagella normally originate from either end of the organism. Ciliated protozoans are covered with short, hair-like appendages known as cilia. These cilia generally are spaced evenly about the entire cell, and they are used for locomotion as well as for feeding purposes. The sporozoans do not have the ability to move, and reproduce by shedding spores. They are typically transferred into the water by already-infected fish or in food.

Juvenile Maculosus Angelfish (*Pomacanthus maculosus*) with marine velvet or amyloodiniosis. Rapid breathing and clouding (1) of fins, eyes and skin are early signs. A dusting of white spots (2) may follow and spread rapidly.

Although not common in home aquariums, they are the cause of several serious infections.

Flagellates and Dinoflagellates

Flagellates are small protozoan parasites, approximately 10–20 microns in size. Characteristic flagella, which extend from either end of the cell, give this group of parasites their name and allow for movement as well as attachment to the host. Most flagellates are endoparasites (internal parasites) and are typically quite small. They are found internally in the intestine, cecum, and gallbladder; sometimes they are found in other organs or in blood. However, there are a

few that are mainly external. Flagellates can be considered normal fauna on fish since they only become a problem during stressful periods. It is thought that healthy fish have the ability to keep these protozoans in check.

Marine Velvet Disease, Coral Fish Disease, Amyloodiniosis, "Oodinium" (*Amyloodinium ocellatum*)

One of the most deadly diseases in marine aquariums is coral fish disease, or marine velvet. Unfortunately, it is far from uncommon, especially in newly imported fish.

Properly known as amyloodiniosis, the disease is caused by the dinoflagellate *Amyloodinium ocellatum*. This parasite is actually an algal protozoan and is responsible for many premature fish losses. Although not directly responsible, *A. ocellatum* is related to the organisms (such as the dinoflagellate *Gymnodinium brevis*) responsible for causing red tides along coastal areas of the world. In advanced cases where

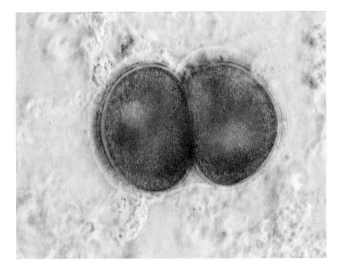

Microscopic view of the *Amyloodinium ocellatum* parasite in cell division (see life cycle, page 149). Rapid proliferation in the right conditions allows this parasite to overwhelm a whole aquarium of fishes within days.

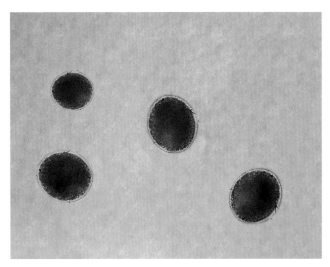

Note thickened cell wall, a clue to the plant-like characteristics of this dinoflagellate. *Amyloodinium* is found worldwide, while a related and less deadly form known as *Miamiensis* is known only in the Caribbean.

water quality is low, nutrition is poor, or other stresses are present, *Amyloodinium ocellatum* is capable of completely wiping out entire populations in as little as 48 hours.

This parasite's life cycle comprises three stages: 1) the parasitic trophont stage—the only time it is visible to the naked eye; 2) the encysted, or palmella (tomont) stage; and 3) the dinospore stage. While in the trophont stage, the parasite is nonmotile and can be found on the host fish absorbing nutrients for its reproduction.

During the encysted or palmella (tomont) stage, the

parasite can be seen dividing while still on the fish. This is the reproductive portion of its life cycle.

Finally, as a dinospore, the newly hatched parasite has emerged from its cyst and is free-swimming and looking for a new host, or has just found a new host.

SYMPTOMS One of the first signs of this disease may be rapid breathing, as the gills, which process great amounts of water, are attacked first if parasites are present. Suspicious clouding of fins, eyes, and skin may soon follow. When fish are heavily affected with *Amyloodinium* they may look as if they have been rolled in powdered sugar. Dr. Edward Noga describes this as a "golden, dust-like sheen." Severe skin infestations can appear velvety, thus the name, marine velvet disease. However, Noga points out that death may occur in as few as 12 hours even without the appearance of noticeable skin lesions. Because of its small size (50–60 microns), *Amyloodinium* will dust fins, skin, and eyes, making these areas appear cloudy or turbid. Fish in advanced stages will show obvious sloughing of their protective slime coating, as they do with other parasitic infestations.

These parasites affect all external areas of the fish and are capable of doing extensive damage to the gill tissue. This impedes breathing, and fish will exhibit rapid gill

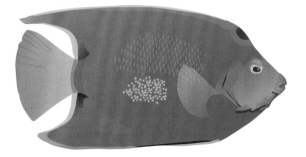

Classic *Amyloodinium* or "*oodinium*" infestation appears as a dusting of powdered sugar. Immediate treatment is warranted for this deadly disease.

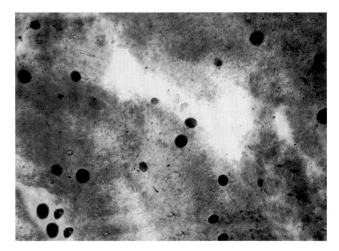

Microscopic view of the causative agent of marine velvet disease: *Amyloodinium ocellatum* seen as dark orbs in mucus of an infected fish's gill tissue. Rapid respiration is an early symptom of this disease.

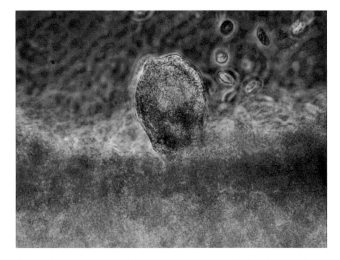

Amyloodinium ocellatum trophont-stage parasite attached to the secondary lamella in the gill of an unidentified fish. Gill tissue can be seriously damaged by *Amyloodinium* before other external signs appear.

movement and have difficulty obtaining oxygen. Irritation to skin and gills may cause fish to "flash" (rub against aquarium décor) or scrape their bodies and gill plates on bottom substrate or other decorations within the aquarium.

Microscopically, it's possible to see large quantities of either round or pear-shaped organisms, often resembling bunches of grapes, although the typical depiction is of a

Chloroquine Treatment

For home aquarists, an effective "new" cure for *Cryptocaryon, Brooklynella, Uronema,* and *Amyloodinium*

One medication used by professional aquarists—but little known in the marine hobby—as an effective remedy for a constellation of marine fish maladies is chloroquine phosphate, or Aralen®.

This drug, once the primary treatment for malaria in humans, can be an effective alternative to the use of copper and formalin. It is both easier to use and less toxic than copper, the traditional treatment of choice.

Many public aquariums—historically on the cutting edge of aquarium science—are now using chloroquine phosphate. Dr. Michael Stafford, consulting veterinarian for the American National Fish and Wildlife Zooquarium in Springfield, Missouri, recommends chloroquine phosphate for the treatment of *Cryptocaryon* and *Brooklynella* infestations, stating that copper and formalin are now "outdated."

Dr. Edward Noga's *Fish Disease* recommends the use of chloroquine at 10 mg/L (or 40 mg/gal) for the treatment of *Amyloodinium ocellatum*. He reports that Ocellaris Clownfish that had been infected with the parasite were cured after 10 days' exposure to a dose of 5–10 mg/L. Apparently there is no effect on tomont division, but dinospores die immediately after exiting the cyst in the presence of chloroquine. Noga notes that therapeutic dosages are nontoxic to fish but highly toxic to microalgae and macroalgae, as well as to various invertebrates, which rules out the use of chloroquine in reef aquariums. One such treatment is generally sufficient, but the fish should be closely monitored for at least 21 days, with repeat treatment performed if required.

Chloroquine is available in bulk crystalline powder form from various chemical supply houses (see Sources, page 223) and no special license or permit is required for its purchase. Aralen® tablets are also available from online human pharmacies or via a prescription from your local doctor. Refer to the "Calculating Drug Dosages" (pages 23–24) to calculate the exact dosage using either the English or metric system. Dissolving 10

Juvenile Highhat with classic *Amyloodinium* infestation, has the appearance of having been rolled in powdered sugar. Compare to *Cryptocaryon irritans*, page 152, which presents itself with relatively larger and fewer white spots. Differentiating the two is not absolutely critical, as the treatments for these potentially lethal ectoparasites are identical.

mg of pure chloroquine powder in one liter of water will yield a 10 mg/L dosage, which is equivalent to 38.5 mg per gallon, or almost the same as 40 mg per gallon.

When initiating chloroquine treatment, remove activated carbon from the filter system or the carbon will remove the medication from the water. Turn off the protein skimmer during treatment, as it, too, may remove some medication. Also, if ultraviolet sterilization and/or ozone are being employed, turn them off as well, since they can denature or even destroy chemical compounds.

In our experience using chloroquine, we have been impressed with the results when treating ciliated protozoans. In fish-only aquariums, it is safe to treat the entire system, although smaller volumes of water would require smaller quantities of chloroquine, thus lowering the cost per treatment. We have seen no detectable loss of biological filtration with our use of chloroquine. Almost all nuisance algae in the aquariums we have treated were eradicated by the chloroquine treatment.

Perhaps as a result of this toxicity to algae (and remember that zooxanthellae are algae), chloroquine has demonstrated toxic and negative effects on both stony and soft corals, many of which quickly perished in our test systems. Likewise, other invertebrates did not survive exposure to chloroquine. It

maybe assumed that this chemical has deleterious effects on all organisms containing symbiotic algae within their tissues, such as *Tridacna* clams, for example.

As testimony to the effectiveness of chloroquine, a Black Triggerfish, *Melichthys niger*, that we treated for a heavy infestation of *Cryptocaryon* was completely cleared of spots within three days of the start of treatment. Two weeks later, there was no sign of reinfestation. Dr. Stafford points out that using chloroquine along with hyposalinity serves to intensify and improve the results of therapy. We feel very confident in recommending dissolved chloroquine and hyposalinity for the treatment of *Amyloodinium*, *Cryptocaryon*, *Brooklynella*, and *Uronema* in a hospital tank setting.

Chloroquine-treated foods

Some public aquarists have recently started experimenting with using chloroquine in display reef systems, where most antiparasitic drugs cannot be employed. If the fish are still eating, it is possible to mix chloroquine with appetizing foods and create a medicated gel.

Rich Terrell of Pittsburgh Zoo & PPG Aquarium reports using chloroquine-dosed gel foods to halt an outbreak of *Cryptocaryon* in a giant-clam exhibit. He credits Robyn Doege of the Dallas World Aquarium with providing the idea. The formula used calls for mixing 3.7 g of chloroquine phosphate with 300 g of gelatin powder, then mixing equal parts of powder and hot water. As the gel cools, food items are mixed in and the medicated food allowed to chill and set.

Terrell repeated the feeding every three days, using a garlic powder–laced food gel on off days. The worry, of course, is that uneaten chloroquine might dissolve and impact the invertebrates in the tank. Terrell reports that some gel that fell onto a Hammer Coral did cause tissue necrosis, so they shifted the feeding spot to another part of the tank. They also used water changes and various filter media (such as Poly-Filter® pads and ferric oxide sponge or granules) to absorb any stray chloroquine or phosphate from the tank water. He reports that the fish recovered nicely and the soft and stony corals were unaffected.

CAUTION: Chloroquine phosphate can cause death if ingested by humans at higher than recommended dosages. Always keep it and other drugs and chemicals out of the reach of children and pets.

Microscopic view of damaged fish gill lamellae affected by hyperplasia. The tissue is swollen and red due to an increase in the size and number of small blood vessels, a condition known as telangiectases.

which give them their mobility. It has been reported that this parasite can colonize the guts or esophagi of many fish, such as the Porcupine Puffer, *Diodon holacanthus*, and the Porkfish, *Anisotremus virginicus*, making it somewhat difficult to control at times.

THERAPY AND CONTROL This is a virulent parasite that demands immediate attention and treatment. Because the characteristic profusion of tiny white spots is not always easily noticed, be very aware of the other symptoms and start treatment promptly. (It is most easily spotted on thin, transparent areas of the fins, or on the skin if the fish is viewed at angle.)

A number of courses of action are possible, each having its own staunch proponents.

• Repeated dips in freshwater, usually dosed with methylene blue plus formalin or formalin/malachite green.

• Treatment for 21–30 days with copper sulfate or citrated copper. Hyposalinity can enhance the effectiveness of this treatment, but the water parameters must be monitored regularly, especially pH.

• Treatment with chloroquine phosphate. Hyposalinity can enhance the effectiveness of this treatment.

Freshwater baths are recommended if you can easily remove the fish from the aquarium. It has been reported that freshwater baths will cause the parasite to fall off the fish, yielding almost immediate results. A bath shorter than 15 minutes in freshwater may dislodge some of the trophonts on the fish, but usually not all of them.

To make the dip significantly more effective, formalin or malachite green (or a combination of the two, such as

teardrop shaped organism attached to tissue at the pointed end with rhizoid extensions. The parasites become round at this point and can grow considerably (up to 125 microns) prior to leaving the host. It has been suggested that damage may occur as a result of a toxin produced by the parasite.

The life cycle of the parasite is 6–12 days, depending on temperature, but quarantine of three to four weeks is advised to keep it from entering a display aquarium.

Microscopically, it's possible to see maturing dinospores within the cell wall. The dinospores are released after a short incubation period of three to six days once a mature cyst drops off the fish. These dinospores have flagella,

Kordon's Rid-Ich®), can be added to the water. Formalin helps dislodge the trophonts attached to the fish. As always, follow the dosage recommendations of the drug's manufacturer.

Whether a freshwater bath is administered or not, treatment of the hospital aquarium with ionic copper sulfate at 0.18–0.20 mg/L for three to four weeks will usually eliminate this disease. The copper level should not be allowed to fall below the manufacturer's directions, as lower levels are often virtually ineffective against this parasite.

Gill damage due to hyperplasia may occur at copper levels higher than .18 mg/L (or higher than the manufacturer's recommendations), so care must be taken. However, hyperplasia can occur with almost any level of copper, usually at the site of penetration of individual trophonts in the gill tissue. If bacterial infections follow, antibiotics may be required.

There are reports that chloroquine antimalarial drugs have shown good results, particularly during the trophont stage. In fish, chloroquine can be ingested with food or absorbed through the skin and gills. It then travels through the bloodstream. As the parasite derives its nutrients from the fish's blood, it also takes in the medication. (See Chloroquine Treatment, page 146–147.)

Whatever treatment is employed, it must be carried through until all life stages of the parasite are killed. Many times a hobbyist will end the treatment too soon and after a few days of apparent cure, the parasite will reappear and infect fish once again. It has also been reported that dinospores may live without a host for an extended period of time (in excess of three to four weeks). Therefore, it might be wise to continue treatment for at least 10 days after the last signs of the parasite have been observed.

Although *Amyloodinium* may not be as sensitive to lowered salinity as other parasites, we highly recommend that the SG of the aquarium be lowered during treatment for these parasites. Some authors recommend lowering the SG slowly, but we suggest a radical and immediate drop in SG

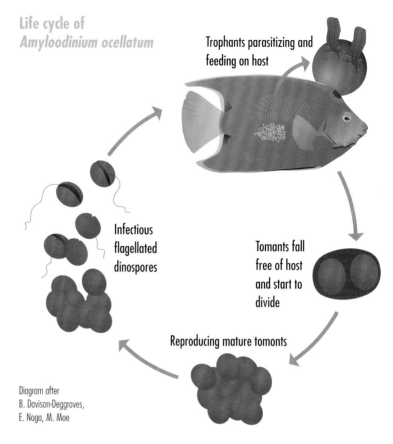

Life cycle of *Amyloodinium ocellatum*

Trophants parasitizing and feeding on host

Tomants fall free of host and start to divide

Reproducing mature tomonts

Infectious flagellated dinospores

Diagram after
B. Davison-Deggraves,
E. Noga, M. Moe

Parasitic trophonts are seen speckling the victim and feeding on its tissues. These drop off in 3–7 days as free-swimming tomonts that, after about 18 hours, form cysts, divide prolifically, and then break apart as infectious dinospores after 3–28 days, depending on water temperature. The dinospores can survive for just 1–2 days while trying to find a host, and are most vulnerable to drugs at this stage.

to a level as low as 1.010–1.013. We have not seen any ill effects on the fish diluting the salt content in this manner. We have, however, seen dramatic results in controlling these parasites. They cannot control the osmosis through their semipermeable membranes, so they begin to absorb water as the cells involuntarily try to equalize the osmotic pressures within and outside of their walls. Eventually they explode, like balloons filled with too much water, when their cell walls can no longer withstand the pressure of the water they absorb. However, some strains of *Amyloodinium* reportedly are less sensitive to hyposalinity than others.

Hole-in-the-head disease is characterized by pitting of the flesh on the forehead and around the eyes. Compare to head-and-lateral-line erosion, page 190.

If the water temperature is raised to 80.6–82.4° F (27–28° C), it is possible to increase the rate of reproduction of the parasite and shorten the life cycle. However, you will also increase the fish's metabolic rate, raising its demand for oxygen and placing added stress on its already compromised gills. Raising temperature is now regarded as a questionable tactic that has fallen from grace with many aquarists.

When the treatment period has ended, be sure to raise the SG slowly, as we have seen osmotic shock and imbalances as a result of raising the salt content too quickly. We recommend an adjustment of .002 per 24 hours. For example, if the SG is 1.010, raise it to no more than 1.012 in the first day, then from 1.012 to 1.014 the following day, and so on. For obvious reasons, this procedure must never be applied in an aquarium containing invertebrates.

Hole-in-the-Head Disease (*Hexamitosis* and *Spironucleosis*)

This syndrome may manifest itself as pitting in the flesh around the head, although the offending parasites are actually most concentrated in the digestive tract. It is most commonly seen in marine angelfishes and tangs.

There is little known about *Hexamita* and *Spironucleus*, the organisms that cause hexamitosis and spironucleosis,

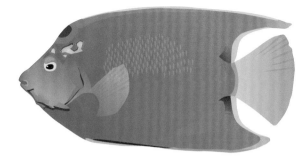

Hole-in-the- head disease may be caused by a dinoflagellate intestinal parasite, and treatment calls for feeding with foods mixed with metronidazole and, if necessary, improving water quality in the aquarium.

respectively, except that they are flagellated parasites that are often found in the gastrointestinal tracts of apparently healthy fish. When symptoms are noted, their populations have usually swollen out of control. Very small and difficult to identify, these flagellates have been implicated in hole-in-the-head disease. This should not be confused with head and lateral line erosion (HLLE), which has many other possible causes. Both *Hexamita* and *Spironucleus* are mentioned here since they appear not to have been clearly differentiated. Their link to hole-in-the-head disease has been reported anecdotally in the aquarium literature but has not been confirmed scientifically.

Microscopically, a spoon-shaped or oval organism, with six anterior flagella and two on the posterior end of the organism, each measuring about 6–8 microns wide by 10–12 microns long, can be seen.

Under a microscope, *Spironucleus* has a spoon-shaped appearance as opposed to the full, round or teardrop shape seen with *Hexamita*. Problems associated with these organisms commonly occur when fish are exposed to high levels of stress, such as from poor water quality, cold temperatures, high levels of organic waste, etc.

SYMPTOMS When fish suffer an overgrowth of these parasites, they begin to lose their color and become pale or, on occasion, darkened. As with mycobacteriosis, fish will lose their appetites and subsequently lose body weight and become emaciated. They seek dark corners of the aquarium, lie on the bottom, and become listless. Many

times as the infestation progresses, the excretion of slimy white feces can be observed. Microscopic or post-mortem examination of fecal intestinal contents is needed to make a confirmed diagnosis.

THERAPY AND CONTROL If you have determined or suspect that your fish has *Hexamita*, the first order of business is to do a thorough assessment of your water quality. You may need to change the water more often, clean filters and substrate, increase filter power, and use chemical filtration to decrease dissolved organic matter. Enhanced circulation and skimming may help.

The treatment of choice is to feed medicated foods containing metronidazole. (It is sold as Flagyl® in human medicine, where it is used against various bacterial infections and internal parasites.) If fish are still eating, feed them with medicated foods for three days, then non-medicated foods for three days, then again with medicated foods for three more days. Metronidazole is not very soluble and should first be dissolved by shaking vigorously in a separate container with a small amount of water.

Simultaneous treatment with metronidazole in the tank water at a concentration of 9.1–10.4 mg/L for three days may also be effective. In our experience, this combination of medicated feed and treated hospital tank water usually rids fish of these flagellates very effectively.

Anecdotally, Mike Breen, a fish farmer in West Palm Beach, Florida, believes that regularly feeding foods containing *Spirulina* powder or flakes causes his fish to purge such parasites from their intestines.

CILIATES (Ciliated Protozoans)

The ciliated protozoans represent one of the more frequently encountered parasite groups that affect our marine fishes. This, and their impact on fish populations (numbers of fish deaths attributed to them), makes them the most significant group of parasites.

Known as ciliophorans, they all possess cilia, cirri, or tentacles—short, hairlike appendages that are used for locomotion and/or feeding. The ciliates are some of the largest protozoans aquarists encounter. Saltwater ich, or

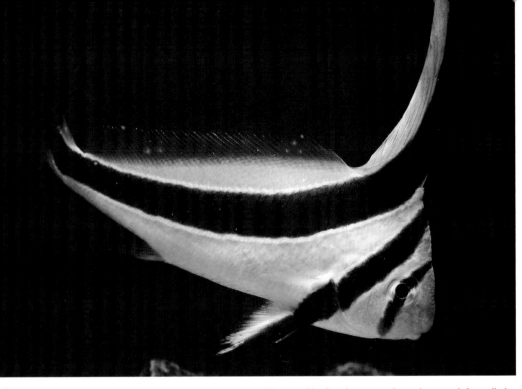

Early stages of *Cryptocaryon* attack on a juvenile Caribbean Jackknife Fish (*Equetus lanceolatus*), with first telltale spots appearing in the translucent dorsal fin. The parasites can be difficult to see on white and light-colored fishes.

host fish is stressed from poor water quality, poor nutrition, radical temperature fluctuations, and the like, resulting in a lowered resistance, these parasites can reproduce explosively and reach epidemic populations.

Ciliates are ectoparasites (external in nature), and will primarily affect the skin, fins, eyes, and gills. Rapid breathing and "flashing" (dashing against objects in the aquarium to relieve irritation) are common symptoms. Ciliates can create openings in the slime coat and epithelium (skin) where more dangerous pathogens, such as bacteria, can enter.

Cryptocaryon irritans, for example, reaches 350–450 microns in diameter.

It would appear that many of these parasites are ubiquitous, and may be ever-present in our marine systems. They can proliferate in organic debris and are transmitted from tank to tank by infected nets and/or wet hands. When a

The most important microscopic characteristic of the ciliates is that they posses two nuclei: a macronucleus, which controls cell functions, and a micronucleus, which controls sexual or reproductive functions.

Saltwater Ich, White Spot Disease, Cryptocaryonosis (*Cryptocaryon irritans*)

Cryptocaryonosis, commonly known as marine ich or saltwater ich, has been known to attack all marine fish except the elasmobranchs (sharks and rays). *Cryptocaryon irritans*, the causative parasite, is probably the most common plague encountered by marine fish enthusiasts. (Freshwater aquarists have to deal with a very similar ciliated parasite, *Ichthyophthirius multifilis*, known as ich.)

These parasites, due to similar appearance, have been variously misidentified as sporozoans, lymphocystis, and *Amyloodinium*, just to mention a few. Fortunately, the treatment is the same for several of these problems.

This disease will often manifest itself when fish are exposed to stressful conditions, such as extreme temperature

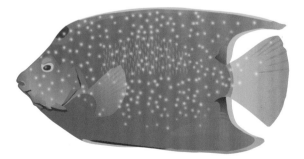

Cryptocaryonosis or marine ich is caused by the ectoparasite *Cryptocaryon irritans*, and the primary external symptom is distinct white spots. It is often said that the afflicted fish appears to have been dusted with salt crystals.

fluctuations, poor water quality, or poor nutrition; stress allows this (and many other diseases) to gain a foothold. Ich commonly arrives in an established marine aquarium with a new fish that is stressed from being transported and has not been through quarantine.

However, stress in itself does not cause diseases to occur. It merely compromises the fish's immune system,

New Fish Syndrome:

Marine ich most often breaks out in the home aquarium soon after the arrival of a new fish that is introduced without going through quarantine. Transport stress can trigger the disease.

lowering its resistance and immune response to disease organisms that may be present within the system. Of course, as professional aquarist David Vaughan points out, there must first be a window of opportunity for the "…parasite to reproduce and manifest itself in larger numbers, which can no longer be maintained by the immune system. This outbreak becomes the exponential increase in number we know as epidemic…." Also, as Vaughan so accurately reminds us, it must be understood that these parasites are actually introduced into the aquarium along with infected fish and are not always "part of the environment, which would only be true in nature…."

Saltwater ich bores under the fish's skin, causing a thickening and buildup slime. Also, if a parasite remains in one spot for any length of time, a fish's natural immune response can cover the trophont with mucus and slime. This results in a whitish appearance, giving the disease its familiar name, white spot. *Cryptocaryon* may not always be seen on a microscope slide sample of skin slime scraping; the fin or gill tissue harboring the

parasite must also be examined. The parasite will appear as a round to pear-shaped organism displaying cilia, as well as a horseshoe-shaped macronucleus.

Vaughan reports that he typically sees trophonts slowly moving around, even through the secondary lamellae, while feeding on tissue. They tend to "tumble over themselves in a very classic rolling fashion," using their cilia for locomotion. He goes on to say that *Cryptocaryon* parasites are almost always in motion, even when covered by the mucus of the fish, unlike *Amyloodinium* parasites.

Cryptocaryon's life cycle can extend upwards of 28 days or more and undergoes three stages: 1) the trophont stage, 2) the tomont stage, and 3) the tomite stage. The trophont, or feeding, stage is the period when the parasites are embedded in the fish's skin and gills and doing their damage. Next, during the tomont (dividing) stage, the parasites fall from the host and form cysts to reproduce. Finally, after as few as three and up to 28 days, the cyst breaks open and tomites are released in swarms; the newly hatched parasites seek their own hosts (tomite stage). Because the parasite is either under the skin of the fish or encysted during the two

Tomato Clowns (*Amphiprion frenatus*) with white spots typical of the trophont stage in the parasite's life. Such fish can be saved with quick treatment using hyposalinity and/or one or more drugs.

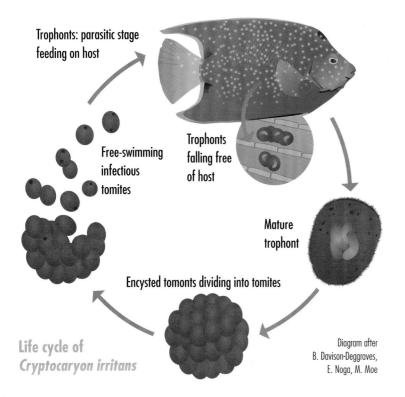

Trophonts: parasitic stage feeding on host

Free-swimming infectious tomites

Trophonts falling free of host

Mature trophont

Encysted tomonts dividing into tomites

Life cycle of Cryptocaryon irritans

Diagram after
B. Davison-Deggraves,
E. Noga, M. Moe

Parasitic trophonts are seen speckling and feeding on the victim. These drop off in 3–7 days as non-infectious trophonts that, after about 18 hours, form cysts that divide prolifically and then break apart as infectious tomites after 3–28 days, depending on temperature. The free-swimming tomites survive for 1–2 days while trying to find a host. At this stage they are most susceptible to copper and other treatments.

previous stages, it is only during this final swarming stage that medications such as copper or formalin can actually kill the parasite.

SYMPTOMS Fish infested with *Cryptocaryon irritans* appear to have distinct white spots on the skin, fin tissues, and eyes. These are considerably larger and more widely spaced than those seen in *Amyloodinium ocellatum*. Initially a few white spots will appear, becoming progressively more abundant over time. Fish with affected eyes may become blind, particularly in advanced stages. Closer microscopic examination of gill lamellae may reveal parasites embedded within both the lamellae stalks and the secondary lamellae, although the parasite does not always bore into the lamellae.

According to David Vaughan, the fish will eventually exhibit difficulty in breathing as a result of "… extensive physical damage to the gill tissue, which the trophonts are capable of causing. The function of respiration is impaired by the gill tissue damage with subsequent anemia, and the host's response to this problem is to try to maintain normal levels of respiration by increasing its frequency…."

Similar symptoms may be observed when *Amyloodinium* and other gill diseases affect fish.

Other symptoms, such as cloudy eyes, ragged fins, sloughing of the slime coat, and secondary bacterial infections, may appear as well. As with infestations by *Amyloodinium*, flashing may also be observed.

THERAPY AND CONTROL As with *Amyloodinium* (page 144–152), treatment options include:

• Repeated dips in freshwater, usually dosed with methylene blue plus formalin or formalin/malachite green.

• Treatment for 21–30 days with copper sulphate or citrated copper. Hyposalinity can enhance the effectiveness of this treatment.

• Treatment with chloroquine phosphate. Hyposalinity can enhance the effectiveness of this treatment.

The control of *Cryptocaryon* outbreaks is most often achieved with the use of ionic copper sulfate in a bare-bottomed hospital tank at a concentration of 0.18–0.20 mg/L for at least 21–30 days. This is the recommended therapeutic level, but, according to experts, including George Blasiola, gill hyperplasia may occur if copper concentrations exceed 0.18 mg/L, so care must be exercised. However, it is also thought that hyperplasia can be a result of damage to surrounding tissue caused by the parasite, and not just from higher concentrations of copper.

We suggest that treatment last a minimum of 28 days, because it has been reported that the life cycle of *Cryptocaryon* may stretch to 28 days (or even longer at low temperatures). If the copper concentration has been allowed to drop below 0.15 mg/L (or below the manufacturer's recom-

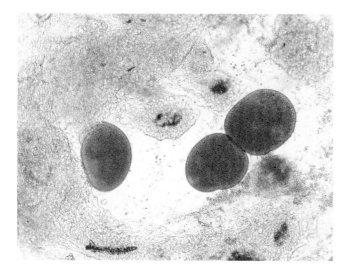

Cells of *Cryptocaryon irritans*, the causative organism in marine ich, moving freely in a fish's gill tissue where they feed and cause serious damage.

Marine ich on a Purple Tang (*Zebrasoma xanthurum*) in a reef tank, where the only possible treatment is the use of medicated feeds (see page 147).

mendation) for any length of time, which would allow the parasite to reinfect fish, the treatment must go a full four weeks or longer. To eradicate the parasite completely, the treatment must exceed 28 days at the optimum reproduction temperature of 76–78°F, or close to it, according to David Vaughan.

As in the case of *Amyloodinium*, we recommend that hyposalinity conditions be established as first aid, if at all possible. (Hyposalinity can be combined with any of the other treatments used to kill *Cryptocaryon*.) To reiterate, hyposalinity conditions means specific gravity of 1.010–1.013, which is equivalent to a salinity of below 16 ppt. Obviously, neither hyposalinity nor the drugs and chemicals listed below should be used in a living reef aquarium.

Formalin and malachite green can both be used against *Cryptocaryon*, either in repeated baths using freshwater or in a hospital tank over a period of weeks. The combination of formalin and malachite green is more effective than either of them alone. Some aquarists who choose to avoid copper and its potential longterm effects, including possible interference with reproductive abilities, prefer to do repeated freshwater or saltwater dips, using formalin and/or malachite green and repeatedly changing the hospital aquarium water to prevent reinfestation.

Matthew Wittenrich, a marine fish researcher at the Florida Institute of Technology and author of *The Breeder's Guide to Marine Fishes*, is a proponent of formalin dips. "When we were importing our own broodstock from the Philippines," he says, "I ran into a world of problems associated with disease from compromised immune systems. The Ocellaris and Maroon Clowns, angels, and *Meiacanthus* blennies all broke down with varying ailments from *Brooklynella* to *Amyloodinium*. The only thing that worked was formalin baths. I perform saltwater baths in 5-gallon buckets three separate times every other day for 45 minutes under brisk aeration. The dosage is one ml per gallon of full-strength formaldehyde (37 percent)." (This is ten times the usual dosage for continuous treatment.)

"I prefer not to treat the quarantine tank," Wittenrich adds, "as the chemicals often render the bio-filter useless and the fish's immune system then breaks down as a result of treatment. Then, you have to treat the fish. Kind of an oxymoron, I guess."

A newer treatment that may be easier and less stressful than copper for the afflicted fish is chloroquine phosphate (pages 146-147). Although it will take more effort to get the drug, which is not commonly available in the pet trade, a single dose usually works very effectively.

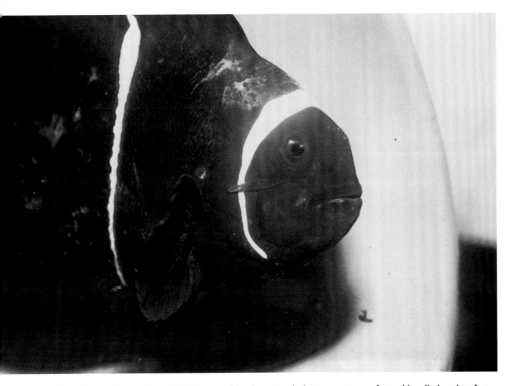

Large female Maroon Clownfish (*Premnas biaculeatus*) with classic symptoms of *Brooklynella hostilis* infestation: spots, bumps, skin lesions, and milky patches of slime caused by proliferating ciliated protozoans.

Whatever the treatment, vigilance and patience are essential. In most cases the fish will only exhibit a few spots during the initial stages of infestation. Soon after a hobbyist recognizes the problem, treatment can quickly cause the spots to disappear. The hobbyist may then terminate the treatment, thinking the problem has been cured. However, a few days later the parasites return in greater abundance than originally encountered, as previously pointed out in the section on *Amyloodinium*. Therefore, to reiterate, the treatment duration should not be terminated for at least 28 days.

Finally, although many sources recommend raising the aquarium temperature to 85°F, we do not suggest doing so. Even though this may work for freshwater ich by preventing the uptake of oxygen through the cell membrane, it serves to stress the saltwater ich, *Cryptocaryon irritans*, to the point where the parasite will encyst and go dormant. According to George Blasiola, it will remain encysted until the temperature is returned to normal, at which time it will seek a new host, reinfesting the aquarium. Actually, we have seen *Cryptocaryon* lie dormant in a reef aquarium for over 90 days, only to reinfest newly introduced fish that had been in quarantine for over 60 days. To avoid this, leave the temperature within the aquarium at the normal level, approximately 76°–80°F.

Interestingly, David Vaughan and aquatic pathologist Dr. Kevin W. Christison have discovered new strains of *Cryptocaryon* while working on fish diseases in South Africa. They report that they have identified significant genetic and physiological differences between three new isolates, but the practical implications are not yet known.

Brooklynella hostilis, although known as clownfish disease, actually occurs in many families of marine fishes and is known for its virulence and ability to spread rapidly in a community aquarium if not promptly treated.

Brooklynellosis, *Brooklynella*, Clownfish Disease, "Brook," *Brooklynella hostilis* Infestation

During most of the late 1990s, one of the most common diseases we witnessed was clownfish or anemonefish disease, caused by the ciliated protozoan, *Brooklynella hostilis*. (A freshwater version of the parasite is *Chilodonella* sp.) This obligate parasite appeared to be the cause of death in more fish than *Amyloodinium* and *Cryptocaryon* combined, based on the authors' personal observations in some aquarium stores, although others have reported it to be uncommon in home aquaria.

Brooklynella is often quite virulent; its simple cell division occurs quickly, making it very contagious, and it can cause speedy deaths in a tankful of marine fishes. As the name indicates, clownfishes are exceptionally susceptible to this illness, as are seahorses. However, it appears to affect all marine fish: We have isolated it in bony fishes of all families with the exception of the scaleless, thick-skinned elasmobranchs (sharks and rays).

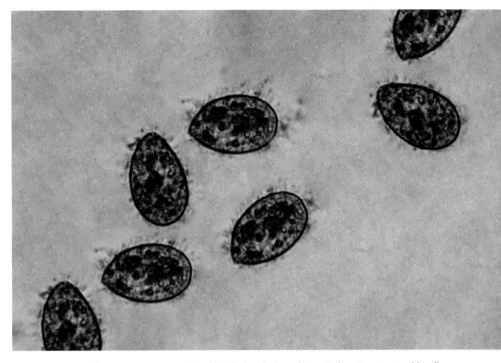

Microscopic view of the protozoan parasite *Brooklynella hostilis*. According to Nelson Herwig, *Brooklynella*, unlike other similar parasites, has nine micronuclei rather than a single nucleus.

This parasite is opportunistic in that it will affect fish that have been stressed by shipping, wide or sudden fluctuation of temperature, tankmate aggression, poor water quality, or an inadequate diet. Once a fish has been stressed, it easily becomes a host for invaders such as *Brooklynella*.

The fishes at greatest risk appear to be those living in overcrowded conditions and/or with poor water quality. Typically, this disease will enter an established aquarium on a previously infected fish. Once in an aquarium it can reach epidemic proportions within a few days, given the right conditions. Infected fish can die within a few days.

The particular stages of *Brooklynella*'s life cycle have not been described as those of *Cryptocaryon* have. The parasite simply divides right on the host and matures, and daughter cells spread directly to other fish. The parasite feeds on the skin and blood cells of its host, and due to the potential for great numbers of parasites, can cause serious and extensive damage to skin, gills, and fin tissue. Death usually occurs as a result of dehydration, tissue damage, and sometimes secondary bacterial infection, in that order.

SYMPTOMS Initially, there may be no outward signs of this disease, although small whitish spots may become visible on skin and fin tissue. Within a short period of time, the aquarist will be able to see rapid gill movement as the parasite causes damage to the epithelial layers and lamellae, making breathing difficult.

Soon thereafter, characteristic white patches will be visible on the skin, caused by a buildup or thickening of the slime coat on the areas of the body affected by the parasites. There will be a cloudiness of fin and eye tissue as the slime coat thickens, as well as a general sloughing of the mucus, appearing as slimy strings hanging off the body.

Over time, fish will begin to flash, or rub against objects (common in cases where skin and gill tissue is irritated), lose their appetites, display labored breathing, exhibit a shimmying behavior, and eventually lie on the bottom. Severe infestations may cause skin lesions that act as sites for dehydration and the introduction of secondary bacterial infections. Bacterial infections may also lead to fin and tail rot. In some species of fish, the parasite can enter the blood system of a host and possibly invade internal organs, as *Amyloodinium* does. Death may soon follow and if immediate steps are not taken, entire populations of fish can perish.

Microscopic examination of an external skin scraping on a wet mount at 100x magnification will show fairly large, round to pear-shaped or kidney bean–shaped adult parasites measuring 50–80 microns. However, it may be possible for much larger mature cells to exist, some as large as *Cryptocaryon*, in the range of 350–450 microns. Daughter cells are much smaller, somewhere around 20–25 microns, and may appear teardrop-shaped. In both cases you will see large numbers of cilia, which give this parasite great mobility. It might be worth mentioning here that although teardrop-shaped daughter cells may look like *Uronema* cells, *Brooklynella* moves much more slowly and deliberately than *Uronema*.

THERAPY AND CONTROL Hyposaline conditions (lowered specific gravity) have yielded good results as first aid in treating *Brooklynella* outbreaks, since the parasite is not osmoregulatory. We recommend freshwater baths, at least for the stronger specimens, to help reduce the number of parasites present.

It also appears that freshwater baths containing formalin are more effective than freshwater baths without it. We have performed baths with a range of concentrations from 25–250 mg/L (two drops per gallon to 20 drops per gallon of water with a 37 percent formaldehyde solution) with

Formalin Dips:

If using a formalin dip for any of the ectoparasites, be sure to aerate the water vigorously, as formalin tends to rob oxygen.

good success. Keep in mind that the higher the concentration of formalin, the shorter the bath time should be. Also, always aerate the bath vigorously as formalin tends to rob oxygen from the bath solution. Observe the fish carefully, and terminate the bath if fish begin to show excessive stress. Refrain from such formalin dips in cases where fish

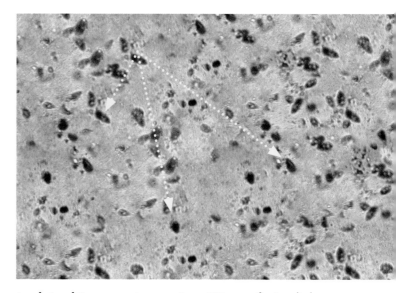

A profusion of *Uronema marinum* parasites at 200x magnification, displaying a characteristic sharply defined oval shape in many of the dark cells.

have severe lesions or skin damage.

There is wide agreement that the drug of choice in combating a *Brooklynella* outbreak is formalin or a formalin/malachite green solution. A dose rate of 15–25 mg/L formalin (1.25–2 drops per net gallon) combined with 0.05 mg/L malachite green is recommended for at least three treatments, every other day. Formalin treatment should be performed in a separate hospital tank to avoid "pickling organisms that you do not want pickled," in the words of Martin Moe.

Moving a tankful of fish is very stressful to the inhabitants, so we feel it is best not to expose the fish to daily capture from a display tank for bathing. Daily dips with specimens kept in bare quarantine/hospital tanks are easier. Also, it is our observation that formalin can interrupt or otherwise inhibit nitrification, and ammonia poisoning may result. We are not strong advocates of using formalin in a show tank, even if it is fish-only system.

Some experts say this parasite is not vulnerable to copper treatment. A combination of drugs may work, however. We have had good results treating *Brooklynella* with ionic copper sulfate at 0.18–0.20 mg/L for 28 days when combined with hyposalinity conditions in the range of

1.010–1.013 SG. Martin Moe suggests that for copper to be effective, a co-treatment with formalin, quinacrine, or malachite green may be in order.

A newer, simpler protocol being used in public aquariums is the use of chloroquine phosphate (see page 146).

Additionally, it may become necessary to include antibiotics in the treatment procedure to prevent or treat secondary bacterial infections. We have had very good results using kanamycin sulfate, but other drugs, such as neomycin, nifurpirinol, or sulfonamides, may also be effective.

Uronema, Uronemosis (*Uronema marinum*)

This is yet another opportunistic ectoparasite and it appears that all marine teleosts (bony fish) are somewhat at risk, as we have seen *Uronema marinum* on all of the fish families typically kept in marine aquariums. Other species of *Uronema* may exist; many authors refer to some parasites as "*Uronema*-like," indicating that *U. marinum* may be only one of an unknown number of still unidentified species.

As with most diseases encountered, stress from shipping, poor water quality, sudden changes of environment, overcrowding, poor nutrition, and poor handling will allow this parasite to get a foothold and flourish.

It appears that this ciliate is ubiquitous and is almost always present, since it is part of the fauna of decomposition associated with closed systems. Typically, it can be found on the decomposing tissue of uneaten foods or dead fish.

SYMPTOMS The most common symptoms of this illness appear externally, although, like some of the previously mentioned diseases, it has been reported to reside within the gut of marine fish. Initial signs include loose or missing scales and a buildup of slime in affected areas. Such areas quickly develop into lesions surrounded by reddened, hemorrhagic rings, with tissue and musculature exposed, as the parasite begins to embed itself deep under the epithelium. These symptoms have led many aquarists to erroneously treat for a bacterial infection. Fins become ragged and the fish start to flash when the parasite begins to create irritation. There is rapid and labored breathing. Noga says that this is unlike most other common ectoparasites, as it will invade internal organs and create ulceration of the muscles,

liver, kidneys, bladder, and spinal cord.

As a result of the lesions, dehydration may occur. Fish may die from suffocation due to gill damage. Fish with such advanced symptoms as large open lesions are usually beyond saving.

Under 100x magnification, a wet mount prepared from a skin scraping of the affected area will usually reveal large numbers of small, teardrop- or pear-shaped (pyriform) parasites, which multiply explosively by simple cell division. They measure approximately 10–15 microns wide by 30–35 microns long, are very agile, and can move quickly through the field of view. Often, these parasites will attack areas already compromised by other pathogens, such as fungus. We have seen many cases where fungus and

Maroon Clownfish (*Premnas biaculeatus*) with characteristic wounds surrounded by pale skin caused by a severe *Uronema marinum* infection.

Uronema are found concurrently, living in a loose, commensal relationship of sorts.

THERAPY AND CONTROL Treating this illness can be somewhat difficult, as this parasite tends to be unaffected by standard copper sulfate treatments.

As recommended above for the treatment of *Brooklynella hostilis*, a formalin or formalin/malachite green combination is the treatment of choice, either in repeated baths or in a treated hospital tank.

Cloroquine phosphate has been used effectively in treating this as well as other ciliated protozoans, as demonstrated repeatedly by aquarists at public institutions.

As with other parasitic ciliates, freshwater baths can be helpful, but the treatment should not be used on fish with severe lesions, lest it cause osmotic shock.

Keeping fish in hyposaline conditions has also shown good results. Such treatments should be geared to saving fish that appear non-infected or are in the initial stages, since fish exhibiting advanced stages of this disease are usually terminal.

The best approach with *Uronema* is to keep it from getting started in your system. Avoid stress from poor husbandry conditions, keep water quality high and the aquarium free of excessive organic detritus, remove dead organisms immediately, and quarantine all newly acquired specimens. Being proactive will go a long way toward preventing the outbreak of ubiquitous, opportunistic parasites such as *Uronema*.

SPOROZOANS

Although not commonly seen, sporozoans do infect marine fish on occasion. They are often visible externally, manifesting as a small, white to gray, tumorous mass known as a *xenoma*, or highly enlarged host cell.

These xenomas are usually embedded in the skin or fin tissue. Sporozoans may sometimes be considered host- and tissue-specific, since they have a unique propensity for specific hosts and for specific tissues in that host. We have noticed that xenomas typically show up on the forehead and along the lateral line of Naso Tangs and angelfish after a short period of time, although the fish may start out looking clean and healthy. We have also witnessed this problem affecting butterflyfish, in whom xenomas show up under the scales and are visible as small white bumps that lift the scales from underneath.

Many sporozoans can exist internally in muscle tissue or internal organs as well, and all types of tissues are af-

fected. At this time we believe all fish are susceptible to infestation by sporozoans. In the early stages, it looks very similar to and may be mistaken for other diseases, such as lymphocystis and *Cryptocaryon*. Generally speaking, there are two primary groups of sporozoans—microsporidians and myxosporidians—that we need to be concerned with, each containing many genera and many species.

Microsporidians

The microsporidian, *Glugea heraldi*, has been identified as the cause of what is commonly known as seahorse disease, which causes dense white patches of spores on the bodies of seahorses and other species of fish with hard body plates, such as boxfish and pipefish.

As the cysts begin to enlarge due to binary fission reproduction and sporogeny, and as the tissue surrounding the cysts breaks down, they may erupt, releasing large numbers of spores into the water. Direct ingestion, either of the spores or of foods containing spores, will cause the disease to spread.

Under microscopic examination, a wet mount of a cyst that has been squashed reveals large numbers of small spores ranging in size up to 7.5 microns long by 3.5 microns wide. One polar capsule may be visible at the anterior end of the spore in microsporidians, and two polar capsules can be seen in myxosporidians.

SYMPTOMS Besides the obvious cyst embedded within fin and skin tissue, fish may appear lethargic, become emaciated, hide in the corners of the aquarium, and exhibit abnormal color changes in body tissue, all of which may indicate advanced disease. Sometimes, muscle tissue necrosis will occur, causing the body to appear wavy or display an uneven undulation. This could even lead to a curvature of the spine, as in the case of mycobacteriosis.

THERAPY AND CONTROL Depending on the species and the area of the fish affected, microsporidians can kill fish. There is no known cure or effective treatment at this time. If fish are suspected of being infected with this parasite, it may be wise to isolate them and ultimately destroy the affected specimens to prevent an epidemic. Remove

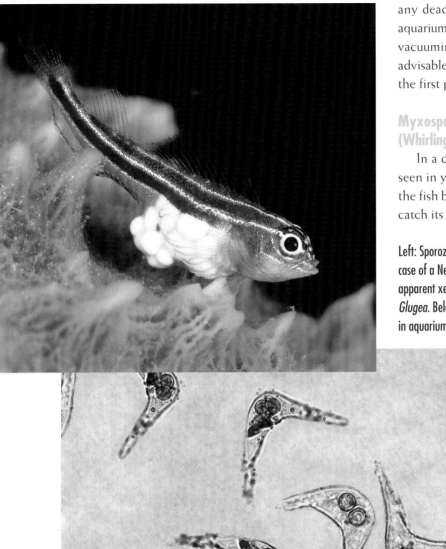

any dead fish before they are eaten by other fish in the aquarium. General maintenance should be stepped up and vacuuming of the gravel to remove any organic waste is advisable. Try to prevent the introduction of the disease in the first place by quarantining all new acquisitions.

Myxosporidians, *Myxobolus cerebralis* (Whirling Disease)

In a classic case of whirling disease, most commonly seen in young fish, the animal's tail first turns black; then the fish begins spinning crazily and appears to be trying to catch its own tail. The parasites attack the spinal cord and

Left: Sporozoan parasites attack both external and internal organs, as in the case of a Neon Triplefin Blenny (*Helcogramma striatum*) with a bellyful of apparent xenomas or pseudotumors like those caused by the microsporidian *Glugea*. Below: Microscopic view of myxosporidians. Although not common in aquarium fishes, these parasites are difficult or impossible to treat.

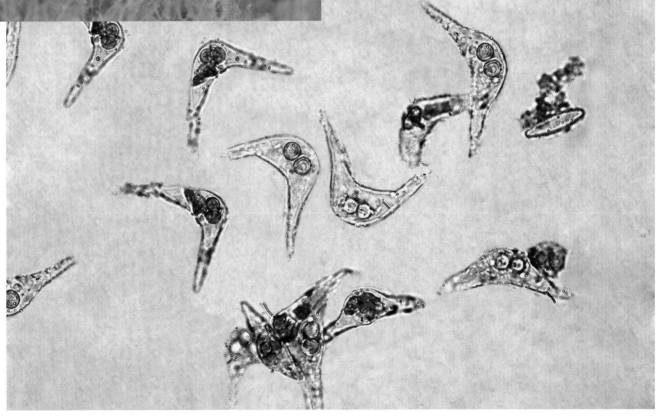

cartilage in the auditory capsule where a fish's sense of balance is normally maintained. Death is often the result.

Like microsporidians, myxosporidians may affect any marine fish. Some species of myxosporidians cause small, white, pointed eruptions on or around the head and lateral line areas, while others form a white cyst under the scales, creating a milky appearance. Microscopically, myxosporidian spores contain two polar capsules and look very similar to microsporidian spores. Like microsporidians, myxosporidians have been found both internally and externally.

SYMPTOMS Many of the symptoms of myxosporidian infection are similar to those listed above for microsporidians. In addition, small white cysts may appear in gill and skin tissue, and again, this sometimes leads to a misdiagnosis of lymphocystis or *Cryptocaryon*. In the case of whirling disease, it seems to depend on the age of the fish and the severity of infection. Affected fish will carry the spores for life. Darkened pigmentation around the caudal peduncle and tail may be visible. Chronically ill fish will swim in erratic circular patterns, thus the name. It appears that the head and lateral line areas are particularly susceptible.

THERAPY AND CONTROL As with microsporidians, there is no known cure for myxosporidian infestations. It would be advisable to isolate suspected specimens and destroy all known carriers before it spreads to other fish. Quarantine all new acquisitions and follow the procedure recommended for microsporidians. However, anecdotally, the use of 35 percent hydrogen peroxide at a dose rate of 1 ml/10 gallons for five consecutive days seemingly cured an Emperor Angelfish of a very advanced case of myxosporidian infestation. By the time the treatment was complete, the fish displayed no symptoms. In fact, where there had been scars from the parasite, the epithelium actually healed and the fish appeared perfectly healthy.

METAZOANS

Of the many metazoan (multi-celled) parasites affecting our marine fish, there are only a few of concern to most home aquarists. Most of them belong to the categories of worms and crustaceans.

Many of the metazoan parasites require specific intermediate hosts (such as birds, crustaceans, and mollusks) in order to complete their life cycles. This makes it difficult, if not impossible, for them to reproduce and cause problems in a home aquarium.

Worm Parasites

It is normal to find between 70 and 85 percent of all marine fish examined to be affected by some sort of worm infestation, because exposure in the wild is very common. Common worm parasites, such as nematodes (roundworms), usually do not threaten the well-being of our fish. Therefore, minor infestations normally do not require treatment. Of importance to us are just a few of the more commonly encountered ones that have the ability to reproduce in our aquariums, thereby creating the potential for severe infestations and substantial damage. Tang turbellarians, as well as flukes such as monogeneans (*Benedenia* sp. is one commonly encountered worm parasite), fit these criteria.

Tang Turbellarian, Black Ich, Black Spot Disease

The most common worm parasite among marine aquarium species is the tang turbellarian, also known as Black Ich or Black Spot Disease. Caused by a parasitic planarian (free-

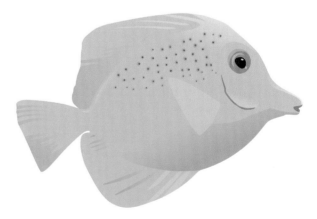

Tang turbellarians are parasitic planarian flatworms that attach to skin and gill tissue of fishes and show up as tiny black pinpoint spots. They are most common in systems with high levels of dissolved organic wastes.

living flatworm), this disease is easily diagnosed by black spots that are clearly visible on the bodies of fish such as the Yellow Tang, *Zebrasoma flavescens*. The parasite has not yet been officially classified, but may eventually end up in the genus *Paravortex*. It is common in systems with high levels of organic waste, which typically goes hand-in-hand with poor water quality.

The tang turbellarian gets its nutrition from its host's blood, and the stored hemoglobin appears black, thus the name. The parasite frequently occurs in the Yellow Tang, where the black color is especially visible, although we have seen it on many other types of fish, such as butterflyfish, wrasses, and angelfish. Because these turbellarians are monogenetic, they are capable of completing their life cycle on a single host within the aquarium and therefore must be controlled.

Initially, a small, free-swimming worm locates a host fish and attaches itself to skin or gill tissue, taking in blood for nourishment. After a few days the worm leaves the host to mature on the bottom of the aquarium. Then, after a few more days, it splits, releasing a swarm of many free-swimming worms that begin the cycle all over again. The life cycle of this parasite lasts approximately 10 days at 76°F (24.5°C). In this manner an infestation of epidemic proportions may occur in just a short period of time if left untreated. According to Dr. Edward Noga, a single mature parasite can develop upwards of 160 juveniles, which could result in one fish carrying up to 4,500 parasites in as few as 20 days, at which time death is imminent.

SYMPTOMS On lightly colored fish it is fairly easy to see many small black spots on the body and fins of an affected fish. Fish will flash, scratching themselves on hard objects. In advanced cases, they may exhibit rapid breathing, become listless, and eventually stop eating. Under microscopic magnification it is easy to see a pear-shaped flatworm with two characteristic eyespots at its anterior end, gliding slowly across the slide.

THERAPY AND CONTROL Most worm parasites are susceptible to formalin and these turbellarians are no differ-

Although most commonly seen on Yellow Tangs, so-called black ich is known to afflict other tangs, wrasses, butterflyfishes, and angelfishes. Standard treatment calls for offering foods dosed with the dewormer praziquantel or Droncit®.

ent. The formalin or formalin/malachite green in freshwater baths described in the section under *Brooklynella* work quite well. Placing the fish in hyposaline hospital tank water can also be very helpful, particularly if it includes formalin or formalin/malachite green.

Noga recommends formalin as used in the treatment of other ectoparasites, or several treatments with an organophosphate in the hospital tank. Trichlorfon (also known as Masoten®, Dylox®, or DTHP) at 1.0 mg/L daily for three consecutive days has also proved effective, although great care must be exercised when using organophosphates since they can be very toxic to fish and invertebrates. Alternatively, the recent use of praziquantel (tradename Droncit®) in a hospital tank at 1 mg/L has given remarkable results. Mixing praziquantel directly into appetizing food (250 mg/100 grams of food) is perhaps the surest way to administer this broad-spectrum dewormer.

"Deworming should be a part of quarantine husbandry," says Kelly Jedlicki. "It is estimated that at least 70 percent of all fish brought into the hobby have worms. Worm infestations are difficult to detect, and it may take weeks to

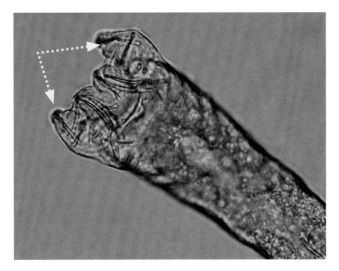

Flukes such as this monogenean (Dactylogyrid) that attack gills, skin, and eyes of fishes are often armed with tail hooks that anchor them to a victim.

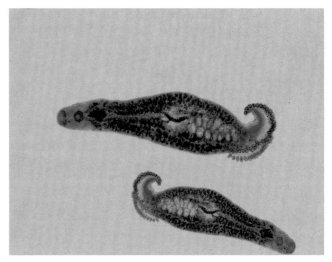

A monogenean fluke that uses suction to attach to fish. Fluke infestations are commonly associated with degraded water quality and lax maintenance.

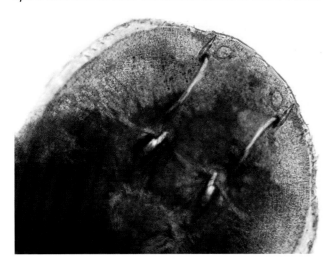

The attaching haptor of a capsalid monogenean, *Benedia* sp., a common parasite of Caribbean fish. It is large enough to be seen with the naked eye.

Monogenean (gill) flukes in a microscopic view of gill tissue. Most monogeneans are specialized to attack a single family or species of fish.

months for symptoms to become apparent. Treating for worms is easier, less stressful, and more successful if done before the fish becomes symptomatic." She advocates the routine use of pranziquantel.

Flukes, Trematodes

There are a few types of fluke that act as parasites on fish. Because digenetic trematodes require an intermediate host or two to complete their life cycle, so are unable to reproduce in aquariums, they are of no real consequence to most fish, though some may succumb to them from time to time. Of greater concern are the monogeneans, since they can reproduce in the aquarium without the need for intermediate hosts.

Some of the flukes (such as most belonging to the family *Dactylogyridae*, subclass *Monogenea*) are equipped with a set of hardened body parts, known as sclerites or hamuli. Collectively, these hooks make up the attachment disc or haptor by which positioning on the host is achieved. The fluke will attach itself by digging these hooks into the host's skin or gill tissue, allowing it to easily get its nutrition. Obviously, the hooks inflict damage on the host and create potential entry points for secondary bacterial infections as well.

Other flukes, such as those of the genus *Benedenia*, possess suction or oral discs in addition to sclerites to achieve attachment. They are characterized by a large attachment disc and two smaller suction cups on the opposite end. The fact that *Benedenia* possess oral discs makes them similar to digenetic trematodes, but since they are capable of reproducing without the need for an intermediate host, they are monogenetic. Butterflyfish and angelfish appear to be highly susceptible to gill flukes. Many fishes from other families are also affected, including sharks and rays.

SYMPTOMS Fish affected with flukes will flash constantly, scratching themselves on available surfaces in the aquarium to relieve the irritation caused by the flukes, oftentimes on the opercula (gill plates), which are favorite targets for flukes. Fish may also swim erratically, shaking their heads from side to side. Rapid gill motion and heavy breathing may be noted as the gills become progressively damaged. Eventually fish will lose their appetites. These flukes primarily spread by crawling from host to host. They are not known for their swimming ability. Therefore, once they have become dislodged, the chances that they will find another host are minimal. Infection of the host is actually through the free-swimming *oncomiracidium* stage, where parasites are attracted to the host by chemical stimuli present in the host and/or detection of host movement.

A small section of gill tissue, along with a skin scraping, placed under a microscope, will usually reveal the parasite attached to the tissue. It can be seen pulsing up and down as it obtains its nutrients. However, sites of infection differ from species to species, depending on the fluke's physiology, its source of food, and the water currents in which host fishes live.

Benedenia, a small, opaque to white parasite normally 3–12 mm in length and 1–4 mm in width, can easily be seen, usually on the eyes, fins, and skin of affected fish. On rare occasions we have even witnessed some as large as 18–20 mm long. As with many other parasites, severe infestation of a fish creates an opportunity for secondary bacterial infections, as well as other ailments, increasing the potential for fish death.

THERAPY AND CONTROL Freshwater baths are the best first aid when dealing with these pests. Carefully remove the afflicted fish from the aquarium and place it in a separate container filled with freshwater. As previously recommended, make sure to first adjust the temperature and pH to match those of the fish's aquarium and neutralize any chlorine present. An airstone powered by a good air pump should also be placed in the bath.

In addition, when formalin or formalin/malachite green has been added to the bath, at a concentration somewhere between 100 and 150 mg/L (8–12 drops per net gallon), the flukes will fall off the fish in short order. However, vari-

▶ **Death for Flukes:**
A five-to-ten minute freshwater dip will cause most flukes to dislodge from a fish. Formalin/malachite green adds impact.

ous authors indicate that certain dosages of formalin may be less effective on one species than another, and therefore may not eradicate all adult flukes. We have been quite successful in controlling these parasites by leaving the fish in the freshwater bath for five to ten minutes, constantly keeping an eye on their condition. As always, one must be prepared to terminate the bath at the first sign of stress to the fish (for example, if they begin to list onto their sides). These baths can be administered on a daily basis if necessary. However, the higher the concentration of formalin, the shorter the bath should be.

Great care should be taken not to dislodge the flukes while capturing the fish, and one should also be careful not to reintroduce them into the main tank (or other aquariums). Refer to the treatments recommended above for tang turbellarians, since they are also very effective in the treatment of skin and gill flukes. Even if you can avoid reintroducing adult parasites into the tank, any eggs that have been laid in the system will still hatch and reinfect the host. The eggs are resistant to treatment and it is therefore imperative to know as accurately as possible the biology of the worm species you're treating for so you can accurately determine the reinfection rate.

Praziquantel has been used effectively against monogeneans as well as tang turbellarians. When administered to an aquarium at a dose rate of 1–5 mg/L (powdered form) once a week for at least three weeks, it can be very beneficial in the treatment of external flukes, providing proper coverage of the life cycle can be accomplished. Such treatments should be confined to quarantine or hospital tanks whenever feasible. A dose of 3.125 mg/L of praziquantel is recommended for external treatment.

To add some further complexity to treatment methods, this compound is available in both liquid and dry forms. It is not very soluble in water. It may be somewhat difficult to obtain, but an aquarium brand called PraziPro is now available in liquid form. Although many consider praziquantel the drug of choice for certain worm parasites, others who have used it recognize its drawbacks. Still, praziquantel is one of the safest and most effective drugs for the treatment of flukes.

Be forewarned: Praziquantel will kill ornamental worms, such as featherdusters, and is best used in a hospital tank.

CRUSTACEAN PARASITES

Isopods

Occasionally, parasites that are large enough to be visible with the naked eye appear on our fish. One of these is an isopod, or fish louse, Livoneca sp., which looks similar to a light-colored sow bug, a terrestrial isopod. The name "isopod" refers to the fact that it has multiple appendages all of the same design (iso = equal or one, and pod = foot).

Although fish lice usually occur singly, they can get quite large (we have seen them as large as 37 mm, or 1.5 inches). In fact, the giant isopod, Bathynomus giganteus, which lives on the ocean bottom at depths in excess of 2,000 feet (610 m), can reach lengths of 12–16 inches (30–40 cm).

These animals are equipped with appendages that look very similar to those of a lobster: sharp and thorny. Therefore they are capable of inflicting serious wounds on fish, and possibly allowing secondary bacterial infections to set in. They can usually be removed manually with forceps or needlenosed pliers. (See Therapy for Parasitic Copepods, page 167.) Swab with iodine or peroxide afterward.

Parasitic Copepods

Another type of crustacean parasite, the parasitic copepod, is large enough to be seen with the naked eye. There are many species of copepods that are parasitic to fish. Some of them are species-specific. Copepods seen moving around on the host are males; only female copepods actually attach to fish, and they are rarely (if ever) seen. Normally, the body of a female copepod is embedded deeply in the musculature under the epithelium of its host, by means of specialized mouthparts. As a rule, the males have the 'Cyclops' appearance of copepods. The underside of a male copepod exhibits the characteristic features of a typical crustacean.

SYMPTOMS An isopod on a fish will be obvious upon sight and quite easy to diagnose. However, a fish affected by parasitic copepods will exhibit one or two filaments extending from the point of entry, which may develop into lesions. These filaments are egg strings, the means of reproduction, and are usually the only visual sign of the copepod's existence. The appearance of these strings varies depending on the species of copepod, and Blasiola has described them as "straight, serpentine, or coiled." The point of entry may appear ulcer-like with a reddened ring around the ulcer, and scales may be raised or missing. Copepods can cause great damage to the host, particularly ones attached to a fish's gills.

Free-swimming parasitic copepods hatch from the egg strings upon maturation, seeking a fish as a host. When the larvae reach adulthood they mate; sometimes the male dies after mating, leaving the female to continue the life cycle. Interestingly, Vaughan has reported that in many common

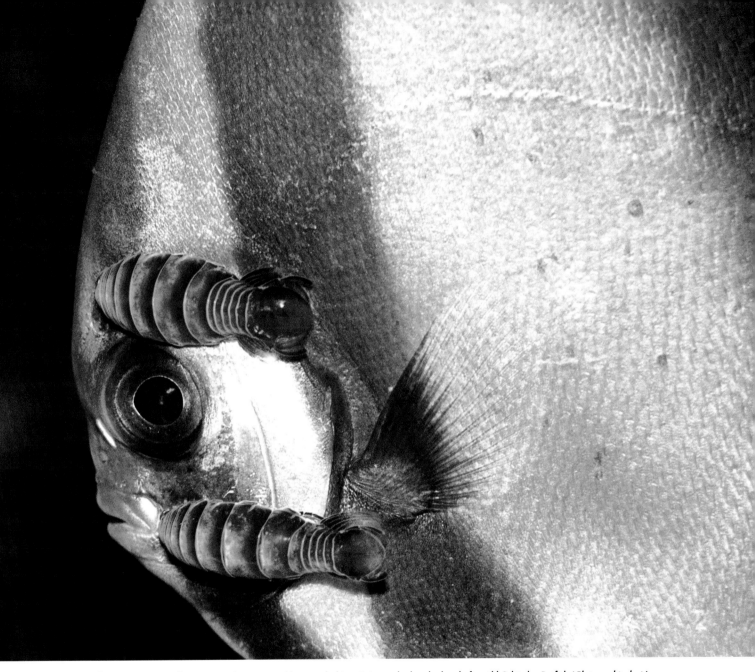

Some isopods can grow to significant size and open a sizable wound; this pair is attached to the head of a wild Orbicular Batfish (*Platax orbicularis*).

calagid copepods, the males and females colonize different parts of the host. On one kingfish, belonging to the family Carangidae, or Jacks, the female copepods were found attached to the back of the host, while the males were found on the anal fin and the ends of the pectoral fins. Vaughan has also found both male and female calagid copepods un-

der the same operculum of oceanic needlefish and tuna, so there appears to be variation among the various calagid copepod species.

THERAPY AND CONTROL Treatment for isopods is usually not required, since all one really has to do is remove the *Livoneca* sp. parasite by hand (tweezers work well for

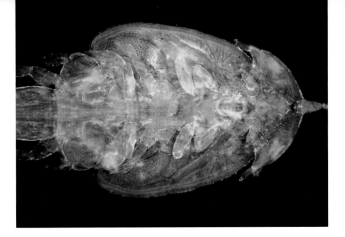

Ventral side of a male copepod, with characteristic crustacean appendages also seen in more familiar crabs, lobsters, and shrimps.

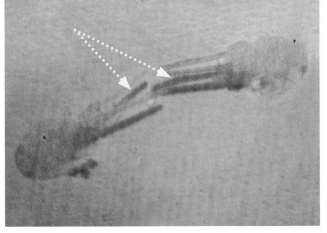

Two full-bodied female calagid copepods removed from a kingfish and displaying filaments, or so-called egg strings.

this). After removal the use of a topical antiseptic such as hydrogen peroxide or iodine is recommended to prevent secondary bacterial infections.

Parasitic copepods, on the other hand, can be difficult to treat, as it is not possible to remove the entire deeply embedded animal without causing a great deal of damage to the fish. As recommended above for the treatment of worm parasites, formalin, a combination of formalin/malachite green at 25 mg/L, or Trichlorfon at 100 mg/100 l are very effective.

The medications will kill young copepods when they hatch; however, they will usually not affect the female since it is embedded. Therefore, several treatments over a period of several weeks are required to eradicate all of the parasites in various stages of the life cycle. Antibiotics should be administered as well, as secondary bacterial infections may ensue where lesions occur. Aquarist David Vaughan reports very good success treating calagid copepods with a formalin bath of 1 ml/20 L.

Greatly magnified female fish louse, a parasitic copepod in the Family Caligidae, with paired egg sacs trailing behind, each containing several dozen eggs.

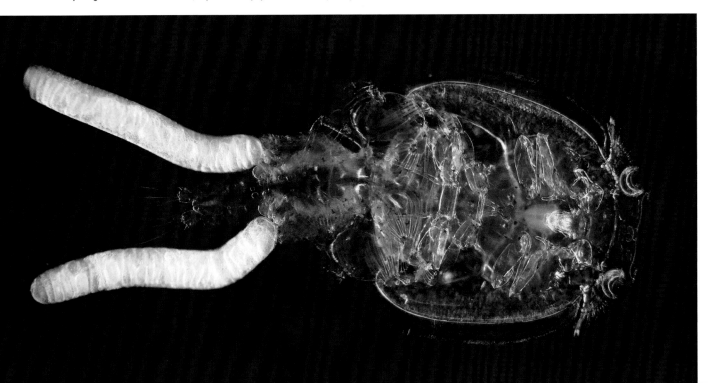

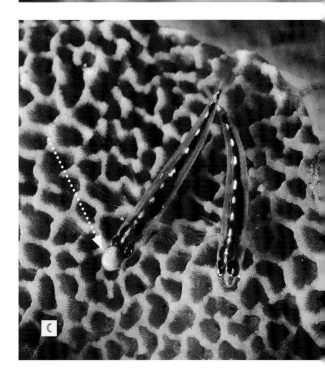

PARASITIC CRUSTACEANS: (A) Toothy Goby (*Pleurosicya mossambica*) with multiple parasitic cope-pods on its side with egg-filled tubules showing; (B) Magenta Dottyback (*Pictichromis porphyreus*) with a parasitic isopod above its eye. (C) Pair of unidentified tiny gobies on a *Favites* sp. stony coral, the fish at left with a parasitic copepod covering its snout. (D) Diminutive Pinkeyed Goby (*Bryaninops natans*) perches on an *Acropora* sp. staghorn coral branch tip and carries a parasitic copepod attached to its back, with trailing egg sacs.

PARASITIC CRUSTACEANS: (A) Unfortunate Clark's Clownfish (*Amphiprion clarkii*) whose tongue has been eaten and replaced by a live isopod, possibly *Cymothoa exigua,* a parasite that attacks many types of marine fishes (note black eye spots) and establishes itself in a prime feeding position where the animal's tongue was once located. (B) Copepod egg sacs (arrows) attached to a Sand Goby (*Coryphopterus* sp.). (C) Blackstriped Cardinalfish (*Apogon nigrofasciatus*) with a parasitic isopod attached. (D)Parasitic fish lice (Isopoda) on the head of a scorpionfish (*Scorpaenopsis* sp.). (E) Three magnified views of a parasitic isopod removed from a larval Pinfish or Porgie (*Lagodon rhomboides*). (F) Young Atlantic Bumper (*Chloroscrombus chrysurus*), a member of the Jack family, struggling with three isopods hangers-on.

Emperor Red Snapper
(*Lutjanus sebae*) with bulging,
cloudy eyes that are often
the symptoms of internal
bacterial infections.

Bacteria, Fungal Diseases, & Viruses

Invisible plagues, with their symptoms and treatments

Unlike the parasitic problems we encounter in our aquariums, diseases and conditions caused by bacteria, fungus infections, and viruses have causative agents that are not visible to the naked eye. We recognize them by the symptoms they cause, but identifying the exact pathogen at work can be difficult or impossible. Fortunately, we can often provide a treatment without a perfect diagnosis.

Bacterial Infections

There are many different genera of bacteria associated with marine fish diseases, and it appears that all marine fish are susceptible to bacterial infections of one type or another. Treatment depends upon the species of bacteria and, particularly, whether they are gram-positive or gram-negative. Most of us are ill-equipped to make this distinction. Fortunately for marine hobbyists, though, the majority of bacterial infections affecting marine fish (95 percent or more) are gram-negative, which somewhat simplifies treatment: One can assume that if a bacterial infection is present, a broad-spectrum antibiotic used to treat gram-negative bacteria will, more often than not, be appropriate. (Gram-negative simply means that a particular bacteria does not absorb a laboratory stain used in identification.)

Since pathogenic bacteria are ubiquitous in nature, most bacterial infections may be considered secondary or opportunistic, usually taking hold after a primary or initial problem (i.e., parasitic infestation, trauma to the fish, poor nutrition,

Group of juvenile Sergeant Majors (*Abudefduf saxatilis*) in sad shape after importation, with signs of infection on tails and napes. For the home aquarist, precise diagnosis of such infections is usually impossible, but quick treatment with a broad-spectrum antibiotic in a quarantine or hospital tank is often effective.

deteriorating water quality, territorial aggression, etc.). Therefore, in order to bring a diseased fish back to good health, one must first treat for the initial cause(s) and add antibiotics for the secondary infections in the procedure.

It is important to know that the beneficial bacteria in an aquarium's biological filter are gram-negative. Many antibiotics, particularly those designed to treat gram-negative bacteria, may inhibit or kill off our carefully cultivated populations of nitrifying bacteria, present on live rock, substrates, and in filter media. If these bacterial populations crash, a system can quickly develop an ammonia problem, which has serious health consequences of its own. Therefore, it is advisable to treat affected fish in a hospital tank whenever possible because bacterial infections normally afflict individual specimens and are not epidemic.

When the protective slime coat of a fish is disturbed, whether by poor handling, parasitic infestation, fungal infection, or trauma, opportunistic pathogenic bacteria will sometimes attack the damaged areas. (A healthy fish has natural defenses against bacteria in its skin, but these can be breached by injury, parasites, or disease.) Once the bacteria begin to colonize, they secrete enzymes and/or toxins that break down and digest surrounding tissue, causing proliferation of the bacteria, deterioration of the tissue, and—if not stopped—the death of the fish.

Sometimes an ulcer will develop. An ulcer normally appears as a clear, distinct, and fairly circular area of tissue with a white center where the digested tissue occurs. This central core will normally be surrounded with tissue that becomes reddened. In other cases, hemorrhages (localized bleeding) on or under the skin will occur. Hemorrhaging areas can be as small as pinpoints (petechiae) or appear as patches or swatches. Most commonly we see damage to the fins where bacteria have eroded fin tissue and fin rays, causing areas to appear white and ragged.

Fin Rot

Because fin tissue is usually the first area to be damaged during collection and handling, fin rot may occur as a result of bacteria invading the damaged areas. Overcrowding and poor water quality also provide opportunities for bacterial overgrowth, and they will help spread the problem. Many genera of bacteria have been associated with fin and tail rot; some of these are *Pseudomonas* sp., *Aeromonas* sp., *Edwardsiella* sp., *Vibrio* sp., and *Cytophaga* sp., all gram-negative.

SYMPTOMS The damage and subsequent rot will occur at the fin edge, working inward to the body. Erosion may be limited to the tissue between the fin rays, exposing the bony rays; sometimes it even consumes the rays themselves. Damaged fins will appear torn and ragged. If the rot progresses into the caudal peduncle (the "wrist" area of the tail), possibly causing swimming difficulties or other muscle tissue problems, fish lose their appetites and appear sluggish. If the bacteria progress to this point, a cure is quite unlikely. (See fish at right.)

THERAPY AND CONTROL The use of wide-spectrum antibiotics, such as kanamycin at a dosage of 50–100 mg/L or neomycin at a dosage of 65 mg/L of water, is an effective cure. (Note: 20 drops equal 1 ml; 1 U.S. fluid ounce equals 30 ml.). Dr. Edward Noga recommends Furanace® at a dosage of .1 mg/L, added to the water for a prolonged period, as effective in treating this condition. Nifurpirinol can also be used at 1–2 mg/L for a 5-minute to several-hour saltwater bath to rapidly elevate therapeutic levels in badly infected tissue prior to the start of normal treatment procedures. We have used kanamycin at 50–75 mg/L of aquarium water for seven to ten days (redosing every 3 days) with excellent results. In marine fishes, there is minimal established resistance to this medication, and since it is absorbed through the gut, it is fast-acting.

To administer the antibiotic (or any other powdered medication, for that matter), mix it with aquarium water in a small, clean glass or a small plastic bag. Once prepared, pour the solution into a treatment bath bucket or into the hospital tank, in the latter case removing the chemical filter media that may extract the medication. Repeat the dose every 24 hours for seven to ten days, monitoring fish behavior, water clarity, and ammonia. If the fish begin to swim erratically, breathe rapidly, or gasp for air at the surface, if the water becomes cloudy, or if the ammonia level begins to rise, remove the fish from the bath or perform a 50–75 percent water change on the hospital tank. (Water exchanges should be done at least every two to three days during such treatments.) Never add antibiotics to a display aquarium.

Lesions

Fish often develop lesions or open sores on the body. They can usually be attributed to a parasitic infestation

Severe fin rot afflicting a Coral Beauty (*Centropyge bispinosa*): This fish needs to be isolated, treated with a broad-spectrum antibiotic, and nurtured back to health with clean water and proper feeding.

Tail rot and sunken appearance of dorsal musculature and abdomen of a Golden Wrasse (*Halichoeres chrysus*) suggest poor care and/or a very long period between being caught on a reef and arriving in a local fish store.

examined under a microscope to see if any parasites are present. Typically, parasites are the underlying cause and the treatment must include the proper antiparasitic medication as well as the proper antibiotic.

This may sound a bit confusing, but some of the same bacteria that cause fin rot, such as *Vibrio* (see photos) and *Pseudomonas*, as well as *Aeromonas*, *Flexibacter*, and *Mycobacterium*, can also be isolated from lesions of the skin. Some experts believe that the primary cause of this disease is *Aeromonas*, and particularly *A. salmonicida*.

Professional aquarist David Vaughan states that treating parasitic and bacterial infections simultaneously is not always feasible, based on his own experiences. He suggests that an aquarist should always "weigh out carefully" which is the most life-threatening of

such as *Uronema*, *Amyloodinium*, or *Brooklynella*, or to a secondary bacterial infection following a parasitic infestation. Sometimes this condition is called "furunculosis," referring to the furuncles or boil-like lesions that develop from the bacterial infection. Monogenean infestations commonly result in open lesions and are often associated with secondary bacterial infections. When lesions appear, quick action must be taken because if an infection is allowed to progress, not only will any parasites present exacerbate the problem, but toxins from the bacteria will diffuse freely throughout the fish's body. Complicate this with dehydration from fluid loss through the open lesion, and you can quickly have a dead fish.

SYMPTOMS The manifestations of this condition are fairly obvious. Within a short period of time (sometimes within two or three days), a red, inflamed area on the skin will develop into an open sore and grow larger and deeper very quickly. These open sores can look quite irritated and will almost always appear red and raw. If at all possible, a laboratory slide of a skin scraping should be prepared and

the two or more diseases present, and treat it first. In his opinion, bacterial diseases should be considered only after the state of parasitic infestation is understood. Treatments, he says, should be "…prioritized according to which ailment will kill the patient first. In most cases, secondary bacterial infections will accompany heavy or long-standing parasitic infections. Parasites should be removed first or controlled using SG reduction therapy (hyposalinity) while antibiotics are being administered in solution. Effectively, if the parasite is controlled in this way, the aquarist can concentrate his or her efforts on the bacterial infection without using antiparasitic chemicals, and once the bacterial infection is correctly treated, then the full treatment for the parasitic infection should be reviewed."

THERAPY AND CONTROL As a rule of thumb, most bacterial infections will respond favorably to a small group of antibiotics against which resistances have not developed. Nifurpirinol and kanamycin are two such treatments for non-resistant bacteria. Also, sulfathiazole at a dosage of .2–.4 mg/ 10 gallons of water for three days has shown good results. Sulfamerazine can be mixed in the feed at a dosage of 220 mg/ kg of fish for 7–10 days to treat bacterial infections. Use the procedures for fin rot (page 175), bearing in mind that depending on the drug, adjustments

must be made to the actual dosages administered based on the manufacturer's recommendations.

Skin Hemorrhage

When a fish's protective slime coat is disrupted and/or the fish is exposed to poor environmental conditions, hemorrhage, seen as red patches or inflammation on or under the skin, can sometimes result. This symptom can also indicate parasitic infestations, but is most often seen when secondary bacterial infections enter the outer layers of the skin as a result of parasite damage. Such a symptom is frequently seen affecting Yellow Tangs, either because they are more susceptible to this condition or, much more likely, because the bright yellow color allows us to see the redness more clearly.

SYMPTOMS This condition may begin as small red spots resembling enlarged blood cells. Most commonly it is seen as a red patch of skin under the scales. Eventually the problem will progress into large bloody and inflamed areas. Sometimes the scales are entirely missing, resulting in lesions or open sores. Since these symptoms occur with many bacterial infections, it is difficult to determine any one cause; however, *Vibrio* and *Pseudomonas* are commonly associated with these symptoms.

THERAPY AND CONTROL Antibiotics such as kanamycin at 50–100 mg/L for seven to ten days, nifurpirinol at 1–2 mg/L for seven to ten days, neomycin at 65 mg/L for seven

Skin hemorrhages: far left, Panther Grouper (*Cromileptes altivelis*) with lesions caused by *Vibrio parahemolyticus* infection; near left, an unidentified Jack suffering from vibriosis, with a characteristic whitish central core (1) to the infection, surrounded by a large area of blood-filled tissue (2).

A severely malnourished and stressed Yellow Tang (*Zebrasoma flavescens*) exhibiting reddening caused by ruptured blood cells pouring their contents into the external mucus—literally "sweating blood," in the words of fish disease expert Nelson Herwig.

pathogens responsible for this infection, which affects many species of fish. Similar symptoms may appear as the result of low pH and may also indicate columnaris disease, which is characterized by degeneration of the tail and posterior of the fish.

SYMPTOMS Beginning stages appear as a lightening of the skin color in localized areas on the body. After a couple of days the light areas will develop into white patches affecting the protective slime coat. Progressively, the slime coat sloughs off, resulting in scale and skin loss to the extent that even fin and tail rot may be exhibited. Once the slime and skin have become affected, raw tissue and musculature become visible, as in the case of lesions. When this disease affects the gills, it is known as bacterial gill disease or gill rot. Fish with gill rot have difficulty exchanging gases, which blocks the uptake of oxygen and the elimination of wastes like toxic ammonia.

THERAPY AND CONTROL If parasites are present, treatment should be adjusted accordingly. One treatment for these symptoms is neomycin at 65 mg/L or nifurpirinol at 1–2 mg/L for seven to ten days. These may be used either alone or in combination. Following this regi-

to ten days, and some sulfonamides at 6.5 mg/L for 10 to 15 days have, in our experience, been quite effective in eradicating bacterial infections. Parasites such as *Uronema* may cause similar symptoms, but for the amateur aquarist it is usually not feasible or practical to isolate a specific bacterium. Therefore, treatment procedures must attempt to eliminate all causes, bacterial as well as parasitic.

White Skin Patch Disease

Sometimes fish will exhibit a white skin patch of varying size somewhere on the body. Fin and tail rot may accompany this symptom. Usually, the protective slime coat will begin to loosen and appear to be sloughing from these areas. Although such symptoms appear similar to those of *Brooklynella* and *Uronema* infestations, *Cytophaga* sp. (formerly *Myxobacterium*) and *Flexibacter* sp. are sometimes the

"Parasites may cause symptoms similar to those of bacterial infection. Treatment procedures may call for eliminating both bacteria and parasites simultaneously."

men, we have seen improvement in many cases.

Sometimes we prefer to use neomycin sulfate at a dosage of 65 mg/L for seven to ten days, redosing every three days, which, in our experience, usually yields good results. Remember to do water changes regularly with antibiotics.

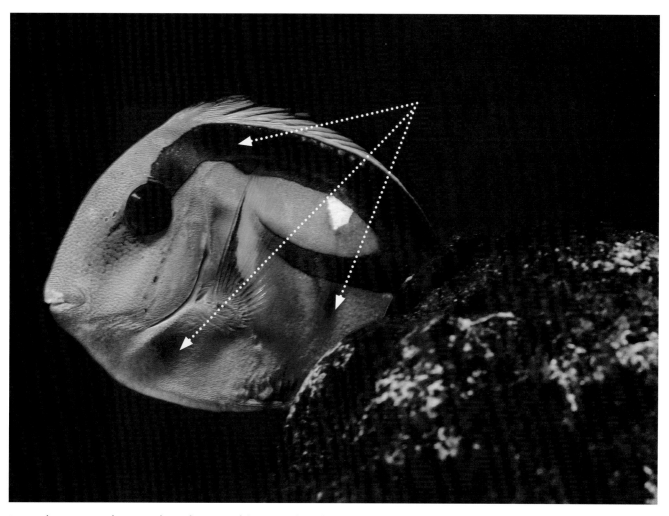

Suspected wasting away disease in a large Blue Surgeonfish (*Paracanthurus hepatus*): Signs include slow loss of body mass along the dorsal ridge and in the abdomen, listlessness, and patchy skin. In confirmed cases of Mycobacteriosis, the aquarist may be infected through open wounds on hands placed in the tank.

Internal Bacterial Infections

When a fish's immune system is compromised, internal bacterial infections may become a problem. Stress, poor nutrition, and poor water quality play important roles as precursors of these diseases. Fish may ingest bacteria or otherwise be easily exposed, as such bacteria are considered to be ubiquitous in the ocean and in aquariums. Typically, internal organs such as the liver and kidneys will be affected. With most internal bacterial infections, redness, indicating hemorrhaging, will be noticed around the mouth and gill covers and at the bases of fins. Inspection of the abdominal cavity of a dead fish often reveals fluid buildup and necrosis or dead tissue in the internal organs.

Mycobacteriosis, "Tuberculosis," Wasting Away Disease

Of all the internal bacterial infections affecting our wet pets, mycobacteriosis seems to be the most prevalent—though not especially common—disease encountered by fishkeepers. At this time it appears that several species of *Mycobacterium* may be responsible for what is (though somewhat erroneously) called piscine tuberculosis.

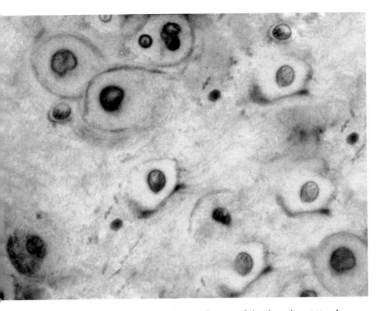

Magnified tubercles or granulomas of marine fish tuberculosis (*Mycobacterium marinum*) in the liver of a Green Chromis (*Chromis caeruleus*).

This loose association is due to the fact that *Mycobacterium* sp. is also the etiological agent known to cause tuberculosis in humans. As such, this fish malady is one of the few fish diseases that can be contracted by humans. We have personally known individuals who have been affected by this disease, sometimes known as fish tank granuloma (see precautions below).

Since this disease is normally chronic, it is also known as wasting away disease, and the death of a fish occurs after an extended period of time.

SYMPTOMS Initially, an affected fish will begin to lose weight and overall emaciation will become obvious. The area just behind the head (along the dorsal ridge), as well as the abdominal area, will appear sunken or emaciated. Conversely, the area just behind the pectoral fins (corresponding to the general location of the liver) will bulge and become pronounced. This symptom is generally a result of the liver becoming enlarged, typically due to the formation of characteristic white nodules (granulomatous lesions) within the liver, kidneys, and other organs. These lesions will appear as gray or white shapeless nodules, which are easily visible under magnification, within various organs

and tissues. One or both eyes may protrude (unilateral or bilateral exophthalmia), scale loss may occur, and white skin patches or lesions may become prevalent as the disease progresses. Fish will become lethargic and withdrawn, seeking the corners of the aquarium. Eventually, we have even observed curvature of the spine in chronic cases of this disease.

In humans, if the bacteria enters a cut or wound, a lesion may develop, particularly in individuals with compromised or depressed immune systems or those whose resistance is lowered for some other reason. This open sore will not heal and can remain for a long time, no matter what treatment is applied to it.

Therefore, if you are a fishkeeper and notice a cut that does not heal or worsens after a week, you should consider going to the doctor. Tell the doctor that you work with marine fish and you suspect mycobacteriosis could be the problem. Unless specific antibiotics are taken for an extended period of time, this disease can last for many months. Try to refrain from exposing an open wound to water from the aquarium. Use long-sleeved rubber gloves if you wish to protect yourself from this bacterium.

THERAPY AND CONTROL In the case of mycobacteriosis, the best course of action is to euthanize the affected or carrier fishes and sterilize the aquarium. The use of kanamycin

❗ Fish Tank Granulomas:

Mycobacterium, related to tuberculosis, can attack humans, usually getting started when an aquarist puts hands or arms with open cuts into an infected tank. For protection, wear rubber gloves and seek treatment for any sore that does not heal.

at a dosage of 20–40 mg/L for three to five days has shown some effectiveness. You can also try Isoniazid (a tuberculin drug) at a dosage of 10 mg/L for seven to 10 days, or streptomycin at a dosage of 20–40 mg/L for three to five days. However, subsequent doses at 30–60 days may be required for a complete cure. Rifampin (also known as rifampicin) at a dosage of 6 mg/100 g of food has also been suggested as a possible cure. Some suggest adding vitamin B6 in the

Tail rot in a Bicolor Goatfish (*Parupeneus barberinoides*) completely missing its caudal fin, perhaps as a result of injury or attack by another fish followed by bacterial infection.

form of baby vitamins to the hospital tank at the rate of one drop per 5 gallons as an initial dose, repeating after every water change.

Typically, though, by the time most people recognize this disease, it has advanced to a point where the fish is beyond saving. In chronic cases, it causes deformities within the fish's integument structure, making it impossible for it to accept any food. As a result, death can occur from starvation, so positive identification of the cause of death is difficult.

The best way to handle this ubiquitous disease is to prevent it, a good reason to quarantine new fish. However, since the disease's progression is chronic, rather than sudden, a limited quarantine may not offer any respite. Fresh, raw fish flesh can be a vector for spreading the disease. To be safe, you may want to cook or microwave any fish flesh being fed. Be careful to sterilize nets and other tools with hydrogen peroxide (equal parts 3% peroxide and water for at least 10 minutes).

Swollen Abdomen and/or Raised Scales

This malady is fairly common and can affect all species of fish. Although this bloating condition, known as ascites (possibly erroneously), may seem to be caused by trapped fluid in the abdomen, it is more commonly the result of an infection by *Pseudomonas* or *Cornebacterium* sp. Some authors believe that ascites in marine fish does not exist, as marine species dehydrate rather than absorb fluids, owing to the osmoregulatory function of their kidneys. Remember, marine fish must take in water continuously in order to avoid becoming dehydrated. Ultimately, this is the main reason why true marine species die when placed in freshwater and freshwater species die when placed in saltwater. (They must urinate continuously in freshwater to avoid ascites.)

SYMPTOMS At first, scales will appear raised, typically in areas around the intestinal cavity. As the condition progresses, scales may be raised over the entire body. Often, gas and/or fluid buildup within the intestinal lumen will cause the scales to puff up and the fish begins to look bloated. As the bloat progresses, anal distension becomes obvious. Unilateral or bilateral exophthalmia (popeye) soon follows, and fish stop eating. Sometimes, hemorrhaging will occur in the affected areas as well.

THERAPY AND CONTROL Isolation of the affected specimen is always a prudent idea. We recommend treatment with nifurpirinol (Furanace) at a dosage of 2-3 mg/L for seven to ten days, repeating as required after each water exchange. Oxytetracycline at a dosage of 20–30 mg/L for three to five days, or erythromycin at a dosage of 10 mg/L for three days, have shown some effectiveness in treating

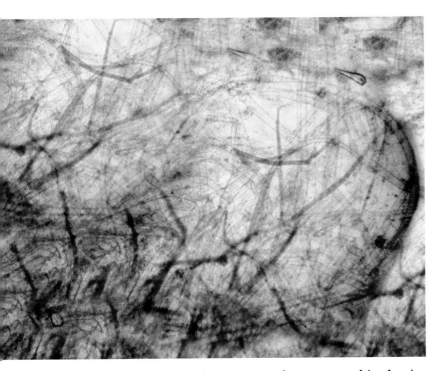

Typical fungus threads illustrated in a microscopic magnification (100x). In fishes, fungal infections often follow injury, parasitic infestation, or bacterial infection. They are also much more common in aquariums with yellowed water and high levels of dissolved organics.

certainly uncommon, but not unknown. (See facing page for a photo of a clownfish exhibiting a typical external fungal infection analogous to freshwater *Saprolegnia* sp.)

External Fungus

When fungus is encountered in marine aquariums it is usually secondary to parasitic infestation, bacterial infection, or traumatic injury, since the fungus will attach to areas where the protective slime coat has been disturbed or skin damage has occurred. Typically it is found in aquariums with yellowed water signifying high levels of organic waste and generally poor water quality. It especially affects various species including seahorses, clownfishes, and butterflyfishes. External fungal infections are also often seen in fishes that have been poorly handled.

It is interesting to note that while fungus can exist independently of any other problem, this condition is not common. Fungal infections are almost always accompanied by *Uronema* infestations, regardless of which came first. A general lack of maintenance, deficient filtration, overcrowding, or overfeeding may also lead to this problem.

SYMPTOMS   Typically, you will see a slightly raised, light-to-dark pigmented area on the skin, sometimes resembling a cottony tuft. This may be on the body and/or the fins (and sometimes on the mouth or eyes), and can be somewhat difficult to recognize. Usually the affected areas on the body will appear somewhat circular in shape. Fungus on the fin is usually white to light brown in color and appears circular, but can also be darker in color and have an elongated shape.

Under microscopic examination, it is possible to see mats of hair-like strands of filaments containing spores. The brown coloration is a result of the dark-colored spores contained within the ends of the filaments, known as sporangia, as well as debris that is trapped within the threads. Fish usually do not act abnormally until the disease has reached its advanced stages, when open lesions may be noticed.

this condition, particularly when administered in food. Oxolinic acid, at a dosage of 15 mg/L for five to seven days, has helped resolve this problem as well.

FUNGAL INFECTIONS

Fungal infections rarely affect healthy fish, even though the spores that cause them may always be present. Fungal infections are common in freshwater fish and quite uncommon in marine aquariums. In fact, some claim that external fungus does not exist in seawater, since most fungi pathogenic to fish cannot survive even a mild exposure to saltwater. However, we have often seen fungal hyphae (filaments) closely resembling the freshwater *Saprolegnia* sp. (external fungal infections) isolated from marine fish, and cases of *Ichthyophonus hoferi* (formerly *Ichthyosporidium hoferi*, or internal fungal infection) have also been visually isolated on occasion. Fungal infections in marine fishes are

THERAPY AND CONTROL To cure a fungal infection, which can be difficult if not impossible, try to find and eliminate the cause. Start by examining the filtration system and making sure the equipment is adequate and functioning properly. Since good water quality can all but eliminate this disease, refrain from overfeeding, consider reducing the fish population (or getting a bigger tank),

Formalin Side Effects:

Using formalin to treat fungus or other problems can seriously interrupt nitrification in your biological filter. Monitor ammonia levels during treatment and do water changes as needed.

perform more routine water exchanges, and remove excess organic waste. Improving a fish's natural immune system can usually help ward off such infections. And since fungus is normally associated with other more primary problems, treatment of those initial problems must be included in the procedure: antibiotics for bacterial infections, formalin/malachite green or copper sulfate for protozoans, etc.

We have had relatively good success treating fungal infections using sulfa drugs, including sulfathiazole (.65–1.3 mg/L daily for seven to ten days); sulfonamide in the same dosage; and even combinations of sulfa drugs such as Triple Sulfa, which includes sulfamerazine. Also, a treatment with zinc-free malachite green at a dosage of 0.15 mg/L (three treatments, three days apart, for a treatment period of nine days) has been shown to be effective. A commercially prepared formalin/malachite green combination solution, using two drops per net gallon every other day for 10 days, can be quite effective.

Look for commercially prepared formulations at your local aquarium shop, as it is not recommended that you handle the raw ingredients yourself. Formalin (37 percent formaldehyde) can be used at 25 mg/L (2 drops per net gallon) dosed every 48 hours until signs of the infection are gone. Always monitor water quality and be prepared to do water exchanges (between 50 and 75 percent if necessary) at two- to three-day intervals. (Formalin is banned in California and may be hard to find in other places.)

Be aware that formalin has been known to interrupt nitrification, so monitor ammonia levels throughout the treatment procedure. Formalin combines with ammonia to form hexamine and water, denaturing the formalin and rendering the treatment ineffective, so any formalin-based treatment should be used only in cases where there is no ammonia present. Fish should be allowed to purge their digestive systems for at least 24 hours prior to treatment, with no feeding until routine water exchanges can take place. For the therapy to be successful, feeding should be severely restricted during formalin treatment. Formalin also reduces oxygen content in the bulk water, so it is highly recommended that you increase oxygenation by adding a vigorously bubbling airstone to the treatment vessel when using this chemical.

Copper sulfate has also shown some effectiveness at or near the maximum dosages recommended by the manufacturers for a minimum of seven days. Discontinue the use of ozone and UV, since they can electrochemically alter the medications and may cause the formation of free radicals that are extremely harmful to fish. Also, such devices can

Fungal infection appears as a brown, fuzzy area around the region of the vent on this Pink Skunk Clownfish (*Amphiprion perideraion*).

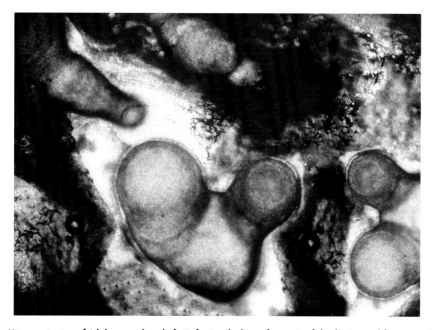

Upon completion of the procedure, place the fish in the untreated container with the airstone. Generally the fish will recover within three to five minutes once it is placed in the recovery container. If MS-222 is not available, clove oil may be substituted, and recent research seems to suggest that this natural anesthetic may be more effective and allow for quicker recovery. A dosage of 25 mg/L to 50 mg/L is recommended. The oil may be diluted slightly with ethanol (or vodka) before being mixed into the water. At very high doses, clove oil can be used to euthanize a fish or put it into a very deep sleep before freezing.

Microscopic view of *Ichthyosporidium hoferi* infecting the liver of a marine fish. This internal fungus can manifest itself externally as exopthalmia ("popeye"), reeling or sandpaper diseases.

Internal Fungus (Exopthalmia, Popeye, Reeling or Sandpaper Disease)

Ichthyophonus hoferi (formerly *Ichthyosporidium hoferi*) affects fish internally, invading the organs. It is sometimes referred to as reeling disease or sandpaper disease. The term "reeling" refers to an unsteady whirling or dancing motion, and "sandpaper" refers to the look of skin and visceral tissue, which resembles the rough, bumpy surface of coarse sandpaper.

artificially raise the toxicity of copper.

Monistat®, a medication developed to treat fungal infections in humans (active ingredient: miconazole nitrate), applied directly to the affected area daily until a cure has been effected, has also shown promise. If topical treatments are to be administered, exercise care while removing the fish from the aquarium to avoid stress and further injury.

Once a fish is removed, it would be very wise to sedate it using an anesthetic such as MS-222 (sold as Finquel® or tricaine methanesulfonate) or clove oil (eugenol). Typically, we set up two containers of tank water at a workstation, and have on hand a soft, wet towel saturated with a prepared water conditioner to place the fish on. MS-222 is added to one of the containers. (Depending on the size and species of the fish, 50–100 mg/L of MS-222 is used.) Add an airstone to the untreated container, which will be used for the recovery of the anesthetized fish. Start at the lower dosage and gradually increase it until a complete sedative effect is achieved, which is usually within one to three minutes. Once the fish has been anesthetized, a topical ointment or preparation can be swabbed on the affected area.

Unlike external fungus, *I. hoferi* affects marine fish more commonly than freshwater species, and all marine fish appear to be susceptible to this disease. It has been observed in and isolated from primarily liver, kidney, and spleen tissue. Fish are infected by eating infected feeder fish or fish flesh. We feel it prudent to refrain from feeding raw fish flesh and raw fish by-products.

SYMPTOMS Unfortunately, once the symptoms appear the fish is usually beyond saving. Fish infected with internal fungus will quickly become emaciated and swim abnormally, in a corkscrew pattern. In some cases they will eventually exhibit unilateral or bilateral exophthalmia, or "popeye" (see photos), and areas of darkened pigmentation will appear on the skin. In other cases, the surface of the skin may take on a granular appearance. As the fish weakens, secondary bacte-

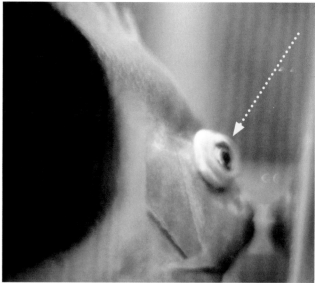

Unilateral exopthalmia or "popeye" in a Lionfish (*Pterois volitans*), below, affecting only one eye (arrow). The exopthalmos or bulging eye of a Rock Beauty Angelfish (*Holacanthus tricolor*), right, was caused by an internal fungal infection (*Ichthyosporidium hoferi*). Prognosis is questionable.

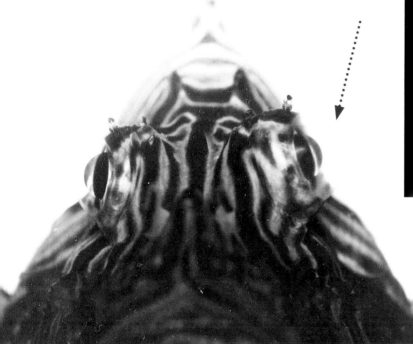

rial infections may occur, resulting in fin damage as well as reddened skin patches (hemorrhaging).

If a laboratory slide is prepared with affected tissue, it is possible to see white to gray cysts in a somewhat disorganized and shapeless mass, forming what is termed the quiescent or resting stage. As the disease advances, pseudopodia-like hyphae or plasmodial extensions (filament-type cells) emerge from the mass, signifying germination.

THERAPY AND CONTROL Prevention is the key to dealing with this disease, and proper nutrition, optimal water quality, and the avoidance of stress can usually avert losses. Quarantine will not always reveal a problem, as it takes a fair amount of time for this disease to manifest itself.

Phenoxyethanol, when added to a hospital aquarium using a 1 percent stock solution at a dose rate of 12.5 ml per 4 liters of water, can be used to treat internal fungus. Mix a standard solution using 1 ml phenoxyethanol to 99 ml of water, then dilute it at a rate of 10–20 ml per liter of tank water. Soaking food using a 1 percent stock solution can be an effective treatment against *Ichthyophonus*, although results are not always favorable.

If you suspect that a fish is infected with internal fungus, be sure to isolate it immediately in your quarantine or hospital tank. Carefully observe the remaining population for symptoms to make sure the disease has not spread. The symptoms may appear similar to those of mycobacteriosis, but in either case it may become necessary to euthanize affected specimens humanely in order to protect all the healthy individuals remaining in the system.

VIRAL DISEASES

Of all the diseases that afflict our aquarium livestock, viral diseases are the most difficult to identify. Many symptoms of viral infections are similar to those of bacterial infections, but viral infections will not respond to antibiotic treatments. Viral infections kill many fish, and unexplained deaths are probably often the result of viruses. But without the availability of an electron microscope and a well-trained virologist, hobbyists will never be able to see, much

Classic lympocystis or nodule disease disfiguring a juvenile Queen Angelfish (*Holacanthus ciliaris*). Caused by a virus, its appearance is often a mystery and it sometimes disappears over time.

less identify, most of these disease-causing pathogens.

However, one viral disease in particular—lymphocystis, or nodule disease—can be identified by casual observation and is encountered from time to time.

Nodule Disease (*Lymphocystis*)

This disease, caused by an iridovirus, appears to be very common in fish that have been exposed to rough handling and/or shipped under stressful conditions. It has even been reported that excessive exposure to copper can incite this disease. When the protective slime coating of fin and skin tissue is disturbed, the tissues become vulnerable to the virus.

Our experience indicates that all marine fish are suscepti-ble to this disease, though certain families, such as angelfish and butterflyfish, seem to be particularly vulnerable. Tangs and wrasses are somewhat resistant to the virus, although

they have been observed with this dis-ease on rare occasions. Regardless, we have seen lymphocystis in species from all areas—even from freshwaters—so it is likely a pandemic virus.

We have observed a shipment of Three-Striped Damselfish (*Chrysiptera tricincta*) that arrived from Sri Lanka looking good, but broke out with lymphocystis just one day later. This might indicate that exposure occurred during holding at the shipper's facility and that with the stress of transport, visible symptoms developed rapidly, putting the entire group into a dis-eased state literally overnight.

SYMPTOMS As the virus enters the tissue cells, it causes gross enlargement of the cells (from several hundred to many thousand times the normal cell volume and size). In its initial stages, lymphocystis can be mistaken for white spot disease (*Cryptocaryon irri-tans*), as both diseases show as a few small white spots in the early stages. This similarity in ap-pearance can easily lead to incorrect diagnosis.

Lymphocystis can usually be identified by a salt-like appearance of the fins and/or body. In advanced cases, clusters of giant cells resembling cauliflower or bunches of grapes can be clearly seen under 100x magnification. It ap-pears that the virus spreads from the fins to the areas where they join the body, since it is uncommon for the disease to appear first on the body areas. Sometimes, the growths will appear on the mouth or gill areas, which may interfere with feeding, oxygen uptake, and waste elimination. As you can imagine, this causes great difficulty for a fish.

THERAPY AND CONTROL Since infected fish can be considered carriers, isolate them in a hospital tank. Un-fortunately, as viruses have no known cure, not much can be done with medications, although some manufacturers claim to have a cure for lymphocystis.

In the past we have cut away portions of the affected fins with a clean, sharp pair of scissors, cutting just past the affected areas and taking some good tissue as well to avoid the release of virions, which would exacerbate the problem. We have had some favorable results using this method and fin regeneration usually takes place quite rapidly in healthy fish. If tissue removal is undertaken, be sure to disinfect the area with an antiseptic to prevent the introduction of bacterial infections. Also, we highly recommend first anesthetizing the affected fish with MS-222 or clove oil, as previously described in the section on treating external fungus infections (page 185). Always use rubber gloves for handling fish out of water, but this virus is not transmitted to humans.

You can also treat affected areas with a swab of tincture of merthiolate or mercurochrome, and/or a 10 percent stabilized solution of silver nitrate, twice a day for four days. Let the treated areas dry for 30 seconds. Anecdotally, we have also heard that good results can be obtained by treating affected areas with Visine®, which contains the active ingredient tetrahydrozoline. It has been reported that treatment with ganciclovir, a drug used in the treatment of herpes virus, has shown some effectiveness, particularly at slowing the spread of lymphocystis. Lately, we have been experimenting with a topical preparation known as Virac-

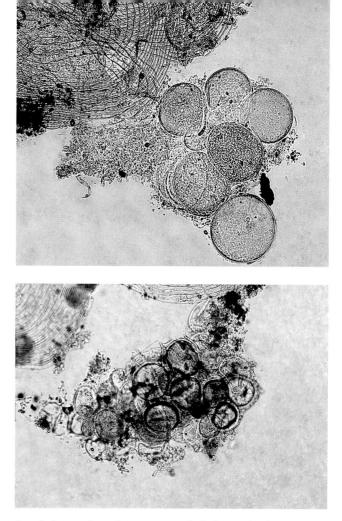

Magnified views of *Lymphocystivirus* sp. cells displaying what diagnosticians refer to as a "bunch of grapes" appearance. Note the curious lack of nucleus and other typical cell structure (nuclear membrane, vacuoles, mitochondria).

❗ Experimental Cures:

There is no known cure for the lymphocystis virus, but possible treatments include surgical removal of the growths followed by application of an antiseptic or topical application of mercurochrome, Visine® or ganciclovir sodium, a drug used against the herpes virus. The fish should be anaesthetized with MS-222 or clove oil when being handled.

tin®, a human cold-sore remedy available over the counter, with promising results.

And, as previously mentioned, we successfully used 35 percent hydrogen peroxide at a dose of 1 ml/10 gallons of water to cure lymphocystis in a Koran Angelfish.

More often than not, with lymphocystis no action

is taken. Sometimes, by allowing the virus to run its course, an apparent immunity to further outbreaks is developed and affected fish seem to fight the virus on their own. Due to the nature of their growth, viruses may block their own uptake of nutrients and die. Sometimes it will take from several weeks to a few months for disease symptoms to be completely eliminated. On the other hand, the disease can advance to the point where the affected fish has to be euthanized. This is particularly true for fish affected around the mouth and gills.

Fortunately, lymphocystis does not seem to be a fish killer, so the primary concern is one of aesthetics. ↩

Kole Tang (*Ctenochaetus strigosus*) with early signs of head and lateral line erosion (HLLE): Note faded coloration and pits forming around eye and along lateral line behind eye.

Non-Pathogenic Conditions
A roundup of other diseases & maladies of concern

Sometimes, fish succumb to conditions or diseases that are not traced to pathogens or disease-causing organisms such as bacteria or parasites. The cause of such deaths are sometimes difficult to pinpoint unless the diagnostician possesses a full understanding of water chemistry and the associated mechanics. Here are some of the conditions that can result in the loss of an individual fish or even the catastrophic loss of a whole tankful of fishes.

Gas Bubble Disease (Supersaturation)

Gas bubble disease is a condition that typically occurs when fish are exposed to water that has been supersaturated with gases. When a pump develops a leak on the suction side, air is taken in through the impeller under pressure. As the air comes in contact with the impeller, which is usually rotating very rapidly (in most cases, up to 3500 RPM or more), the air becomes "atomized" and is forced into solution at concentrations much higher than those found under normal atmospheric conditions. Because air is approximately 80 percent nitrogen, the most common condition to result from such an air leak is nitrogen supersaturation. Although oxygen may also be supersaturated, nitrogen presents the greater problem.

This condition can also be caused by a rapid rise in water temperature or rapid depressurization of water, particularly when it is taken from deep wells. Cold water, drawn up from a deep well, contains a greater concentration of gases and is usually under higher pressure than surface water, so supersaturation of gases in solution is more likely to occur.

Gas bubble disease in an Olive Tang (*Acanthurus olivaceus*), an often fatal or irreversible condition usually caused in the aquarium by supersaturation of air (oxygen and nitrogen) created by a faulty water pump.

SYMPTOMS As the gas is absorbed directly into its tissues, a fish will display gas bubbles in the eyes, gills, skin, and fin tissue. Death can result from gas bubbles forming in the gill lamellae, blocking the uptake of oxygen and preventing elimination of carbon dioxide. Embolisms can also occur when fine gas bubbles block the bloodstream. Also, since oxygen shares space in solution with other gases, oxygen depletion can result from excess nitrogen being forced into solution, resulting in death by asphyxiation (lack of oxygen). Entire collections of fish have been lost due to supersaturation in short periods of time, so the situation must be corrected immediately.

THERAPY AND CONTROL If the problem is a result of an air leak on the suction side of a pump, the pump must be shut down immediately and repaired or replaced before restarting. A cracked volute or impeller housing must be replaced. If the air leak is from a threaded joint, the joint must be disassembled and the threads retaped with Teflon®.

If using deep well water, it is recommended that such water be aerated or "sparged" to allow the gases to escape and the partial pressures to return to normal. Also, allow the water temperature to equalize to existing tank water conditions before use. Fish that have survived an experience with gas bubbles will usually return to normal in a short time once the cause has been corrected.

For those with large or extremely valuable collections of fish, a decompression chamber can successfully reverse gas bubble disease as well as embolism and decompression problems (bends) in fish, according to David Vaughan. Perhaps of some interest to engineer types, John Ballard has designed and built a device (known as "the Bomb" in South Africa) that can be pressurized with oxygen, usually around 1 bar (@ 14.5 psi). This device is somewhat akin to a barometric repressurization chamber, used to recompress divers who suffer from the bends. By placing affected fish in this vessel and applying the appropriate pressure, then slowly releasing the pressure over 24 hours, he has been able to reverse the effects of gas bubble disease in seahorses, clownfish, frogfish, and several species of tropical angelfish and butterflyfish.

Head and Lateral Line Erosion (HLLE)

Often more disfiguring than deadly, this condition is quite commonly encountered by marine aquarists, but only very rarely reported in the wild. Among the theories about its cause are nutritional deficiency, pathogens, stray voltage, use of copper therapeutic treatments, poor water quality,

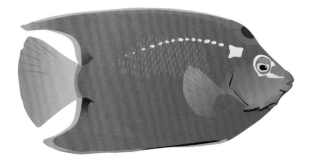

Head and lateral line erosion or HLLE is relatively common in aquarium fishes, but its possible causes (and cures) are still hotly debated.

Blue Tang (*Paracanthurus hepatus*) with HLLE, mostly limited to its head at this stage. Although disfiguring, the condition may not be fatal and may be reversed with improved water quality, a move to another aquarium, better feeding, and, possibly, removal of activated carbon dust from the filtration system.

and, most recently, the use of activated carbon for filtration. Whatever the cause, the symptoms are pitting, fading, and scarring, mostly on the face, around the eyes, and along the lateral line of afflicted fish. (The lateral line is a sense organ running from the head to the tail on each side of a fish. It is faintly visible, more in some species than in others, and its function is to sense movement in the water, helping the fish hunt prey, avoid being eaten, and avoid collisions with objects or other fishes. It is lined with exquisitely sensitive nerve organs called neuromasts.)

The process of degeneration along the lateral lines is far from completely understood. Nutritional deficiencies have been implicated, as many nutrients are involved in building and maintaining skin and muscle tissue. Free electromagnetic fields and stray electrical voltage have been suspected of causing irritation of the sensitive receptors found along the lateral line. The appearance of the condition after exposure to copper has led many to believe this may be one of its causes.

In many cases, fish have developed HLLE in systems employing activated carbon, which will indiscriminately remove vitamins and trace elements from the water. Then there are what appear to be disease-induced symptoms, caused by viruses and protozoans. Also, many feel HLLE always seems to begin with the appearance of small lesions or areas of skin tissue and pigment deterioration on or around the head, yet primarily along the lateral line.

As the condition advances, the lesions travel down the body, still on or very close to the lateral line. Noga (2000) refers to them as "crateriform" and indeed, they look like craters as they deepen. Over time, severe loss of overall body color may take place; we have seen fish so pale one could actually see the internal organs, and almost completely through the body. Advanced stages can also include loss of fin tissue and bony fin rays from dorsal and pectoral fins, operculum (gill cover plate) deformation and reduction to the point of exposing the gills, and even exophthalmia.

Recently, professional aquarist Jay F. Hemdal, curator of fishes at the Toledo (Ohio) Zoo, offered an interesting overview of HLLE. In his book, *Advanced Marine Aquarium Techniques*, Hemdal questions the notions that pathogens may be at work in this condition. Although pathogens, by their very nature, are considered contagious, there has never been any demonstration of HLLE being spread by introducing affected fish into aquariums with unaffected fish.

Hemdal cites case studies where fish affected with HLLE have been moved to new aquariums and fed the same diet, resulting in symptom reversal, while fish not moved to a new aquarium but fed a new and enhanced diet have not had any remission.

As for the use of copper-based medications and activated carbon—so common in marine aquariums, he surmises that the appearance of HLLE could be somewhat coincidental, with no clearly demonstrated cause and effect. He does, however, note "cases of acute HLLE that seemed to coincide with the presence of activated carbon dust" in public aquarium systems. The theory is that carbon's harmful role is not in scavenging nutrients out of the water, but rather that very fine carbon dust gets into the lateral line pores, causing lesions. HLLE is rare in reef aquariums, Hemdal notes, and these systems have both protein skimmers and

A pale Yellow Tang with whitening of the face (1) and clearly delineated lateral line (2), signs that HLLE may be setting in. Better water conditions and feeding may help.

filter-feeding invertebrate life that are known to extract carbon dust from the water column.

The controversy is far from over. David Vaughan offers that, "As with all of these things, there might well be more than one underlying cause of the same symptoms. In the case of hole in the head and lateral line erosion, *Hexamita* are known to be a cause, as is nutrition, and even (activated) carbon." Moe adds, "One simple, single specific cause has never been demonstrated for this condition; however, the strongest evidence implicates poor diet." He goes on to report that author George Blasiola observed an improvement for the condition when enhancing the diet of a Pacific Blue Tang (*Paracanthurus hepatus*) with vitamin C.

As Hemdal points out, not all fish are affected by this problem on an equal basis. We (the authors) have observed that some fish in captivity never seem to come down with the problem, which Hemdal regards as a possible immunity. Also, in many years and thousands of dives, we have never observed a fish in the wild that had been affected with HLLE. Dr. Edward Noga reports that HLLE has been seen in wild-caught as well as farm-raised Atlantic Cod, a coldwater species. Closer examination of the cod revealed that the nerve fibers, running "from the destroyed lateral line to the brain were inflamed," and that their "medullary ganglia were degenerated."

So, with the jury deadlocked, or at the very least uncertain, the general consensus still indicates that there are many possible causative agents of HLLE, perhaps even in combination. Noga, in an unpublished work, suggests that this malady may indeed be "a clinical sign of chronic stress in reef fish."

We are of the opinion that HLLE can be compared to beriberi or rickets in humans, and that a possible vitamin or mineral deficiency can combine with poor water quality and stress to allow infection to attack certain areas of the body. The treatment of HLLE may simply be to eliminate all of the many possible causative agents, provide good water quality, and feed an enhanced, varied, and balanced diet. As with beriberi and rickets, which can rather quickly be cured by providing the missing vitamins (vitamin B_1 and vitamin D, respectively), we have seen severe HLLE turned around by feeding the afflicted fish fresh macroalgae.

To heal the disfiguring wounds, a number of public aquaria have been experimenting with the use of a drug called Reganex® used to treat foot ulcers in human patients with diabetes. It apparently has the ability to encourage new skin growth in fishes, but it is expensive and the long-term results are not yet known.

Malnutrition

Nutritional deficiencies do occur in aquarium fishes, certainly more often than they are observed in the wild. The causes are far more wide ranging than simple lack of feeding on the part of the hobbyist. They include not having access to the proper foods, being out-competed at meal times by aggressive tankmates, having internal parasites that sap their energy, or coming down with diseases that diminish their appetites.

Some species and groups, such as the Sleeper Gobies, have a long, well-documented history of starving in aquariums. They are active foragers of live foods that they sift out of sandy substrates, and many home aquariums cannot provide sufficient grazing to keep them well fed.

Once a fish reaches a certain stage of starvation, there is little chance of recovery. The Sleeper Goby shown here is a sad example, with a disproportionately large head and a body that has been catabolized to provide energy to the nutrient-starved fish.(In tissue catabolism, an animal's body starts feeding on itself until the fish no longer has the energy to eat.) Even a concerted effort to "feed it back to health" will often fail, as damage to the fish's anatomy may be irreparable.

If a fish appears to be losing weight despite having proper access to food,

Starving Twostripe Sleeper Goby (*Valenciennea helsdingeni*) with concave belly and pinched appearance along its dorsal ridge. Causes of apparent malnutrition may go beyond a simple lack of the right foods.

a deworming treatment may be in order. An estimated 70 percent of wild fish are imported with worms, and some hobbyists now strongly advocate routinely deworming all incoming specimens. Praziquantel administered in food is the usual treatment of choice.

There are a few important lessons to be learned from aquaculturists and marine fish breeders. Larval marine fish will starve in droves if not offered foods of an appropriate size. The mandarinfishes (*Synchiropus* spp.) have notoriously tiny mouths and picky feeding habits, and they often waste away unless plenty of live grazing or meaty foods of the correct size are available daily.

Wholesale losses of farmed fish, young stock, also occur when fed rancid dry rations. Rancidity occurs when oils are oxidized—a phenomenon that happens from time to time in every cupboard. Unfortunately, rancid rations are sold every day in the aquarium world from dispensers of bulk feeds. Informed aquarists always buy vacuum-packed or sealed feeds and keep them tightly sealed once they have been opened. Dry foods are best stored in a cool, dark spot, or even the refrigerator or freezer.

See Chapters 4 and 5 for additional information on foods and feeding. The overarching rules are to feed small, frequent meals (at least twice daily) that are fully consumed in three to five minutes and to offer a variety of rations: flakes, freeze-dried, frozen, and, occasionally, live.

Be sure the carnivores, omnivores, and herbivores in the community are all getting enough of what they crave and need to be healthy.

Malnutrition is, in the end, easily avoided with the cornucopia of modern foods available to aquarists. The secrets are not to buy a terminally starved fish in the first place, to know what foods each species in your tank needs to thrive, and, finally, to be sure each fish in the community is getting its share at each mealtime.

Swim Bladder Disorders

Most—but not all—species of fish have a swim bladder, also known as a gas bladder or air bladder. Dr. Edward Noga, in his *Fish Disease: Diagnosis and Treatment*, identifies it as a shiny, gas-filled membrane that is white in color. It can be found high in the peritoneal cavity, just below the kidney. Its function is to regulate and maintain a fish's buoyancy, basically in a neutral or "weightless" state, much like weights worn by divers to regulate their buoyancy and steadiness in the water.

In many fish, the swim bladder also plays an important role in their hearing, which is accomplished through a series of sound-transmitting bones that are attached to it. The bones conduct sound from the swim bladder to the inner ear in the form of pressure. Obviously, the swim bladder is a complex organ and vital to the health of a fish.

Typically, swim bladders are composed of one or two chambers, but the physiology of swim bladders differs widely between various fishes. Hawkfishes, belonging to the family Cirrhitidae, are one group of fishes that lack the organ, allowing them to move rapidly through the water column in a vertical direction but forcing them to perch on a patch of

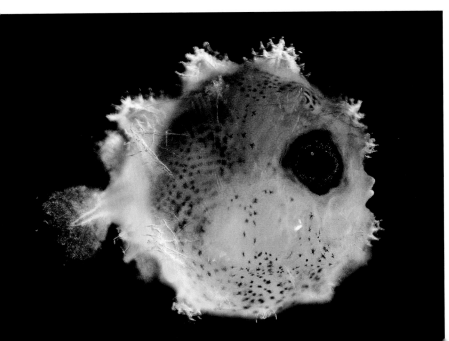

Larval Ocean Sunfish (*Mola mola*): Adults are the largest bony fish known, growing up to 5,070 lbs (2,300 kg), but, like most aquarium fishes, the young must have the right-sized foods of the right types to survive.

The Sargassumfish, an oddity found in subtropical waters worldwide, is the only member of the frogfish family to possess a swim bladder and have the ability to maintain its bouyancy in the water column.

transfer gas to fill the bladder, it can be seen struggling to stay afloat in the water column, only to sink to the bottom once it stops swimming.

Many disease organisms have been identified as affecting the swim bladder. Viruses, bacteria, sporozoans, trematodes, protozoa, and fungi have all been isolated in disorders. Swim bladder disorders also appear in aquarium fishes subjected to improper decompression during the collection process. If caught in deeper waters and not decompressed properly, a fish can suffer a form of "the bends," with gas buildup in the swim bladder. Since the swim bladder is internal, it's impossible to see or test the fish's bladder in order to identify the actual cause of problem while it is alive. Swim bladder disorders remain poorly understood and very difficult to treat.

Therefore, when purchasing a new fish, always note how it is swimming. This behavior should always be easy and effortless, bearing in mind the normal swimming pattern of individual species. The fish should not be listing (tipping oddly to one side or the other), and there should be no bloating in or around the abdomen.

If a problem can be attributed to improper decompression during collection, sometimes "recompressing" a fish by placing it in a closed container and submersing it in a deeper container of water may help. Whenever we find a fish in such a state, we place the fish in a perforated plastic jar (to allow for water exchange) with a tight-fitting lid, then submerse the jar into another aquarium, container, or tall, water-filled PVC pipe at least 24–36 inches (60–90 cm) deeper than the aquarium it came from for at least 48 hours.

Be sure to add some sand as ballast in the container if it floats, and also to aerate the treatment tank, using an airstone producing coarse bubbles. We have seen that lime-

substrate rather than hovering in the water column.

Fish regulate without effort the amount of gas (oxygen and nitrogen) retained by the swim bladder, thus controlling their buoyancy. Something known as the *rete mirabile* system allows gas exchange between the blood stream and the swim bladder, causing more or less buoyancy as required. However, when diseases or other maladies affect the swim bladder, fish often experience debilitating disorders.

When a fish cannot remove excess gas from its swim bladder, it will typically float to the top of the water. Most of the time, fish float in an upside-down position, with their bellies bloated and facing up. Sometimes, if the disorder is not as severe, the fish may swim erratically with its nose pointed down and tail up. In either case, there is a tremendous amount of stress imparted to the fish, and much of its energy is spent just trying to stay upright and in the water column. Conversely, if a fish is not able to

Better adapted to walking than swimming, a Combearing or Whitefingered Frogfish (*Antennarius nummifer*) is one of relatively few aquarium fishes that lacks a swim bladder. An organ vital to the survival of most fishes, the swim bladder can be damaged during collection or impacted by disease and parasites.

wood and other airstones that produce ultra-fine bubbles have the potential to cause gas bubble disease in sensitive fish and should be avoided. This "recompression" treatment is successful many times when the problem is actually improper decompression, although the sooner it is applied after collection, the better the results.

If disease affecting the swim bladder is suspected, remove the fish from the main show tank and treat it in a hospital tank whenever possible. Generally, antibiotics, such as kanamycin sulfate at 13–19 mg/L or oxolinic acid at 6.5–13 mg/L, may be used, and have shown some effectiveness in cases where the problem was suspected to be bacte-

Beyond that, there does not seem to be much anyone can do for swim bladder problems with their myriad possible causes. In the future, we can hope for more protocols to correct what is a life-threatening condition for any fish. Humane euthanasia may be called for if a specimen is suffering and no treatment appears effective.

Doctor-Caused Problems (Iatrogenic Diseases)

Sometimes, in trying to deal with health or maintenance issues, we ourselves cause problems in our aquariums. We may mistreat with improper medications or treat with too much medication. There are times when we overfeed our fish or overclean our aquariums. One might say we sometimes kill our fish with kindness. By far the most common causes of iatrogenic death are the misuse or overdose of medication and treatment with the wrong medication.

SYMPTOMS As the causes of iatrogenic problems vary greatly, so do the symptoms. If the problem is caused by overtreatment, look for rapid gill motion, a sloughing of slime, cloudy fins or eyes, fish gasping at the surface of the water, lying on the bottom or facing into a corner. If you suspect the cause is overtreatment with antibiotics or formalin, test for ammonia, since it is possible to inhibit or outright destroy biological filtration with many medications. When treating with any medication, always look for symptoms of ammonia toxicity, no matter what the particular medication or dosage. Overfeeding can also be harmful, as food will break down to ammonia. However, sometimes an elevated nitrite level will be the only indicator of overfeeding, short of seeing piles of uneaten food on the bottom or in the decorations of the aquarium. Overcleaning an aquarium may also result in ammonia toxicity if too many bacteria are removed. When this occurs you may notice a cloudiness to the water. If the cloud looks solid

rial. If protozoans are suspected, chloroquine phosphate at 10 mg/L in solution may be used, although it might be more effective to feed a medicated ration containing the chloroquine, as long as your fish is still eating.

For a more detailed recipe of chloroquine-medicated food, see the discussion on pages 138–139.

and homogenous, it is probably due to bacteria dying. If the cloud appears to be "rolling," resembling clouds in the sky, suspect a bacterial bloom.

Overdosing of medications can lead to organ failure, particularly the liver and kidneys. Overusing or misusing antibiotics can lead to drug-resistant bacteria, an alarming problem in commercial fish culture and human medicine.

THERAPY AND CONTROL As with gas bubble disease, there is generally no medication to counteract an iatrogenic problem. If overmedication is the problem, try a high-volume water exchange; adding activated carbon will enhance the removal of most medications.

A water exchange will also help in cases where ammonia toxicity is the culprit; the addition of bacterial cultures may be of benefit as well. Finally, be careful when handling medications, and always follow the manufacturer's recommendations and cautions.

Disinfecting A System

If all practical means fail to cure a disease problem in the aquarium, tearing down and sterilizing the entire system may be necessary. First, any animals that you wish to save should be removed. Because these animals could be carriers, it is best to house them in a separate new home and never return them to the aquarium you are about to sterilize and possibly reuse for new animals.

If the aquarium to be disinfected is quite dirty, or contains excess algae, detritus, or organic deposits, these should be removed before proceeding. (Any clinging algae or scum will interfere with the bleaching process.) Any nets, equipment, sand, or live rock that were in contact with the system should be included in the sterilization process. (Do not leave nets soaking in bleach, as they will disintegrate.) If there are any decorative plastic or hand-painted items in the system, it is best to remove them as they may fade. Because chlorine bleach usually damages carpets and clothing, the whole procedure is best done outdoors or in a work area far removed from family living quarters.

To proceed, use one half cup of common household bleach per 10 gallons of water. (Concentration is less important than a sufficiently long contact time with the bleach.) Aerate the system during the disinfecting process. You may want to replace all sand or gravel, but if not, be sure to soak it in this solution and stir it repeatedly to expose all surfaces to the bleach. Live rock can easily harbor diseases and parasites. The best approach with live rock may be to bleach it along with everything else and consider it "base rock" for rebuilding your reef structure. The whole system, tank and contents, should be allowed to "cook" in bleach for at least one day. If everything does not look clean and white, then add another dose of bleach and wait another day. When finished, drain the system and continue to flush with freshwater until no smell of bleach remains. Allow everything to dry for a couple of days and then refill the system with freshwater and allow it to stand for a day or two. Once again, drain the system and allow it to dry thoroughly before reusing.

Once the bleaching process is complete, and upon thorough rinsing of all objects that have come in contact with bleach, the final step should be dechlorination. Chlorine can be quickly and safely neutralized with sodium thiosulfate (STS or $Na_2S_2O_3$). Look for dechlorinating treatments at any aquarium store.

Our experience indicates there is no set formula for dechlorinating bleached objects, as there is for dechlori-

■
● **Hopeless Tank?**
After a whole-tank wipeout caused by infectious disease, the best course of action may be to tear the system down, sterilize everything with bleach, and start over.
....

nating a known concentration of chlorine in water. Typically, a stock solution is prepared by mixing one pound of crystals to one gallon of purified water. Do not mix it in hot water, as the compound is rendered useless. We use the stock solution according to this method: If you used one half cup of bleach to 10 gallons of water for five minutes for the chlorination, use 1 cup of stock solution to 10 gallons of water for 10 minutes. In other words, we normally double both the dose rate of dechlor solution to bleach

Healthy, beautiful marine fishes: the ultimate reward of being a watchful, informed aquarist, ready to catch problems before they spin out of control.

and the dechlorination time to neutralize chlorine when bleaching objects for sterilization or cleaning purposes. Upon completing the dechlorination process, thoroughly rinse with freshwater. Use your sense of smell for the final test: If you can still smell chlorine, repeat the rinse, dechlor, and rinse steps again. Due to the dangerous and volatile nature of chlorine, every effort should be made to keep from introducing it into an established aquarium, as

it will kill bacteria, fish, and invertebrates very quickly. A cheap OTO test kit, used by pool and spa owners, can be used to confirm if there are any traces of chlorine still present. Always handle chlorine and test chemicals with care.

Finally, here's wishing you never have to deal with a whole-tank wipeout. Once is enough, as many of us have learned the hard way, and we hope this book guides you and your fishes around such an event. ∿

Staff inspects and begins
the acclimation of a new
shipment of marine livestock
at a local fish store.

Professional Notes

*A final message to marine fish sellers—the gatekeepers for healthy
fish and the future of the aquarium hobby*

It was once thought the world's oceans were a source of endless bounty, and their profound resources would never be depleted. Sadly, we now have come to understand that this is not so. An estimated 90 percent of the biggest fish in the world's open seas have disappeared in the past 50 years due to overfishing, while in shallower waters coral reefs are under pressure from climate change, coastal development, deforestation, and destructive harvest methods such as dynamite and cyanide fishing. Critics of marine aquarium-keeping have accused us of being "raiders of the reef" and of trading in fishes and corals that have very poor survival records after collection.

Although brighter minds now believe that the marine aquarium trade is a force for protecting reef environments and providing livelihoods to local fisherfolk, there are still periodic calls to ban all harvesting of wild reef fishes, corals, invertebrates, and live rock.

A good livestock retailer is the final gatekeeper between the home aquarist and the sometimes unsavory world of collecting, shipping, and distributing marine animals. It is a calling full of challenge and responsibility. Retailers must deal with demanding live animals on the one hand, and, on the other, clients who very often need to be educated in how to care for them. It is hardly the easiest career, but we think that professional marine fish retailers will play a key role in preserving the future of our hobby.

Elsewhere in this book, we have strongly urged aquarists to seek out the healthiest fishes possible and to be wary of cheap and mail-order specimens bought sight

Filling bag with oxygen in preparation for shipping. Some larger retailers provide this service for clients who travel long distances to acquire marine livestock.

the consumer and thus help ensure that marine aquarium keeping is regarded as the "green," sustainable pursuit that it can be, and not as a drain on coral reef ecosystems.

Selling Good Stock

Because aquarium shop owners are usually the first to have access to imported livestock, they have a responsibility, not only to those animals, but also to those who will eventually purchase them.

In the first place, a forward-thinking shop owner will work to offer his or her customers hand-caught stock from suppliers who are actively trying to avoid dealing in cyanide-captured fishes. (See pages 76–77.) Some of the marine trade's leading importers and livestock suppliers (e.g., Sea Dwelling Creatures, Quality Marine, Seagrest Farms) have already earned certification from the Marine Aquarium Council for providing sustainably harvested, cyanide-free livestock, and more suppliers are sure to follow.

Captive-bred fishes have also come along way in both quality and variety in the past few years and ought to be promoted and sold. As just one example, anyone who has dealt in wild-caught clownfishes knows that they have a much lower rate of survival after arrival than the many species and color morphs of aquacultured clowns.

Appearances also count. Critics of the aquarium hobby like nothing better than to relate tales of unkempt retail shops with dead fish on display. A good shop, we believe, should present a clean and orderly appearance, with tanks clean and teeming with healthy-looking fish and invertebrates. An awareness of health issues will translate into immediately removing any specimen that appears sick to a hospital tank behind the scenes. Moribund fishes need to be removed from the display system as soon as spotted.

Newly arrived specimens must be scrutinized carefully. If a fish appears to have any condition or symptoms that

unseen. We believe that hobbyists whose fishes thrive are the most likely to become lifelong aquarists—your best customers and the best ambassadors for marine aquariums in general and for your business in particular.

In turn, we would like to see more local fish stores aspire to standards that will deliver better, healthier fishes to

require isolation and possible treatment, it should be moved to an individual hospital tank (typically, a 10–20-gallon bare glass tank with heater and air-driven sponge filter is sufficient, depending on the size of the fish) for observation, diagnosis, and appropriate treatment.

Any serious marine fish dealer should have some references on fish disease identification and a microscope on hand. Because many disease-producing organisms encountered are visible only under a microscope, and it is important to identify a pathogen in order to treat it effectively, we always rely heavily on this tool. Learning how to use the microscope effectively is extremely beneficial for dealers, and a working microscope for the store will be an invaluable investment.

Dealer Quarantine

We know that only a relative minority of North American marine fish retailers have quarantine systems in place for all incoming shipments.

The word quarantine is derived either from the Italian for "40 days" (*quaranta giorni*) or the French *quarantaine*. Webster defines quarantine as "restraint on the movements of persons or goods to prevent the spread of pests or disease." No matter how long a fish is kept in quarantine, such a procedure takes time, is labor-intensive, requires sales floor space, and ultimately adds to the cost of the fish. But the dealer who quarantines his or her fish is adding a great deal of value to the animals, and should be able to sell them for a higher price.

We would like to assure skeptical dealers that quarantine can be good for business. One of us was a dealer for many years and saw first-hand the benefits of quarantine and the savings in time that would have been spent diagnosing problems and treating for diseases. Routine quaran-

tine truly paid off. Fish loss was greatly reduced, and our customers were far more successful with the quarantined fish they purchased.

Our shop procedure was an "all in, all out" process whereby all of the fish that came in with a particular shipment were held for a minimum of two weeks in a quarantine system and given a prophylactic treatment of anti-parasitic and/or antibiotic medications. The "all-in" fish were kept separate and never mixed with other animals from previous

Holding tank in a Manila fish market provides a glimpse of the diversity of species being harvested from reefs in the Philippines, as well as a clear picture of the crowding that can induce stress in just-caught fishes.

shipments. The "all out" half of the process meant that all animals were removed from the quarantine system prior to the introduction of new animals from incoming shipments. During the quarantine period, water quality was carefully monitored on a daily basis and medications administered and their levels adjusted as required.

As for those medications, ionic copper sulfate (non-chelated) was typically used during the quarantine process. We did not use chelated coppers. Chelation makes the copper safer for the fish, but it also renders the copper safer for parasites. It is also difficult to test for chelated coppers, since most copper test kits are designed for ionic coppers. It has been our experience that most test kits designed for testing chelated coppers at the hobby level remain somewhat unreliable. (Exceptions are certain brands that sell both chelated copper and matching test kits.) Furthermore, the concentration of chelated copper must be kept much

"Routine quarantine truly paid off for our business. Fish loss was greatly reduced, and our customers were far more successful with the quarantined fish they purchased."

—*Lance Ichinotsubo*

higher than that of ionic copper, and it is also much harder to remove from solution. Therefore, our choice has always been to trust ionic copper sulfate in cases where copper treatments are needed.

We performed routine water exchanges as required, then brought medications back up to therapeutic levels. Fishes were kept at 1.010–1.013 SG in quarantine, and 1.017–1.018 in the sale tanks. When the treatment was nearly complete, the fish were acclimated to a higher specific gravity (SG). This was accomplished by adding small quantities of salt to the quarantine systems, with a rise of

Back room holding tanks where incoming marine fish are isolated, observed, and, if necessary, treated before being offered to the public.

no more than .002–003 SG per 24 hours; this process took approximately 48–72 hours. Once the SG was adjusted to within .002–003 of the sale tanks' SG, the fish would be moved to sale tanks and sold.

We believe that copper treatments should be maintained in fish-only sale tanks because the life-cycle of some of some common parasites can exceed the length of time fish are generally held in quarantine. A copper concen-tration of approximately 0.18–0.20 mg/L (or at the rec-ommended dosage of the drug manufacturer) should be maintained routinely on a prophylactic basis, with daily testing and adjustments. Copper-sensitive fishes should be isolated and kept in systems without copper, albeit under careful observation.

It is important to note that, while the fish are in quaran-tine, customers are often happy to purchase them and wait

"...while the fish are in quarantine, customers are often happy to purchase them and wait until the quarantine period is over to take them home. This creates good will and loyal customers who come in frequently to visit with their new pets."

until the quarantine period is over to take them home. If the fish should die while still in quarantine, the purchase price is credited towards the purchase of another fish. This creates good will and loyal customers who often come in frequently to visit with their new pets. Repeat visits often result in additional sales.

We always thoroughly cleaned the systems (at times, complete sterilization was required) upon the completion of a quarantine process and performed 100 percent water exchanges before introducing a new batch of fish.

We believe all dealers would stand to gain tremendously by investing in a quarantine set-up as the best way to ensure quality and prevent the spread of disease. Quarantine can be done quite simply or in a sophisticated manner. It's as easy as the use of a bank of small glass tanks outfitted with sponge filters, or as elaborate as the use of complete systems with built-in biological and mechanical filters, and perhaps ozone and/or ultraviolet sterilization.

! Attention Fish Buyers:

A cheap fish that dies or brings disease into your home aquarium is no bargain. Support your local aquarium dealers who know what they are doing and who care about the quality of the animals they sell.

The willingness to quarantine animals demonstrates a dedication to customer satisfaction of the highest degree. In the long run, the slightly higher price charged for properly quarantined animals will work in your favor. And those who do have quarantine facilities should display them to the public, as it's something to be proud of.

Professional Acclimation

Here is a method of handling incoming fishes that we have found results in maximum survival and healthier animals.

If a shipment of fishes has been bagged for an extended period of time (10–12 hours or more), we recommend this acclimation procedure. The following is a list of things to have on hand:

- Acclimation bins—plastic Rubbermaid® containers sized according to fish size and quantity work well
- Accurate thermometer
- Air pump with airstone for each bin
- Sodium bisulfate or equivalent acidifier
- Gram scale (to measure chemicals used)
- Rubber or latex gloves
- Pre-mixed water with a temperature somewhere between the bag temperature and the quarantine tank temperature (Assume the bag temperature will likely be much lower than that of the quarantine tank)
- pH meter or pH test kit

When the fish arrive, take a pH and a temperature reading from a couple of small, medium, and large bags, and then calculate an average. Of course, if there is only one bag, it does save some time. Adjust the new saltwater pH to within 0.1–0.2 of this average by adding sodium bisulfate. Be careful to wear gloves when handling the sodium bisulfate, since it is a strong acid buffer made for use in swimming pools. Generally, 2.5 grams of sodium bisulfate will lower the pH of 10 gallons of water by approximately one pH unit (e.g., from 8.3 to 7.3). Put the chemical first into a suitable container, add freshwater, and dissolve completely. Then mix the solution into the new saltwater, monitoring the pH constantly. Adjust the new saltwater temperature to a midpoint between the bag average and the tank temperature. Once the adjustments have been made, place the adjusted new saltwater into the acclimation bin or bins, aerating vigorously.

Remove the fish from the bags and place them into the acclimation bins. (Use a sterile net or carefully pour off the bag water into a bucket or sink, then let the fish slip into the bin with the last few drops.)

Some experts suggest that formalin or formalin/malachite green (as well as other medications, such as antibiotics) may be introduced at this point. David Vaughan, senior aquarist at uShaka Marine World aquarium in Durban, South Africa, cautions that most medications should not used on new arrivals that have been in shipment for extended periods of time (more than two to three hours). As he puts it, the fish are already in stressful conditions and any such treatments will only serve to add to the stress and prove detrimental. Additionally, he allows at least 24 hours of rest before beginning to treat fish that have been shipped from transcontinental or international points of origin.

Discard the bag water. Do not mix bag water with acclimation bin or tank water. The bag water might contain pathogens and/or large amounts of ammonia. Since the pH of the bag water will be much lower than normal, most, if not all, of the ammonia will be ionized ammonium, which is non-toxic to fish. If one were to drip tank water (at a higher pH) into the bag water, the pH would rise, causing the ammonium to shift over to un-ionized ammonia and greatly raising the toxicity of the ammonia. This could cause ammonia poisoning in an already stressed fish.

Once the fish are in the acclimation bins, a drip from the receiving tanks can be initiated. While the aeration will cause the pH to slowly rise, since the sodium bisulfate only temporarily lowers the pH, a drip will help to accelerate the pH adjustment. Once the pH has risen in the acclimation bins to within 0.2 of that in the quarantine tanks, it should be safe to transfer the fish into these tanks. Such a process may take one to two hours—or even longer, but this is time well spent.

If the fish have been in transit for 18 hours or more (international shipments or transshipments), follow the above procedure unless a medicated bath is planned. If no bath is desired, lower the pH in the quarantine holding tanks directly as described above, deleting the newly mixed saltwater and acclimation bin step. In this case, the tanks must not contain any fish prior to the introduction of the new arrivals, since the radical drop in pH would have definite deleterious effects on the pre-existing fish population due to pH and osmotic shock.

After making all of the necessary adjustments mentioned above, place the fish directly into the quarantine tanks. However, if you wish to give your newcomers a medicated bath, do not delete the acclimation bin and new saltwater step. Add the medication to the acclimation bins (only for those animals that have not been in transit for extended periods of time) as previously stated above and complete the bath before placing the newcomers into their

Fishes being moved short distances or by overnight express may not require extended acclimation; some experts advocate floating to equalize water temperatures and then "getting them into good water as soon as possible."

quarantine tanks. Again, it is recommended that fish be allowed at least 24 hours of recovery time before beginning any treatment regime or adding any medications. This is particularly true for those animals that have been on long trips or under especially stressful conditions, such as high levels of ammonia, high concentrations of carbon dioxide, low or high temperatures, low levels of oxygen, etc.

Once your new fish arrivals are released into quarantine

tanks, care for and maintain them as you would do with fish in any other aquarium, but with added vigilance and all the observation time you can spare. If, after a period of two to four weeks, these fish show no signs of disease, as detailed previously in this book, they are ready to be transferred to your show tanks. In theory, the conditions in both your show tanks and your untreated quarantine tanks should be the same, so simply netting and transferring your fish is possible. In practice, however, you will want to make sure this is the case and make adjustments accordingly, so as not to stress the fish with any sudden changes. If you do find evidence of disease during the quarantine period, you will need

Prophylactic Dips:

Fishes coming in after extended periods in bags usually need 24 hours of recovery time before receiving freshwater or medicated dips or starting drug treatments.

to treat your fishes, as described in detail in Chapters 8–10. When you begin to treat your fish, your quarantine tank can become the hospital or treatment tank.

In the case of acclimating corals and other invertebrates, the same Rubbermaid® bins described above will work well. Lugol's solution, along with some clean saltwater that has aged for a few days, will be required. (Many invertebrates are very sensitive to freshly mixed artificial seawater.) In this case, a pH adjustment is not initiated, as the intent is to prevent further stress and pH shock by getting the invertebrates into their final home as quickly as possible. Add the saltwater to the acclimation bins and put two to four drops per gallon of Lugol's solution into the water and mix thoroughly. The water temperature should match that in the final receiving tank, whether quarantine or show tank, and the bags floated in the bins (or in the receiving tanks) to help adjust the temperature.

Once water temperatures equalize, place the corals and invertebrates into the acclimation bins, discarding the bag water. Rinse the coral pieces well, looking for such things as turbellarians, parasitic organisms, or any other potentially damaging hitchhikers. Brushing off the corals using a very soft toothbrush (doggie toothbrushes work well for this purpose) may eliminate such undesirable organisms. Remove any decaying tissue now as well.

Caution is advised when transferring shrimp from one environment to another, as they are very sensitive to SG differences; be sure to adjust specific gravity slowly before any transfers are attempted. Whether these animals are put into a special holding facility or display aquarium depends much upon their individual condition. Healthy looking specimens can go directly in the sale aquarium, whereas questionable looking animals should be placed in a quarantine tank until they appear to have recovered.

Surprise Species

Unfortunately, shop owners are sometimes sent animals they did not order and may not feel comfortable selling. Although deplorable, it's simply part of a business that depends on the skills, education, and luck of local fisherfolk many thousands of miles away. Because some of these animals have little or no chance of surviving in aquariums, they should not be offered for sale unless the buyer is fully aware of the situation. Obvious examples are certain butterflyfishes and file fishes that are obligate corallivores. These virtually always starve in captivity, where they are not likely to have constant access to unlimited live coral polyps. Others don't ship well and need expert care to get them back into healthy condition. Some very desirable species, such as the Moorish Idol, have still-misunderstood care and feeding requirements.

Simple ethics calls for warning would-be purchasers that a particular fish is going to need special attention. Some hobbyists truly do have proverbial blue thumbs, and you will feel better about selling a challenging fish if it goes home with someone who has the skills and persistence needed to keep it alive.

Dealer Proficiency

There are a number of areas that we think are key to making local aquarium shops more competitive and helping

Dealer feeds butterflyfishes for a prospective buyer. Well-informed and helpful local retail owners and staff are often a home aquarist's best ally.

their customers succeed and keep their fishes alive. Many shops already do these things, but those that don't may want to consider them as insurance policies for preserving the hobby—and their own livelihoods.

EDUCATION Fortunately, a degree in ichthyology, marine biology, or microbiology is not required to make one a proficient and responsible marine livestock seller. It should, however, be every dealer's desire to continue his education and do as much as possible to help his staff become caring and knowledgeable about their charges.

"If your customers can rely on you to help with diagnoses and recommend appropriate drugs and treatments, you will be cementing your relationship with your most valuable clients—those who are most involved in their hobby."

Having at least one person on staff who has taken a course in fish disease is a tremendous asset. If your store has a microscope and someone who knows how to use it, you will save many more of your incoming stock, particularly when problems arise. Just as important, if your customers can rely on you to help with diagnoses and recommend appropriate drugs and treatments, you will be cementing your relationship with your most valuable clients—those who are most involved in their hobby.

REFERENCE SHELF There are many excellent books that offer valuable information for all who want to learn about animal husbandry, and we recommend that all dealers acquire and maintain a library as part of their arsenal of tools. Education has always been and will always be one of the best avenues to dealer success, particularly since our hobby includes so many ever-changing technical and scientific disciplines. Since no one person can know everything about biology, nutrition, chemistry, physics, engineering, microbiology, and other facets of the hobby, reference books must be relied upon. Dealers who keep current will be more apt to offer accurate and proper information, and

Two young Volitans Lionfishes (*Pterois volitans*) spar in a retail display tank: the allure of exotic species is a cornerstone of the marine aquarium hobby.

also more likely to provide their customers with the appropriate animals and supplies to make them successful.

PROFESSIONAL DEVELOPMENT Aquarium conferences, industry trade shows, and seminars offer great opportunities for professional development. These gatherings of aquarium experts and colleagues are an excellent means of acquiring and exchanging knowledge, experience, and information to increase dealer proficiency. Such topics as

❗ Sustainability Counts:

Buyers and sellers of marine livestock who support sustainable harvesting practices help ensure the future of the hobby. A number of leading importers and wholesalers of marine livestock are now MAC-certified to sell fishes and corals collected and handled with the utmost respect for both reef ecosystems and the lives of the animals being collected.

animal husbandry techniques, water chemistry, lighting, nutrition, disease recognition, and treatment (among many others) are covered by some of the world's top experts. Based on our experiences, your investment of time and money will be repaid in ways unimaginable—as soon as you return from a conference full of new ideas, and in the long term as well.

CARING It seems ironic that simple caring—something not often taught in business schools—can make such a big difference between success and failure in selling aquarium livestock; however, it is so true. Those who care to do their best almost always fare better than those who do not.

Most of us are motivated by our own interest in fish and healthy aquariums, but there are outside forces at work that this hobby can no longer ignore. More and more countries are beginning to take a harder look at the declining conditions of their local environments—and some are taking bolder and bolder steps to regulate, legislate, and in some cases, prohibit aquarium industry activities. Of course, this directly and indirectly affects dealers and their customers.

For example, live rock removal has been banned in Hawaii for over 20 years, with Florida following suit. It is now illegal to remove corals from many areas in the Indo-Pacific region, including some areas in the Philippines. And many countries in Europe have banned the importation of certain families and species of fish and invertebrates (including marine angelfishes, for example) as a stop-gap measure to protect those animals that they perceive do not survive well in captive environments.

Dealers who act responsibly in an effort to preserve the industry we all hold dear become a part of the solution instead of perpetuating the problems that attract critics and regulators. This is a hobby that brings unique rewards to those who pursue it, but it also is a powerful tool in exposing others to the beauty and complexity of coral reef animals and environments.

Finally, we have tried to make the information we have provided as complete and accurate as possible while presenting it in a manner that both shop owners and aquarists can embrace. We hope this book will make it clear that marine fishkeeping is a wonderful challenge, and—with all the new technology, foods, and better livestock options available to us—much easier than at any time in history.

If you have comments, questions or additions you'd like to see addressed in future editions of this book, contact either of the authors at:

www.microcosm-books.com

Glossary

activated carbon: a filter medium used in both internal and external filters to remove toxic substances from water.

adsorption: the process whereby atoms and molecules are attracted to and concentrate upon the surfaces of solids or liquids.

aerobic: requiring oxygen to survive.

Aeromonas: a gram-negative bacteria, ubiquitous in fresh and brackish water, that causes infections in fish.

alkalinity: a measure of the ability of a solution to neutralize acids to the equivalence point of carbonate or bicarbonate.

ammonia (NH_3): a pungent, colorless, gaseous alkaline compound of nitrogen and hydrogen; the primary end product of protein metabolism and the breakdown of living or formerly living matter.

amphipod: a small crustacean such as *Gammarus*, typically introduced into aquariums via live rock; may be used as aquarium fish food.

Amyloodinium ocellatum: a commonly occurring dinoflagellate that affects marine ornamental fishes and causes the disease called **amyloodiniosis**, **coral fish disease**, or **marine velvet**.

anaerobic: able to survive without oxygen; anaerobic bacteria, some of which consume nitrate, live in oxygen-poor environments, such as in the deeper areas of sand beds or in porous live rock.

anthelminthic: one of a variety of drugs used in the control of flatworms, flukes, and tapeworms.

antibiotic: a substance, either one derived from a living organism or a synthetic, used to inhibit or kill another microorganism.

antiseptic: a chemical used to inhibit or kill microorganisms, usually applied topically but in some cases internally.

aquarist: one who maintains an aquarium.

aragonite: a naturally occurring porous mineral high in calcium carbonate that tends to dissolve slowly at a pH slightly below 8.2.

ascites: the abnormal accumulation of serous fluid in the abdomen.

autotrophic: capable of synthesizing its own food from inorganic substances, using light or chemical energy.

Bathynomus giganteus: a giant, deep-water isopod that attacks fish.

Benedenia: a common worm parasite found in fish.

bicarbonate ion (HCO_3-): the main buffer in water under a pH of 9; over pH 9, carbonate becomes predominant.

bilateral: involving or occurring on both sides, such as the eyes or pectoral fins of a fish.

bio-filter: a filter that uses nitrifying bacteria to detoxify nitrogen wastes in aquarium water.

bioload: the demand placed upon the life-support system in an aquarium by the living organisms present in the tank.

black ich: a disease caused by tang turbellarians (worm parasites thought to be of the genus *Paravortex*), also known as **black spot disease**.

black spot disease: see **black ich**.

bloodworms: the red larvae of a non-biting midge; used as fish food.

brackish: slightly less salty than normal seawater.

brine shrimp: a species of aquatic **crustaceans** of the genus *Artemia*.

broad-spectrum: able to be used to treat a variety of illnesses.

Brooklynella: an infestation of the ciliated parasitic protozoan *Brooklynella hostilis*. Also called **Clownfish Disease**.

buffer: a substance capable in solution of neutralizing both acids and bases, thereby maintaining the original acidity or basicity of the solution.

calcium (Ca++): one of the major cations in water and a principal component of hardness.

calcium carbonate (CaCO₃): a commonly found mineral (a.k.a. limestone) contributing to water hardness; the major component of seashells and bones.

carbohydrate: any of a group of organic compounds that includes sugars, starches, celluloses, and gums and serves as a major energy source in the diet of animals; they are produced by photosynthetic plants and contain only carbon, hydrogen, and oxygen.

carbon dioxide (CO₂): a product of carbon oxidation in aerobic metabolism and combustion. Dissolves in water to form carbonic acid and bicarbonate ion.

carbonate ion (CO₃): an anion that will accept a proton (H+) to become HCO₃-.

carnivore: a flesh-eating animal.

caudal: of, relating to, or being the tail.

caudal peduncle: portion of a fish between the body and the tail.

Caulerpa: leafy marine macroalgae used to feed herbivorous fishes; regarded as a noxious, invasive weed in some areas.

cell: the fundamental single unit of structure and function in organisms.

chelated: bonded, typically to a heavy metal, for stability.

chloramine: any of several compounds containing nitrogen and chlorine, especially an unstable colorless liquid, NH₂Cl, used to make hydrazine. Sometimes used as a disinfectant or water purifier.

chloroquine phosphate: a medication used to treat parasites in fish.

cilia: hair-like structures used for food collection or locomotion.

ciliate: a **protozoan** that has **cilia**.

clownfish disease: see **Brooklynella**.

copepods: very small crustaceans of the class *Copepoda*; some are fish food sources, some are disease-causing ectoparasites of fish.

copper sulfate: a crystalline copper salt used to treat a variety of bacterial infections, fungi, and parasitic infestations in fish.

coral fish disease: see **amyloodiniosis**.

crustacean: an aquatic arthropod of the class *Crustacea*, including lobsters, crabs, shrimps, and barnacles; characteristics are a segmented body, a chitinous exoskeleton, and paired, jointed limbs; also parasitic forms, including isopods and copepods.

Cryptocaryon irritans: a common ciliated parasite that infests marine fishes, causing a disease called **cryptocaryonosis, marine ich, white spot disease,** or **saltwater ich**.

cryptocaryonosis: a disease caused by the parasite **Cryptocaryon irritans**.

cyanide: any of various salts or esters of hydrogen cyanide containing a CN group, especially the extremely poisonous compounds potassium cyanide and sodium cyanide.

cyst: a protective capsule a parasite forms around itself in the **trophont** stage.

die-off: dying of numerous aquarium inhabitants.

digenea: a subclass of **trematode** worms in which sexual reproduction as an internal parasite of a vertebrate alternates with asexual reproduction in a **mollusk**.

dinoflagellate: a one-celled aquatic organism with two dissimilar **flagella** and a complex cell covering.

dinospore: the infectious, **motile** stage in the life cycle of certain **protozoans**, e.g., *Amyloodinium*.

dormant: having biological activity suspended.

dorsal: relating to or situated on or near the back or upper surface of an animal.

Droncit®: a trade name for **praziquantel**, an **anthelmintic** effective against **flatworms**.

Dylox™: a trade name for an organophosphate used in the treatment of certain metazoan parasites such as **trematodes**.

ectoparasite: an external parasite.

elasmobranch: a fish of the class *Chondrichthyes*, characterized by a cartilaginous skeleton and placoid scales and including the sharks, rays, and skates.

embolism: the sudden obstruction of a blood vessel by an embolus, an abnormal particle (such as an air or gas bubble) circulating in the blood.

endoparasite: an internal parasite.

enzyme: any of numerous complex proteins that are produced by living cells and catalyze specific biochemical reactions at body temperatures.

epithelium: a membranous cellular tissue that covers a free surface or

lines a tube or cavity of an animal body and serves especially to enclose and protect the other parts of the body, to produce secretions and excretions, and to function in assimilation.

erythema: abnormal redness of the skin due to blood vessel congestion.

euthanize: to kill painlessly to relieve suffering or to contain the spread of disease.

exophthalmia: abnormal protrusion of the eyeball (**popeye**).

feeder fish: certain types of inexpensive fish commonly fed as live prey to captive animals.

filter media: the substance within a filter that removes pollutants from water, including sponges, pads, sheets, etc.

fin rot, tail rot: the decomposition of fin or tail tissue due to bacterial overgrowth; often caused by damage to protective slime during collection and handling of fish; causative bacteria are *Pseudomonas* sp., *Aeromonas* sp., *Edwardsiella* sp., *Cytophaga* sp., or *Vibrio* sp.

fish louse: *Livoneca* sp., an **isopod** that infects fish.

flagella: whip-like extensions of certain cells that facilitate movement, such as in the case of **dinoflagellates** like *Amyloodinium*.

flagellate: a **protozoan** that has whip-like **flagella** for propulsion.

Flagyl®: see **metronidazole**.

flashing: rubbing against objects in the aquarium due to irritation of the skin.

flatworms: simple invertebrates (phylum *Platyhelminthes*) including the parasitic **flukes**, tapeworms, **monogenea**, and *Turbellaria*.

fluke: a **trematode**, a type of parasitic **flatworm**.

formalin: a saturated solution of formaldehyde (usually 37%), water, and typically another agent, most commonly methanol.

gas bubble disease: a condition that occurs when fish are exposed to water that is **supersaturated** with gas.

gill: the organ that fish and some other water animals use to breathe, consisting of a membrane containing many blood vessels through which oxygen passes.

granuloma: a mass or nodule of chronically inflamed tissue with granulations, usually associated with an infective process.

grass shrimp: a species of small, transparent shrimp often sold for freshwater aquariums and as food for other fish.

head and lateral line erosion (HLLE): a disfiguring condition of unknown etiology that causes ulcerations of the **lateral line** and head pores of fishes.

hemoglobin: the oxygen-carrying pigment found in red blood cells.

hemorrhage: bleeding, usually due to secondary bacterial infection.

herbivore: an organism that consumes vegetable matter as its primary food source.

heterotroph: an organism that is capable of deriving energy for life processes only from the decomposition of organic compounds, and incapable of using inorganic compounds as sole sources of energy or for organic synthesis.

HLLE: see **Head and lateral line erosion**.

Hole-in-the-Head Disease: a term for hexamitosis or spironucleosis, diseases caused by the parasites *hexamita* and *spironucleus*, characterized by pitting of the flesh around the head.

hydrogen peroxide (H₂O₂): a unstable chemical compound consisting of hydrogen and oxygen; added to water, it disassociates to form water and oxygen.

hydrometer: a calibrated instrument used for measuring the **specific gravity** of a liquid.

hyperplasia: an abnormal or unusual increase in the elements composing a part (as cells composing a tissue).

hypobromous acid (HOBr): An acid, the aqueous solution of which possesses oxidizing and bleaching properties; formed when natural sea water (or artificial salt mixes), typically containing high concentrations of bromine, is exposed to ozone; acts as an oxidizer, much like chlorine, and is detrimental to fish and **invertebrates**.

hyposaline: having a **specific gravity** lower than that of normal seawater.

hypoxia: a deficiency in the amount of oxygen reaching body tissues.

hyphae: thread-like filaments that represent the vegetative, or assimilative, stage of a filamentous fungus.

hypoxemia: a condition caused by an inadequate supply of oxygen.

iatrogenic: physician-induced; an example of an iatrogenic disease might be one caused by overdosing with medications in a trial-and-error attempt to treat undiagnosed disease.

Ichthyophonus hoferi: a fungus that attacks the internal organs of fish and causes **reeling disease (sandpaper disease)**.

immunostimulant: an agent that stimulates the immune response.

intestinal lumen: the space within the intestine.

invertebrate: an animal that has no backbone, such as a worm, insect, or **mollusk**.

isopod: a parasite that has multiple similar appendages, or feet.

kanamycin: a wide-spectrum **antibiotic** medication used against a variety of bacterial infections.

krill: shrimp-like marine **invertebrates**, a large part of the diet of baleen whales, seals, and some seabirds.

lamella (pl. lamellae): a thin plate or scale; **gill** tissue of **teleost fish**.

larva: the early form of an animal that at birth or hatching is fundamentally unlike its parent and must metamorphose before assuming adult characteristics.

lateral: of or relating to the side.

lateral line: a sensory canal that runs along the side of a fish.

lesion: a wound or injury; an infected or diseased patch of skin.

lipid: any fat-like compound.

live rock: highly porous rock consisting of dead and washed-away coral, overgrown with a multitude of organisms, used to establish biological filtration (**nitrification**).

Livoneca sp: the **fish louse**, an **isopod** that infects fish.

lymphocystis: the **virus** *Lymphocystis*; also the disease caused by this virus—**nodule or cauliflower disease**.

macroalgae: large-celled **algae** that can be seen by the human eye.

malachite green: a toxic chemical used in dilute form to treat parasites, fungi, and bacterial infections.

malady: a psychological or physical disorder or disease; illness.

marine ich: see *Cryptocaryon irritans*.

marine velvet: see *Amyloodinium ocellatum*.

melanin: the yellow, brown, or black pigment that gives skin, eyes, and fins their colors, produced by cells known as melanocytes.

metazoan: any of a group (Metazoa) that comprises all animals having the body composed of cells differentiated into tissues and organs and usually a digestive cavity lined with specialized cells.

metronidazole: an antibiotic drug used against certain bacteria and parasites.

microalgae: unicellular, photosynthetic aquatic plants.

Microsporidia: spore forming, small, obligate, intracellular living eukaryotes with one polar capsule, infecting a broad range of vertebrates and invertebrates.

mollusk: any of numerous chiefly marine invertebrates of the phylum Mollusca, including the edible shellfish and the snails, typically having a soft, unsegmented body, a mantle, and a protective calcareous shell.

monogenean: Any of various **trematodes** of the order Monogenea that typically pass the entire life cycle as **ectoparasites** on a single fish.

motile: exhibiting or capable of movement.

MS-222: see **tricaine methanesulfonate**.

mucus: the viscous, slippery substance that consists chiefly of mucin, water, cells, and inorganic salts and is secreted as a protective lubricant coating by cells and glands of the mucous membranes.

mulm: undecomposed fish waste and other solid matter that collects in the aquarium as a brownish, fluffy material.

mycobacteriosis: an internal bacterial infection in fish, also known as **wasting away disease** or piscine tuberculosis; caused by *Mycobacterium* sp. It is transmittable to humans.

Mysis: a small, freshwater shrimp used as a nutritious fish food.

necrosis: the death of cells or tissues through injury or disease.

neomycin: a **broad-spectrum antibiotic**.

New Tank Syndrome (Toxic Tank Syndrome): the period in which **ammonia** and then **nitrite** levels rise to dangerous quantities in an aquarium before being converted into relatively harmless **nitrate**.

nifurpirinol: an **antibiotic** that works well on non-resistant bacteria.

nitrate: the final and least harmful phase of the **nitrification** cycle.

nitrification: the biological **oxidation** of **ammonia** with oxygen into **nitrite** and then into **nitrates** by bacterial colonies.

nitrifying bacteria: beneficial bacteria that break down the **ammonia** that results from fish feeding and waste elimination.

nitrite: the second stage in the **nitrification** process; formed by the breakdown of **ammonia** by bacteria.

nodule disease: see **lymphocystis**.

nonmotile: not capable of moving.

nori: a form of dried seaweed that is fed to herbivorous aquarium animals.

omnivore: an organism that eats both animal and vegetable substances.

opercula: the bony flaps covering the **gills** of a fish (singular: operculum).

organelle: a differentiated structure within a cell, such as a mitochondrion, vacuole, or chloroplast, that performs a specific function.

osmoregulation: maintenance of an optimal, constant osmotic pressure in the body of a living organism.

osmosis: diffusion of fluid through a semipermeable membrane from a solution with a low solute concentration to a solution with a higher solute concentration until there is an equal concentration of fluid on both sides of the membrane.

osmotic gradient: Difference in osmotic pressure between two solutions.

osmotic shock: a rapid change in the osmotic pressure (as by transfer to a medium of different concentration) affecting a living system.

oxidation: the chemical process where oxygen is added to an element or compound, changing the general nature of the element or compound, e.g. corrosion.

Oxidation Reduction Potential (ORP): a measure of the effectiveness of the **redox** (oxidation-reduction) process with an oxidation reduction potential meter, using the minute electrical charge it generates in millivolts (mV).

ozone: an unstable gas (O_3) used for killing disease-causing organisims and/or improving water quality.

palmella: see **tomont**.

parasite: an organism that lives on or in the body of a host animal or plant and from which it obtains nourishment, often detrimental to the host.

parts per million (ppm): a measurement in chemistry to quantify the number of elements or constituents per a known volume.

pathogen: an agent that causes disease.

pathogenic: disease-producing.

pectoral fin: a fin found behind the operculum on each side of a fish's body.

pH: A measure of the acidity or alkalinity of a solution, numerically equal to 7 for neutral solutions, increasing with increasing alkalinity and decreasing with increasing acidity.

photoperiod: the duration of an organism's daily exposure to light.

photosynthesis: the process in green plants and certain other organisms by which carbohydrates are synthesized from carbon dioxide and water using light as an energy source.

phytoplankton: the minute, free-floating plant organisms, e.g. one-celled **algae**, which make up **plankton**.

piscivore: a fish or other animal that lives by eating fish.

placoid scales: scales of dermal origin with enamel-tipped spines, characteristic of **elasmobranchs** such as sharks, skates, and rays.

plankton: the collection of small or microscopic organisms, including **algae** and **protozoans**, that float or drift in great numbers in fresh or salt water, especially at or near the surface, and serve as food for fish and other larger organisms.

poikilotherm: a cold-blooded organism, such as a fish or reptile, having a body temperature that varies with the temperature of its surroundings; an **ectotherm**.

Poly-Filter®: a specially formulated filter pad with a synthetic matrix, used to purify aquarium water, remove medications after treatment, etc.

popeye: colloquial name for **exopthalmia**, abnormal protrusion of the eyeball.

praziquantel: an **anthelmintic** effective against **flatworms**.

predator: an organism that lives by preying on other organisms.

prokaryotic cell: an organism of the kingdom Monera (or Prokaryotae), comprising the bacteria and cyanobacteria, characterized by the absence of a distinct, membrane-bound nucleus or membrane-bound organelles, and by DNA that is not organized into chromosomes.

prophylactic: acting to defend against or prevent something, especially disease; protective.

protein skimmer: a device that removes organic pollutants from tank water.

protozoan: any of a large group of single-celled, usually microscopic, eukaryotic organisms, such as amoebas, **ciliates**, **flagellates**, and **sporozoans**.

protozoacide: an agent destructive to **protozoa**.

pseudopodium: a temporary cytoplasmic extrusion by means of which an amoeba or other ameboid organism or cell moves about or engulfs food.

putrefaction: the decomposition of animal proteins, especially by anaerobic microorganisms.

quarantine: the isolation of animals (or people) in order to prevent the spread of contagious disease.

reagent: a substance employed to produce a chemical reaction so as to detect, measure, produce, etc., other substances.

redox: a term created by shortening and combining the terms oxidation and reduction; the chemical reaction whereby electrons are removed (**oxidation**) from atoms of the substance being oxidized and transferred to atoms being reduced (**reduction**).

red tide: discoloration of water caused by toxins released by vast numbers of **dinoflagellates**; the phenomenon causes **die-offs** along shorelines.

reduction: the lowering of toxicity of compounds through **oxidation**, such as the reaction which occurs when **ammonia** is oxidized to **nitrate**.

reef: a ridge of **coral** or rock in a body of water, with the top just below or just above the surface.

reeling disease: see *Ichthyophonus hoferi*.

refractometer: an instrument used to measure the index of refraction of a substance.

refugium: A tank that is separated from the main tank but shares its water supply; used as a refuge for plants and animals that suffer from predation in the main tank.

salinity: the relative proportion of salt in a solution; the degree of saltiness of a given substance, such as the ocean.

sandpaper disease: see *Ichthyophonus hoferi*.

saturation: the point at which water contains as much oxygen as it can hold (about 6.0 ppm in the ocean, especially around coral reefs).

sclerites (hamuli): hooks that some parasitic **flukes** possess, used to attach to host fish.

seahorse disease: a disease caused by the parasite *Glugea heraldi*.

specific gravity (SG): the ratio of the density of a substance to the density of some substance (as pure water) taken as a standard when both densities are obtained by weighing in air.

Spirulina: a blue-green algae that is high in nutrients and other beneficial compounds; used in the formulation of many foods for fish.

sporangium: a spore-producing structure.

spore: a primitive, usually unicellular dormant or reproductive body produced by plants, fungi, and some microorganisms and capable of development into a new individual either directly or after fusion with another spore.

sporozoan: any of numerous parasitic **protozoans** of the class Sporozoa, most of which reproduce sexually and asexually in alternate generations by means of spores.

sulfonamide: any of a group of organic sulfur compounds containing the radical O_2NH_2 and including the sulfa drugs.

tang turbellarian: a worm parasite, thought to be of the genus *Paravortex*, which causes **black ich** or **black spot disease**.

teleost fish: fish with bony skeletons, including most common fish.

tomont: the second, or reproductive, stage in the life cycle of certain **protozoans**, e.g., *Amyloodinium ocellatum* (also known as the **palmella** stage).

Toxic Tank Syndrome: see **New Tank Syndrome**.

toxicity: a condition of being or containing poisonous material, especially that capable of causing serious debilitation or death.

trace elements: minor constituent elements found naturally in seawater that are essential for certain biochemical functions.

trematodes (flukes): parasitic **flatworms**.

tricaine methanesulfonate (MS-222): an anesthetic for aquatic animal use.

trichlorfon: an organophosphate compound used to treat parasites.

trophont: the first stage in the life cycle of certain **protozoans**, e.g., *Amyloodinium ocellatum*, when the parasite is attached to the host absorbing nutrients.

tubercle: small nodule or growth on a fish's body.

ulcer: a lesion of the skin or a mucous membrane, accompanied by formation of pus and **necrosis** of surrounding tissue.

unilateral: having or affecting only one side.

Uronema **(uronemosis):** a disease caused by the parasite *Uronema marinum*.

ventral: situated on or toward the lower, abdominal plane of the body.

vibriosis: a disease occurring mainly in marine fish caused by one of a number of gram-negative bacteria in the family *Vibrionaceae*.

virion: a complete viral particle, consisting of RNA or DNA surrounded by a protein shell and constituting the infective form of a **virus**.

virus: a biological disease-causing agent, smaller than a cell, that can only reproduce in living cells and is unresponsive to **antibiotics**.

wasting away disease: see **mycobacteriosis**.

whirling disease: a disease caused by **Myxosporidia**; affected fish swim in circles as if chasing their own tails.

white skin patch disease: a disease characterized by sloughing of the **slime** coat, usually caused by *Flexibacter* sp. or *Cytophaga* sp. bacteria.

white spot disease: see **cryptocaryonosis**.

wide-spectrum: see **broad-spectrum**.

xenoma: an extremely enlarged host cell filled with **spores** and developmental stages of *Microsporidia*.

Selected Bibliography

Bassleer, G. 1996. *Diseases in Marine Aquarium Fish, Causes – Symptoms – Treatment.* Lannoo Drukkerij, Belgium: Bassleer Biofish, with English translation by Global Communications.

Bassleer, G. 2003. *The New Illustrated Guide to Fish Diseases in Ornamental Tropical and Pond Fish.* Westmeerbeek, Belgium: Bassleer Biofish.

Blasiola, G. 1991. *The New Saltwater Aquarium Handbook.* Hauppauge, NY: Barron's Educational Services, Inc.

Clifton, R. 1993. *Marine Fish – the Recognition and Treatment of Diseases.* McKinney, TX: Peregrine Publishing.

Gratzek, Dr. J. B., Wolke, Dr. R.E., Shotts, Dr. E.B. Jr., Dawe, Dr. D., & Blasiola, G. 1992. *Fish Diseases and Water Chemistry.* Morris Plains, NJ: Tetra Press.

Herwig, Nelson. 1979. *Handbook of Drugs and Chemicals Used in the Treatment of Fish Diseases.* Springfield, IL: Charles C. Thomas, Publishers.

Herwig, Nelson. 1979. *Vibrio, FAMA,* Vol. 2, No. 3 (Mar.): pages 38-39, 83-86.

Kingsford, Dr. E. 1975. *Treatment of Exotic Marine Fish Diseases.* New York, NY: ARCO Publishing Company, Inc.

Moe, Martin A. Jr. 1992. *The Marine Aquarium Handbook – Beginner to Breeder.* Plantation, FL: Green Turtle Publications.

Noga, E.J. 2000. *Fish Disease, Diagnosis and Treatment.* Ames, IA, Iowa State Press.

Nybakken, J.W. 1982. *Marine Biology – an Ecological Approach.* New York, NY: Harper & Row, Publishers, Inc.

Post, Dr. G. 1987. *Textbook of Fish Health: Revised and Expanded Edition.* Neptune City, NJ: TFH Publications.

Schubert, Dr. G. 1987. *Fish Diseases – a Complete Introduction.* Neptune City, NJ: TFH Publications.

Spotte, Stephen. 1992. *Captive Seawater Fishes, Science and Technology.* New York, NY: John Wiley & Sons Inc.

Spotte, Stephen. 1979. *Seawater Aquariums: The Captive Environment.* New York, NY: John Wiley & Sons Inc.

Untergasser, D. 1989. *Handbook of Fish Diseases.* Neptune City, NJ: TFH Publications.

Sources & Contacts

American Marine Inc.
54 Danbury Rd., Suite 172
Ridgefield, CT 06877
Phone: 800-925-4689
www.americanmarineusa.com
Digital water testing equipment and food enrichment products

Aquatic Eco-Systems, Inc.
2395 Apopka Blvd.
Apopka, FL 32703
877-347-4788
www.aquaticeco.com
Aquarium pharmaceuticals, supplies, microscopes

Argent Laboratories
8702 152nd Ave. NE
Redmond, WA 98052
425-885-3777
www.argent-labs.com
Fish anesthetics, therapeutical chemicals, and supplies

Florida Aqua Farms, Inc.
33418 Old Saint Joe Rd.
Dade City, FL 33525
352-567-0226
www.florida-aqua-farms.com
Food supplements, cultures, equipment

Reed Mariculture
520 East McGlincy Lane, #1
Campbell, CA 95008
877-732-3276 / 408-377-1065
www.Reed-Mariculture.com
Live and preserved foods, mysid shrimp and copepod cultures

Spectrum Chemicals & Laboratory Products, Inc.
14422 S. San Pedro St.
Gardena, CA 90248
800-813-1514
www.spectrumchemical.com
Chloroquine phosphate and other aquarium pharmaceuticals

Online Information

Aquarium Geographic™
www.aquariumgeographic.com
Online library of marine aquarium facts and articles, including health and feeding advice

Marine Depot Forums
http://forum.marinedepot.com
Online marine fish disease forum moderated by Kelly Jedlicki

Reefs.org
http://www.reefs.org
Online forums for reef aquarists. Publishers of Advanced Aquarist's Online Magazine (www.advancedaquarist.com)

Reef Central
www.reefcentral.com
Online community forums for hobbyists and professionals

Salt Corner
www.saltcorner.com
Database of articles and information assembled by Bob Goemans

Index

Photography & Illustration Credits

All photographs **by Matthew L. Wittenrich** *unless otherwise indicated.*

Photographers:

Alf Jacob Nilsen (Bioquatic Photo): 20, 32, 34–35, 48, 70–71, 78–79, 94, 109, 121, 126–127, 140–141, 191

David Vaughan: 145 TL, 146 B, 148, 155 L, 164 TL, 164 BL, 168 TL, 168 TR, 177, 185 L, 187

Nelson Herwig: 145 TR, 146 T, 156 T, 157, 161 B, 164 TR, 164 BR, 176 B, 178, 186

Dr. Gerald Bassleer: 153, 158, 159, 163, 175, 180, 182, 183, 184, 185 R, 190

Bob Goemans: 44, 68, 95 (inset), 106, 108, 109 (inset), 192, 230

Denise Nielsen Tackett (tackettproductions.com): 161 T, 169 TL, 169 TR, 169 BR; 170 TL, 170 TR, 170 MR

Dr. Vincent B. Hargreaves (photoaquatica.com): 58, 136, 142, 147 R

Larry Tackett (tackettproductions.com): 167, 169 BL, 171 L

Craig Smith: 53, 67, 134

James W. Fatheree, M.Sc.: 24, 84

Jeff Turner: 31, 56, 58

Kelly Jedlicki: 118

Marc Sitkin/Digital Momentum: 231

Gary Braasch/CORBIS: 77

Ralph A. Clevenger/CORBIS: Front Cover

Key: T = Top; B = Bottom; L = Left; R = Right; M = Middle.

Illustrations:

All illustrations by **Joshua Highter/Microcosm**

Color:

Digital Engine/Burlington, VT

About the Contributors

Gerald Bassleer

Gerald Bassleer has been active in the international ornamental fish trade for over 25 years. As a biologist, he has specialized in fish diseases while studying at various universities in Belgium, Venezuela, the United States, Scotland, and Germany. In 1995 he set up his own import/export business in ornamental fish, BASSLEER BIOFISH, in Belgium. Dr. Bassleer is an active member of Ornamental Fish International, which promotes ethical trade standards that focus on the welfare of fish and nature. He is the author of several books, including *The New Illustrated Guide to Fish Diseases*, and is a regular contributor to trade and fish-keeping magazines.

Dr. Vincent B. Hargreaves

Vincent Hargreaves is a marine biologist, underwater photographer and self-described "avid coral reef conservationist." He is the author of a number of aquarium books, including *The Complete Book of the Marine Aquarium* (2002), and a frequent contributor to a number of magazines.

Nelson Herwig

Nelson Herwig has been in the public aquarium field for the past 35 years—25 years as Curator of Fishes at the Houston Zoo, and 10 years as Aquarium Supervisor at the San Antonio Zoo. In addition, he has been studying and collecting marine fish on the Gulf Coast of Texas and Mexico for more than four decades. Nelson is now Curator Emeritus of the Houston Zoo and is a consultant on new methods of fishkeeping and aquarium husbandry. He is the author of several books, including the *Handbook of Drugs and Chemicals Used in the Treatment of Fish Diseases: A Manual of Fish Pharmacology* and *Materia Medica*, and many magazine articles.

Martin A. Moe, Jr.

Martin A. Moe, Jr., is a marine biologist, a noted aquarist, and a pioneering breeder of marine fishes. He is also the author of many popular books and articles on marine aquariums and fish breeding and many scientific papers on fishery biology. He is the author of *The Marine Aquarium Handbook: Beginner to Breeder* and *The Marine Aquarium Reference: Systems and Invertebrates*.

In 1972, he was the first to commercially breed the Indo-Pacific Clownfish and the Neon Goby, and he established the first commercial hatchery for marine tropical fish, Aqualife Research Corporation.

Martin and his wife, Barbara, now live in an old house on the beach in Islamorada in the Florida Keys. His current project is working with the Florida Keys National Marine Sanctuary to restore the keystone herbivore, the Longspined Sea Urchin, *Diadema antillarum*, to the reefs of the Keys.

Alf Jacob Nilsen

Alf Jacob Nilsen is the co-author, with Svein Fosså, of the authoritative *The Modern Coral Reef Aquarium* series, *Reef Secrets*, and other titles. He is an educator, underwater photographer, and founder of Bioquatic Photo in Hidrasund, Norway.

David Vaughan

David Vaughan is the Senior Aquarist for all aspects of quarantine at uShaka Marine World Aquarium in Durban, South Africa, the fifth largest public aquarium in the world, and runs the largest quarantine facility for fish in the southern hemisphere. David wrote the quarantine protocol manual for Two Oceans Aquarium, in Cape Town, South Africa; the manual has been largely adopted by many aquarists throughout Australia.

Matthew L. Wittenrich

Matthew L. Wittenrich is a marine biologist and author of the recently published *The Complete Illustrated Breeder's Guide to Marine Aquarium Fishes*. He is pursuing a doctorate at Florida Institute of Technology, Melbourne, Florida, where his research focuses on the development of feeding abilities in early-stage larval reef fishes.

About the Authors

Bob Goemans

A prominent figure among marine aquarium enthusiasts, **Bob Goemans** has been keeping tropical and saltwater fishes for more than six decades. He was born and raised in Queens, New York, where he started with freshwater aquariums as a child in 1945 and had his first marine aquarium in 1956.

As a world traveler and diver for 50 years, he has collected specimens for his home aquariums from the South China Sea to the Caribbean.

Bob is well known as an author on the many facets of marine aquaristics, at one point publishing 178 consecutive monthly articles for *Marine Fish Monthly* magazine. He is currently a regular contributor to *Tropical Fish Hobbyist* (TFH) magazine and *Freshwater and Marine Aquariums* (FAMA), and *Seascope* in the United States. His work also appears in *Practical Fishkeeping* and *UltraMarine* magazines in the United Kingdom, where he has been a regular contributor to *Marine World*. He has also authored a series of accessible publications dedicated to the more natural aspects of marine aquarium keeping, and also produced a CD-ROM book explaining the biological aspects of the Jaubert Plenum method and associated microbial processes.

He is a well-known aquarium supporter of local aquarium businesses and groups, often appearing at aquarium shop openings, question and answer sessions, aquarium society meetings, symposiums, school events and on related TV programs.

Bob has a doctorate in Business Management and is a retired Environmental Contracting Manager for a subsidiary of General Motors. In addition to aquarium research and writing endeavors, Bob heads aquarium and environmental consulting businesses, and currently resides in Tucson, Arizona, where he is a supporter of conservation efforts and a Sierra Club member. He considers himself a truly independent voice in the aquarium hobby and takes much satisfaction in helping his fellow aquarists.

Lance Ichinotsubo

Lance Ichinotsubo has been an aquarium hobbyist and professional for over 30 years. He was born and spent his childhood years in Hawaii, where he began keeping freshwater aquariums at an early age, graduating to marine aquariums in 1970.

The marine tropical fish industry is Lance's passion and has allowed him to turn his love for the ocean into a career. While working for one of the largest marine fish wholesalers in Hawaii, he became a certified scuba diver, which led to many years of professional tropical fish collecting. During his years in this industry he shipped and received marine fish to and from many exotic international locations.

In 1982, Lance moved to Las Vegas where he and his wife, Mikki, founded Rainbow Seascapes, one of the foremost marine-life dealers in the country, with clients from many states; its resort hotel and casino customers included The Mirage, Caesar's Palace, the Tropicana, and many others. Lance and Mikki have been featured on local and national TV shows and in many national trade and business publications. They have spoken to numerous aquarium societies, taught classes and consulted for the World Wide Pet Supply Association, the University of Nevada at Las Vegas, the Rainforest Café Restaurant chain, and Big Al's Aquarium Superstores, providing advice to curators and animal care specialists.

While pursuing his studies in water chemistry as it applies to marine aquariums, Lance moved to southern Florida, where he is currently president of Captive Seas, Inc., specializing in design, installation, and maintenance consultation for retail stores, maintenance companies, and individual clients nationally and internationally.

Lance is a founding member of the American Marinelife Dealers Association (AMDA), has been involved with the Marine Aquarium Council (MAC), and has served on the Advisory Council for the International Game Fish Association, based in Fort Lauderdale, Florida. His ultimate goals are to help clients and colleagues become successful in marine aquarium-keeping and to truly make a difference in his chosen field of study.

Further Reading

Microcosm/TFH Professional Series Titles

Reef Fishes
A Guide to Their Identification, Behavior & Captive Care

By Scott W. Michael

Volume I: Moray Eels, Seahorses & Anthias
Volume II: Basslets, Dottybacks & Hawkfishes
Volume III: Angelfishes & Butterflyfishes
Volume IV: Wrasses, Blennies & Damselfishes (2008)
Volume V: Gobies, Triggerfishes & Surgeonfishes (2008)
The Reef Fishes Encyclopedia (2009)

Clownfishes
A Guide to Their Captive Care, Breeding & Natural History

By Joyce D. Wilkerson

PocketExpert Guide™: Marine Fishes
500+ Essential-to-Know Species

By Scott W. Michael

PocketExpert Guide™: Reef Aquarium Fishes
500+ Essential-to-Know Species

By Scott W. Michael

Aquarium Sharks & Rays
**An Essential Guide to their Selection, Keeping
& Natural History**

By Scott W. Michael

Reef Secrets
**Reef Aquariums Made Simpler: Expert Advice,
Selecting Fishes & Invertebrates**

By Alf Jacob Nilsen & Svein A. Fosså

The Conscientious Marine Aquarist
A Commonsense Handbook for Successful Saltwater Hobbyists

By Robert M. Fenner

Natural Reef Aquariums
**Simplified Approaches to Creating Living
Saltwater Microcosms**

By John H. Tullock

Aquarium Keeping & Rescue
The Essential Saltwater Handbook & Log

By Carl DelFavero

PocketExpert Guide™: Marine Invertebrates
500+ Essential-to-Know Species

By Ronald L. Shimek, Ph.D.

The New Marine Aquarium
Step-by-Step Setup & Stocking Guide

By Michael S. Paletta

Aquarium Corals
Selection, Husbandry & Natural History

By Eric H. Borneman

Reef Life
**Natural History and Behaviors of
Marine Aquarium Fishes & Invertebrates**

By Denise Nielsen Tackett & Larry Tackett

**The Complete Illustrated
Breeder's Guide to Marine Aquarium Fishes
Mating, Spawning & Rearing Methods for Over 90 Species**

By Matthew L. Wittenrich

**Adventurous Aquarist Guide™
The 101 Best Saltwater Fishes
How to Choose & Keep Hardy, Brilliant, Fascinating Species
That Will Thrive in Your Home Aquarium**

By Scott W. Michael

Further Information: www.microcosm-books.com